THE INFLUENCE OF BORDER TROUBLES
ON RELATIONS BETWEEN THE
UNITED STATES AND MEXICO
1876—1910

A Da Capo Press Reprint Series

THE AMERICAN SCENE
Comments and Commentators

GENERAL EDITOR: WALLACE D. FARNHAM
University of Illinois

THE INFLUENCE OF BORDER TROUBLES ON RELATIONS BETWEEN THE UNITED STATES AND MEXICO
1876—1910

BY ROBERT D. GREGG

DA CAPO PRESS • NEW YORK • 1970

A Da Capo Press Reprint Edition

This Da Capo Press edition of *The Influence of Border Troubles on Relations Between the United States and Mexico, 1876-1910,* is an unabridged republication of the first edition published originally in Baltimore in 1937 as Series LV, Number 3 in *The Johns Hopkins University Studies in Historical and Political Science.*

Library of Congress Catalog Card Number 72-98181
SBN 306-71833-2

Manufactured in the United States of America

THE INFLUENCE OF BORDER TROUBLES ON
RELATIONS BETWEEN THE UNITED
STATES AND MEXICO 1876-1910

THE INFLUENCE OF BORDER TROUBLES ON RELATIONS BETWEEN THE UNITED STATES AND MEXICO 1876—1910

By

ROBERT D. GREGG
Professor of History
Carnegie Institute of Technology

BALTIMORE
THE JOHNS HOPKINS PRESS
1937

PRINTED IN THE UNITED STATES OF AMERICA
BY J. H. FURST COMPANY, BALTIMORE, MARYLAND

TO MY WIFE

WHOSE LOYAL COOPERATION AND AID HAVE PROVED
VITAL IN THE PREPARATION OF THIS STUDY

PREFACE

The materials for this study have been drawn, in so far as it has been possible, from manuscript sources in the Library of Congress, the archives of the Department of State, and the Rutherford B. Hayes papers in Fremont, Ohio. The General William Tecumseh Sherman papers in the Library of Congress and the diplomatic materials in the State Department proved particularly valuable. In addition many printed sources and secondary works have been used.

The writer wishes to express his deep appreciation of the interest and loyalty of Dr. William Stull Holt in preparing this study. The late Dr. John H. Latané by his kindly guidance and Dr. Charles C. Tansill by his generous introduction to the archives in Washington gave great encouragement and aid. The courtesy and interest of Dr. Curtis Garrison formerly of the Library of Congress are gratefully acknowledged.

R. D. G.

CONTENTS

THE INFLUENCE OF BORDER TROUBLES ON RELATIONS BETWEEN THE UNITED STATES AND MEXICO 1876-1910

CHAPTER I

THE BORDER PROBLEM

For several hundred miles the Rio Grande winds southward and eastward through a region dotted with towns and scattered brick and adobe army posts. Back from the river on each side stretches a waste of mesquite and chaparral giving way in turn to grazing lands. In this vast prairie country of southern Texas and northern Mexico in the latter part of the nineteenth century roamed great herds of cattle and horses, tempting sources of gain to raiders who kept the lower border in turmoil for many years. Smugglers and filibusterers and other adventurous and desperate characters also plied their trade with vigor in this fairly populous district. Above Laredo the country grows rugged and broken and north of San Felipe the mountains come down to the river. Mountains and desert extend with a few breaks to El Paso, thence westward along the artificial boundary of New Mexico, Arizona, and California to the Pacific. Since Spanish days these mountains and wild, remote valleys had sheltered fierce Apaches, Comanches, Utahs, Navajos, Kiowas, and Yumas, who swooped down from their fastnesses, robbing and killing in the white settlements. Much of the story of Mexican-American relations for many years after the Treaty of Guadalupe Hidalgo revolved around attempts to end this state of border lawlessness in which white and red adventurers played their parts and the controversies of Diaz' early administration were largely devoted to it. A brief examination of the various forms in which the border question became a subject of international friction before the advent of Diaz is therefore necessary.

11

Cattle Raids

By 1835 the cattle business had become flourishing in the lower Rio Grande valley with great herds, each containing thousands of animals, feeding in the vast unfenced areas of Texas, north and east of the Arroyo Colorado, and with many other herds in the states south of the river. Severely injured by the Mexican War, the cattle industry revived gradually afterward and by 1860 again was measured in terms of thousands of head.[1] Driven by fierce northers or thirst these cattle in great herds of 50,000 to 75,000 wandered many miles and were usually seen by their owners only when rounded up once a year. Expert thieves could thus separate as many as 1500 cattle from a herd and escape to a safe place of sale without serious fear of detection.[2] Conflicting as to responsibility for this border " rustling " reports by Mexican and American investigators would seem to agree at least: (a) that the practice became especially prevalent during the early '60's and, (b) that by the early '70's it had become an organized business probably overshadowing all other forms of border disorder.[3]

Border Smuggling

Another acute problem when Diaz came into office was the

[1] Report of House Committee on Foreign Affairs on the Relations of the United States with Mexico, 45th Cong., 2d sess., *H. Rept.* No. 701, p. v.

[2] *Report of the United States Commissioners to Texas appointed under the Joint Resolution of Congress May 7, 1872*, p. 4; Extracts from Report of American Border Commission 1872, 45th Cong., 2d sess., *H. Rept.* No. 701, Appendix B, pp. 97-98.

[3] For these conflicting estimates see *Report of the Committee of Investigation sent in 1873 by the Mexican Government to the Frontier of Texas*, pp. 79 ff.; *Report of the U. S. Commissioners to Texas 1872*, pp. 8 ff.; Report of the Permanent Committee . . . of Brownsville, Texas, April 17, 1875, 45th Cong., 2d sess., *H. Rept.* No. 701, pp. 71 ff. For evidence as to contracts for sale of stolen cattle in Mexican and American towns see Ord to Sheridan, November 23, 1875, W. T. Sherman Papers MSS, XLI; *Report of Committee of Investigation 1873* . . . , p. 18; Memo. Mexican Secretary of Foreign Affairs, June 30, 1877, in Memo. of June 23, 1877, by Mr. Foster, American Minister to Mexico, *Memoranda y notas relativas cambiadas entre el Ministro de Relaciones Exteriores y el Ministro Plenipotenciario de los Estados Unidos*, p. 10 (an official Mexican publication, hereafter referred to as *Memo y notas*).

question of border smuggling, growing out of tariff differences between the two countries. For a number of years after 1848 the American tariff was much lower than the Mexican and the American side of the line was marked by absence of sales and excessive excise taxes so usual on the other. As a result, goods and population moved to the American shore and the border towns of Tamaulipas, particularly, declined rapidly. Finally, alarmed, the governor of that state sought to end this condition of affairs by establishing in March 1858 a so-called Free Zone, twelve and one-half miles wide and running the length of the state's northern border. Into this Free Zone foreign goods could be brought free of duty. Unfortunately, however, they were often smuggled then into other parts of Mexico or into the United States. In spite of protests by the American Government and some opposition in the Mexican Congress, the Zone was extended in January 1885, following the border to the Pacific. Thus along a difficult boundary of 1,833 miles smuggling came to be practiced on a large scale, particularly in the Rio Grande valley.[4]

Raiding and Filibustering Expeditions

Still another source of irritation arose from numbers of armed expeditions across the border in both directions especially in the period between the Mexican and Civil Wars, the heyday of filibustering in this hemisphere. Taking advantage of revolutionary conditions in Mexico and difficulties in the enforcement of neutrality laws these raiders descended on the border from the American side and in some cases, notably that of General Juan N. Cortina, raided from Mexico into the United States. Motives were mixed, a restless desire for adventure, the spirit of expansion, eagerness for plunder, pursuit of Indians, revolutionary designs, and many other considerations no doubt entered into these movements. After

---

[4] Matias Romero, *Mexico and the United States*, I, 433 ff. See testimony of William Schuchardt, U. S. Commercial Agent at Piedras Negras before the House Foreign Affairs Committee, January 14, 1878, 45th Cong., 2d sess., *H. Rept.* No. 701, pp. 37, 45-46.

suffering for many years from raiders both countries naturally looked at them askance and one of the issues which quickly developed between Diaz and the United States was the alleged outfitting on American soil of expeditions in support of his exiled adversary, Lerdo de Tejada.

Indian Forays

Finally the whole Indian question, often involving raids across the border, was one of the most vexing with which the two countries had to deal on their common frontier. Given ample cover on both sides of the line by great reaches of country whose "peculiarly wild, rugged, and inhospitable character" was practically uncharted on the maps of the time, these savage tribesmen left a trail of fire and blood along both sides of the border, particularly above Laredo.[5] Small numbers of men available for patrol on each side and friction between civil and military authorities still further complicated the situation.[6] Always in the background, moreover, lurked the sinister shadow of revolution in Mexico and civil strife and reconstruction in the United States making for lawlessness worse confounded.[7]

Faced by all these obstacles in the way of effective law enforcement troops of all types and on both sides would have been more than human if they had not succumbed at times to the temptation to cross into the neighboring country in at-

[5] General E. O. C. Ord, Commanding the Department of Texas, before the House Committee on Foreign Affairs December 7, 1877, 45th Cong., 2d sess., *H. Rept.* No. 701, p. 1; *Report of the Secretary of War for 1876*, p. 487.

[6] W. T. Sherman to Herbert A. Preston, Correspondent of New York *Herald* in Washington, D. C., April 17, 1873, W. T. Sherman Papers MSS, Letterbook 1872-1878; W. T. Sherman to John Sherman, May 28, 1871, *ibid.*, xxx; Sherman to Reynolds, May 18, 1871, *ibid.*; Sherman to J. Q. Smith, after retirement of the latter as head of the Indian Bureau, January 23, 1878, *ibid.*, Letterbook 1872-1878. For a full and accurate account of Indian raiding see J. Fred Rippy, *United State and Mexico*, pp. 68 ff.

[7] For a description of lawlessness in Texas during this period see Summary of the Report of Adjutant General Steele of Texas for 1875, 45th Cong., 2d sess., *H. Rept.* No. 701, Appendix B, pp. 139 ff.; Charles W. Ramsdell, *Reconstruction in Texas*, "Columbia University Studies in History, Economics, and Public Law," XXXVI, No. 1, pp. 36, 67, 135, 175.

tempts to enforce order. Nor can the governments of the two countries, bearing in mind the peculiarly irritating situation, be entirely blamed for their attitudes and the resulting friction. As a matter of fact such crossings took place fairly frequently prior to the time of Diaz. Sometimes American forces, regular or irregular, were the offenders, sometimes Mexican, but by the very nature of the case the Americans more frequently took the aggressive. The resultant diplomatic friction threatened on numerous occasions a complete break.

In general the sinuous thread of border-crossing diplomacy before 1876 lies outside the scope of this study. Suffice it to say that the United States Government, starting in 1836, more or less consistently for the next forty years held to the right of pursuit by United States forces of marauders fleeing into Mexico. This alleged right was based largely upon (a) the preservation of treaty obligations, and (b) the fundamental right of self-defense.[8] As a rule permission was asked for such crossings and when it was not forthcoming—as it never was in the explosive state of Mexican public opinion— crossings were carried out without permission.

For the most part such permission was requested only for the "Indian country" along the upper Rio Grande and the Arizona and New Mexican boundaries. Late in the Grant Administration, however, the apparently greater stability of the Mexican Government and the growing storm of border lawlessness led to a new sweeping proposal by the State Department. This called for *reciprocal* crossing instead of by United States troops alone. Further the agreement was to cover not only the "Indian country" but the *whole* border. Obviously this included the much raided populous lower Rio Grande valley where possibilities of clashes between troops of the two countries or between troops and inhabitants made any crossing attempt a delicate matter.[9] Immediately flames

---

[8] Forsyth to Gorostiza, May 10, 1836; Forsyth to Ellis, December 10, 1836, J. B. Moore, *A Digest of International Law* (1906 ed.), II, 419-420. Later State Department heads merely performed variations on this same theme.

[9] Fish to Foster, May 4, 1875, Mexican Instructions MSS, XIX.

of resentment leaped high in the Mexican press against the hated " Gringo." These were fanned into a blaze when the American Border Commission Report of 1876 was made known with proposal for unilateral action by the United States in case Mexico refused a reciprocal agreement.[10] Fortunately for President Lerdo, hard pressed on all sides, and for peace between the countries the congressional resolution embodying the Report did not pass. But continued raiding and the revolutionary disorders of 1876 in Mexico kept the whole issue of border crossing as well as the others mentioned in a state of uneasy suspense. Here they remained to distort relations between the two countries when Diaz stormed the gates of the capital and began a new era in Mexican history.

---

[10] Foster to Fish, April 25, 1876, also May 4, 1876, Mexican Despatches MSS, LVI. Both despatches carry interesting enclosures from the Mexican press.

CHAPTER II

The Struggle Over Recognition

When Diaz and his tired little army rode into Mexico City two days after the early morning flight of President Lerdo de Tejada relations between the United States and Mexico were in utter confusion. The constitutional government was in full flight,[1] the country in a state of anarchy.[2] No one was able to say how long Diaz could maintain himself in power,[3] and whether he represented a genuine popular protest against Lerdo's reelection or merely the strong arm of a revolutionary group. Nor could the wisest tell what might happen to foreign personal and property interests under the new régime. Diaz' various " Plans " and revolutionary watchwords, however, were anything but reassuring on this point.[4]

Also the Grant Administration looked with dismay on government by revolution in Mexico once again after eight years

---

[1] For Lerdo's evacuation of the capital November 21, see Foster to Fish, November 28, 1876, Mexican Despatches MSS, LVII. Lerdo as Chief Justice of the Supreme Court had succeeded to the presidency of Mexico *ad interim* in 1872 upon the death of Juárez. The succession was in accordance with the Constitution of 1857. He was elected to the office in the autumn of 1872 but when he sought and secured reelection in 1876 Porfirio Diaz and Chief Justice José María Iglesias independently raised the standard of revolt, protesting that the election was illegal. Herbert I. Priestley, *The Mexican Nation, a History*, pp. 369-374.

[2] Beginning with September 27, 1875, when he reported "local revolutions and armed disturbances " as "more numerous and frequent than in any previous period during the administration of Lerdo " the despatches of John W. Foster, United States Minister to Mexico, show a gradual breakdown of the Lerdo Government—political, financial, and military—culminating in the smashing defeat at Tecoac, November 16, 1876, which practically opened the gates of Mexico City to Diaz.

[3] Diaz did not triumph completely over his chief remaining rival, Iglesias, until early in January 1877. Foster to Fish, January 16, 1877, Mexican Despatches MSS, LVIII.

[4] The Plan of Palo Blanco, March 31, 1876, a modification of the earlier Plan of Tuxtepec, had held that Lerdo was sacrificing the country to foreign investors. He was said to be attempting to " rob us of our future, and sell us to foreigners." Foster to Evarts, January 28, 1879, *Papers Relating to the Foreign Relations of the United States 1879*, p. 780 (hereafter cited as *U. S. For. Rel.* with the appropriate year).

17

of constitutional and fairly peaceful administration by Juárez and Lerdo. Both had been greatly respected by the American Government. Indeed Foster, who had served in Mexico during practically the whole Lerdist régime, spoke in glowing terms of the period as almost a golden age—" the most memorable in the history of the country for its peace and order and the uninterrupted sway of the federal authority throughout the nation." [5]   On the other hand his opinion of Diaz, during the early days of the revolution at least, would seem hardly to have been flattering. " The substantial interests," he wrote Secretary Fish, " repose little confidence in General Porfirio Diaz." He went on to describe these " substantial interests " as commercial forces, capitalists, and " respectable public men." [6]   Moreover the State Department apparently shared Foster's view, at any rate so far as Lerdo was concerned. Secretary Hamilton Fish, writing unofficially to Foster somewhat earlier, had said:

> As the present government has inspired greater hopes for its stability and for its efficiency in the right direction than any which of late, at least, has existed there, it is good policy in us to encourage it, and to avoid doing or saying anything which might have a contrary tendency. I am sure both that you will agree to this and that you will carefully cooperate in it.[7]

Whether these " hopes . . . in the right direction " inspired by Lerdo were material or spiritual or both is extremely hard to say definitely. No doubt the United States Government desired Mexican good order both in the interest of the Mexicans themselves and of American merchants and investors. But it is next to impossible to analyze out of this complex of forces—American and Mexican—a particular interest and prove, as some writers seek to do, that it dominated the policy of one country toward the other. To show for instance that

---

[5] D. L. Richardson to Fish, December 22, 1875, Despatches MSS, LV with quotations from a speech by Foster before the New Orleans Chamber of Commerce, November 18, 1875. Foster's speeches, despatches, and papers show his great interest in American trade and investment in Mexico. Perhaps this was one reason for his championship of the Lerdo Government.
[6] Foster to Fish, March 1, 1876 (Unofficial), *ibid.*, LVI.
[7] Fish to Foster, January 16, 1874 (Unofficial), John W. Foster Papers MSS.

pressure was brought to bear on the State Department by American commercial interests to defer recognition of Diaz is relatively easy. To prove that this pressure was the main reason, or even one of the reasons, for deferred recognition is another and much harder matter.

This applies particularly to the activities of Edward Lee Plumb, American railroad and mining executive in Mexico. Plumb had spent twenty years or more in Mexico, spoke Spanish like a native, knew intimately most of the men in public life, and in his various plans for business development travelled widely through the country, becoming thoroughly acquainted with all classes from the wealthy entrepreneur in the city club to the lowly laborer in the rough and tumble of the mining camp.[8] His papers are an important source for Mexican-American relations during the latter half of the nineteenth century. As representative of the International Railroad Company of Texas, Plumb sought a concession from the Mexican Government for a line from Mexico City to the Rio Grande, there to connect with his own system. Through the early '70's he urged his case, but the government finally awarded the contract in November 1873 to the Mexican Company Ltd. purporting to be Mexican in membership.[9]

Renewing his efforts, however, in 1874 he completed a contract for a line from Leon to the Rio Grande which was approved by the Mexican Congress May 29, 1875.[10] The fear of the repudiation of this and other Juárez and Lerdist contracts if Diaz achieved the presidency seems to have developed in Plumb a strong apprehension that Diaz might gain power and be recognized by the United States. As early as 1871 he was inveighing against Diaz and what he considered a possible "return to the days of Santa Anna and the era of military

---

[8] He had also served as United States Secretary of Legation, later as Chargé d'Affaires for several years during the highly important and dramatic period of the French invasion and its aftermath.

[9] Plumb to Pearsall (Treasurer of the International R. R. Co.), November 22, 1873, Plumb Papers MSS, XII; Fred W. Powell, *The Railroads of Mexico*, p. 107.

[10] Foster to Fish, June 10, 1875, *U. S. For. Rel. 1875-1876*, pp. 927-928; Powell, p. 108.

pronunciamentos." [11] At the same time he recognized Diaz as a man of great " prestige " and, with his knowledge of the Mexican mind and spirit, clearly foresaw his gathering power. Dreaming of railroad empire, not merely within northern Mexico and the United States, but " eventually to Minatitlan and across the Isthmus of Tehuantepac and perhaps down the coast still farther south, thus forming a single grand continental line from Halifax to Central America," [12] Plumb desired, above all things, peace. To his way of thinking Diaz meant disorder and repudiation of contracts, Lerdo meant peace.

That Mr. Foster and his predecessor, Mr. Nelson, were in active sympathy with Plumb's efforts to secure precedence over his competitors, American, English, and Mexican, would appear from Plumb's correspondence.

> Although Mr. Nelson has not yet stated to me himself [he wrote in 1873] that he has resigned his position as Minister to this country, yet I learn with much regret that such is the fact.
> . . . But whoever may be appointed here, it would be well, if possible, to have him brought into contact with the Company before leaving New York and fully informed of its purpose here and strong position at home. [13]

It is not clear whether Foster had consulted " with the Company," but he seems to have been on very cordial terms

---

[11] Plumb to J. Sanford Barnes (of the International R. R. Co.), November 18, 1871, Plumb Papers MSS, VIII.

[12] Plumb to Barnes, April 13, 1872, ibid.

[13] Plumb to Barhyde, March 14, 1873, ibid., XI. This confidence in the Company's " strong position at home " may have inspired an earlier significant letter in which Plumb urged Barnes to see the President or, if he could not go himself, to ask " Mr. Dodge " to have " some conversation with President Grant " so that the latter would make " only kind expressions toward Mexico " in his forthcoming Annual Message. Plumb insisted on such a course as " very desirable . . . both on account of the effect that would be produced here, and abroad " and he urged Barhyde to stress to " the President and . . . Secretary of State . . . the importance of our enterprise to the interests of commerce and friendly relations between the two countries " and urged him to act " while the subjects to be treated in the Annual Message are being considered." Plumb to Barnes, October 30, 1872, ibid. An examination of Grant's Annual Message for 1872 does not show Plumb's purported influence. The Message speaks without comment of the American and Mexican border investigating commissions and of the Claims Commission. The only other reference to Mexico is the expressed hope and expectation that the new Lerdo Administration would bring peace and order to the border.

with Plumb. The latter wrote to one of the Company officials soon after Foster's arrival:

On the second inst. Mr. Foster, our new minister here, who earnestly desires our success, informed me that Mr. James Sullivan the Englishman appointed agent of the Union Contract Company [14] by General Palmer, when the latter left there in May had called upon him the day before and had informed him that by mail just at hand . . . he had received full powers from the Union Contract Company of Pennsylvania to act as their agent here with discretion to vary their former proposals or to make new ones and even admitting the standard gauge; that he, Mr. Sullivan, had been appointed a director in the Company, and that Mr. Scott and Mr. Thompson had increased their subscription from $50,000 each to $250,000 each and that the company had by no means abandoned their efforts here, but would now press them more vigorously than ever.

Mr. Foster in kindly informing me of this (of which I communicate to you as well as what I have mentioned from the President [15] only in confidence, as it would be undesirable for the fact of their having spoken to me to become known here) manifested much regret at the renewal of the discreditable and useless warfare which he had trusted was at an end and the only effect of which is to retard and render more difficult the establishment of American enterprise.[16]

This important connection with Foster apparently established and his aversion to Diaz taking firmer root, Plumb, early in 1876, minimized the importance of the revolution in a letter to Secretary Fish. "I have no hesitation," he said, "in asserting that it does not seriously menace either the resistance of the present Government or the permanent establishment of constitutional order in that country." [17] A few months later, when the defeated Lerdo had fled, Plumb returned to the United States, partly, apparently, to urge the administration not to recognize Diaz.[18] From New York he

---

[14] This Company, also American, was seeking to gain a contract for a narrow gauge railroad covering practically the same route as Plumb's proposed contract. Naturally competition between the two companies for Mexican official favor was keen.

[15] Apparently from the context " the President " refers to President Lerdo rather than President Grant.

[16] Plumb to Pearsall, September 13, 1873, Plumb Papers MSS, XII.

[17] Plumb to Fish, April 4, 1876 (Confidential), *ibid.* At this time most of the disorder actually was confined to the neighborhood of Matamoras on the Rio Grande and did not seem so dangerous as later.

[18] Plumb had left Mexico primarily because he considered that Diaz' decree of September 26, 1876, nullifying any contract made by his predecessor " which may result in any burden to the nation " and Diaz' arbitrary acts under this decree made the International R. R. concession for the time being hopeless. Powell, p. 109.

wrote Secretary Fish that in spite of the fact that Lerdo had
sailed from Acapulco and Diaz had assumed the provisional
presidency, " I should not be very much surprised to see him
[Lerdo] recalled to Mexico with acclamation of all the people within a year." His optimism was based on Juárez' experience, during and after Comonfort's coup d'état in 1858
when the former had fled first to Guanajuato, thence to
Guadalajara, then to Manzanillo, then to Panama, and finally
to New Orleans. Returning to Mexico after three months or
so, he had " inaugurated the struggle which was crowned
with so important results." [19]

Further light is shed on this connection in Plumb's own
mind between the fortunes of Lerdo and those of his own
organization by a letter to another official of his company.
" Whenever the pressure of revolutionary force is removed,"
he said, " the country will return to constitutional order that
was so interrupted and we can go forward again with our
enterprise, which lies meanwhile in abeyance. . . . Nothing
desirable or stable or . . . permanent can result from either of
the two revolutionary factions now struggling for supremacy
in Mexico." He stated further in the same letter that he did
not intend to have anything to do with the revolutionary
authorities, nor did he advise anyone else to have.[20] Later
the same month he reached Washington and wrote a series of
vigorous notes to Fish marked " Private." Urging the administration to be very guarded in approaching the question
of recognition he asked if it " would not be wise to leave the
very questionable proceeding of any recognition of the revolutionary authorities in Mexico to the test of at least a short
period of time and to the responsibility of the succeeding
administration [in the United States] by whom the grave
issues which may arise from what is now transpiring in
Mexico, will have to be dealt with." [21] A few days later he
was still more emphatic in his plea for non-recognition of
Diaz. " Can anything," he said, " but evil to the United

[19] Plumb to Fish, January 8, 1877. Plumb Papers MSS, XIII.
[20] Plumb to R. S. Hayes, January 12, 1877, ibid.
[21] Plumb to Fish, January 29, 1877 (Private), ibid.

States result from the success of such revolutionary attempts, and if we are swift to give to this the reward and approval of our recognition, will not such a course on our part hold out hope of the same reward to further revolutionary proceedings and thus be a stimulant to disorder? " [22]

Whether swayed by this verbal bombardment and that of other American business men who may have been writing similar letters or, as seems more likely, influenced by the domestic situation with the United States in an uproar over the Hayes-Tilden disputed election, the administration soon decided upon a cautious policy toward recognition of the new Mexican Government. In his instructions of December 19, soon after Diaz became provisional President,[23] Secretary Fish said in part: " It would be premature under the circumstances officially to acknowledge the Diaz Government. Still there is no sufficient reason why you should not hold personal intercourse with the individuals composing it, so far as this may be convenient or mutually agreeable." [24] Foster determined, therefore, to " assume the responsibility of establishing unofficial relations with it [the Diaz Government], and to postpone the formal and official recognition until after the elections had been held and Diaz installed as constitutional president. On consultation with my diplomatic colleagues, they agreed to pursue the same course." [25]

In the ensuing weeks one matter in particular worried Foster as he waited for Diaz' constitutional election: that is, acceptance or non-acceptance of the first claims award due to

---

[22] Plumb to Fish, February 2, 1877, *ibid.* Another note dated February 6, stressed reports of renewed revolutionary activities in Mexico and the consequent instability of the Diaz régime.

[23] Diaz proclaimed himself provisional president November 28. Foster to Fish, November 29, 1876, *U. S. For. Rel. 1877*, Enclosure, pp. 385-386.

[24] Fish to Foster, December 19, 1876, Mexican Instructions MSS, XIX.

[25] John W. Foster, *Diplomatic Memoirs*, I, 86. Foster as dean of the diplomatic corps in Mexico City exercised considerable influence over his colleagues. See Foster to Fish, November 28, 1876, Despatches MSS, LVII for a meeting of the representatives of various governments in the American Legation after the collapse of the Lerdo Government to map out a common line of action.

the United States under the Treaty of 1868. Would acceptance constitute recognition of Mexico's new government?
Foster felt that it would.[26] This Vallarta, Minister for Foreign Affairs in the Diaz Government, denied. He asserted
"unhesitatingly" that the payment "was made in the name
of the Republic of Mexico and not of any particular government in compliance with a solemn Treaty stipulation; that
the subject of recognition of the General Diaz government
was an independent question and that in this latter question
he had confidence the United States would act with sound
and liberal judgment, being governed by the condition of
affairs or occurrence of events with a desire to maintain
friendly relations between the two Republics."[27] The Grant
Administration was in a dilemma. Should it accept the payment and, if so, through a Diaz representative or through the
regularly accredited representative of the Lerdo government
in Washington, Mr. Mariscal?[28] In this new perplexity "it
was decided to give Foster full discretionary power to grant
recognition." Apparently, Mr. Fish argued, Diaz no longer
faced any important adversary in the field and "might be
regarded as the actual ruler of the country. Inasmuch therefore as we cannot receive from a government we do not
acknowledge, the installment of indemnity payable by Mexico
on the 31st inst. on this account especially you would be warranted in recognition of the government of Porfirio Diaz,
unless, before this reached you, such a step should be made
inexpedient by events which are not now foreseen. You will
exercise your best discretion in the matter."[29] But happily

---

[26] Foster, I, 86.

[27] Foster to Fish, January 16, 1877, Despatches MSS, LVIII.

[28] Diaz agreed to pay through Mariscal, thus obviating the necessity of recognition of his government. See below, note 30.

[29] Fish to Foster, January 19, 1877, Instructions MSS, XIX. Fish
in the same despatch lectured Diaz through Foster on the inexpedi-
ency of "disowning official contracts." He thought such contracts
"in the nature of things must be more or less indispensable for
strengthening his [Diaz'] power, nor will the tendency to repudiate
be towards enabling him to obtain better terms from those with
whom he may bargain." Foster was to refer "informally" to these
matters in any interview which he might have with Diaz and to
"express the regret" which the United States would feel "at the

means were found to solve this difficulty of accepting the indemnity without recognizing the Diaz Government. With the consent of Diaz payment was made by Mariscal as minister and in the name of the Mexican Republic.

That question disposed of, a new note was introduced into the problem. In his despatch of February 12, Secretary Fish for the first time mentioned border considerations as a possible force with which to reckon in the question of recognition.

> In your intercourse with prominent men in public life [he wrote] you will endeavor to leave the impression that the United States would expect repeal of the "Zona Libre," so-called, and efficient measures towards checking inroads into their States and territories adjacent to Mexico. Though these measures might not in the end be deemed indispensable to formal recognition of that government they are deemed so important to the preservation of friendly relations between the two countries that our earnestness upon the subject must not be left in doubt.[30]

Meanwhile the situation in Mexico was rapidly becoming more favorable to Diaz. Opposition practically disappearing, in February he was elected constitutional president of Mexico for four years.[31] Lerdo and Iglesias had both left the country. Only General Alvarez with a small force in Guerrero continued the conflict and he was reported by the United States Consul at Acapulco as opposed to the state government and as ready to surrender to Diaz.[32] These facts coupled with his instructions of January 19, now made Foster believe that the time for recognition was at hand. "I regard it as my duty to recognize the government of General Diaz as the *de facto* government of Mexico, and I have therefore to notify you that I will proceed to do so. My formal declaration to that effect will however be delayed a few days,

---

effect of these measures upon those interests of citizens of the United States who may have entered into contracts with the Lerdo Government." But he added: "If, however, the policy avowed should be insisted on and carried into execution, it is not expected that, for the present at least, you will regard this as an international question."

[30] Fish to Foster, February 12, 1877, *ibid.*
[31] Foster, I, 87. His inauguration did not take place until May 5.
[32] Foster to Fish, February 19, 1877, Despatches MSS, LVIII.

to enable me to hold a preliminary interview with General Diaz as seems to be contemplated in your despatch." [33]

However Foster's decision to recognize Diaz for some reason underwent a change in the next few days. He had decided to communicate unofficially on routine matters and to ask Diaz in writing for consular exequaturs, thus granting *de facto* but giving " no formal or written declaration of recognition." To this end he had made calls on President Diaz and his cabinet which they had returned. Foster said that he was influenced in his action " by prudential considerations in the conviction that a few weeks' time would develop manifestations as to the strength and permanence of General Diaz' Administration and as to its acceptance by the country. I was also influenced by the diplomatic precedent established by the government of Mexico in its relation with Spain upon the change of government and the assumption of power by King Alfonso in 1875." At that time the Mexican Minister for Foreign Affairs had refused official recognition until the king's letter noting the latter's assumption of power reached him. He now made the same suggestion to Vallarta, the diplomatic corps agreeing. Vallarta, he said, showed a marked desire for official recognition and in order to secure it as soon as possible the Foreign Minister promised to send a letter for transmission by this " present mail." [34] Promptly the next day Vallarta sent Diaz' letter to the representative of every country having a diplomatic delegation in the capital. Thereupon the other diplomats, according to Foster, thought it better to await formal declaration by the Mexican Congress later in the month " on the recent elections." [35] At

[33] *Ibid.* On Foster's despatch Mr. Hunter, for many years Chief Clerk of the State Department and one of the most experienced and best informed men in the Department, noted: " After an examination it appears to me that the course of Mr. Foster in this matter may be approved."

[34] Foster to Fish, March 3, 1877, Despatches MSS, LVII. Hunter noted on this despatch that Foster's " acts and views as set forth in this despatch may be approved." It reached Washington, of course, after the Hayes inauguration.

[35] Foster to Fish, March 4, 1877, *ibid.* Hunter's notation is interesting. He thought that it " may not be necessary to answer the autograph letter at once, but may be preferable for us also

the same time he sent a telegram post-haste to Secretary Fish pledging " no official recognition till receipt and action by our Government on Diaz autographed letter mailed today to you." [36] Thus Foster had deferred the recognition issue for a few weeks at least while Diaz' letter was being sent and answered and President Hayes was being sworn into office.

There the matter might well have stood for some time. For entering office with a disputed title and distraught by perilous post-Civil War issues the Hayes Administration must have been tempted to leave well enough alone in Mexico. But this soon proved to be out of the question. Diaz' constitutional inauguration to the presidency in May and continued raiding soon forced some decision on the questions of recognition and the protection of the border. In addition a host of conflicting counsellors, representing every shade of interest in and opinion on the Mexican question, were urging their views upon the new administration. Diaz enthusiasts and Lerdo supporters each had their inning. Foster soon warmly advocated recognition of Diaz while Texan influences close to President Hayes urged that it be deferred until Diaz' stability be proved and until he should make guarantees as to the border. American business interests active in Mexico were divided on this and other questions of Mexican policy but were none the less vociferous and in the general clamor rose the voices of some members of the Army group demanding the right to pursue raiders into Mexico and in some cases going so far as to urge the occupation of Mexican territory.

Foster, dubious as to Diaz' intentions and capacities in the early stages of the revolution, seems to have become more and more enthusiastic as the months passed. He had already established unofficial relations with the Diaz Government as the *de facto* power in Mexico before the Grant Administration left office. With the constitutional election of Diaz to the presidency in February and his prospective inauguration

---

to await proceedings of the Mexican Congress which was about to meet."

[36] Foster to Fish, March 4, 1877 (Telegram), *ibid.*

early in May,[37] Foster became convinced that he should be recognized by the United States. He admired Diaz' rugged simplicity, feeling that he ". . . manifested none of the boastful spirit of the victorious general, but was modest in the assumption of civil executive duties, plainly showed that he was walking in an untried path, and welcomed counsel and encouragement in the establishment of a government of law and order." [38]   Furthermore Foster felt that lack of American recognition " was a source of much embarrassment to the new Administration in Mexico." [39]

When also late in April he found himself sadly handicapped in adequately representing American interests Foster respectfully requested reconsideration of the administration's cautious recognition stand.[40] He noted that previously under Fish he had been given discretionary powers and that he had then suggested postponement of recognition until the " revolutionary government was supplanted by a constitutional form—in other words to await the result of elections to be held for Federal powers." He now asserted: " These events have occurred—almost uninterrupted peace has prevailed— for more than three months—and the authority of Diaz is everywhere recognized." He felt that Lerdo and Iglesias were unable to make headway against Diaz, that the latter was popular, had great military prestige, a large army, and " was regarded as a man of integrity, candor and good habits, qualities often wanting in a Mexican public man." He was certain that the choice in Mexico lay between Diaz and anarchy. The practical embarrassment of lack of recognition also weighed heavily in his reckoning. In referring to

---

[37] The Decree of the Chamber of Deputies May 2, 1877, declared " Citizen Porfirio Diaz . . . Constitutional President of the United Mexican States by virtue of having obtained in the elections lately held, an absolute majority of the votes cast by the total number of electors in the Republic. . . ." Foster to Evarts, May 7, 1877, Enclosure No. 4, Despatches MSS, LIX. For the report of Diaz' inaugural on May 5, see *ibid.*, Enclosure No. 5, *El Monitor Republicano* for May 6.

[38] Foster, I, 87.

[39] *Ibid.*, p. 88.

[40] Foster to Evarts, April 28, 1877 (Unofficial and Confidential), Despatches MSS, LIX.

the Diaz régime he said: "The government has been in peaceful control of the entire country for four months and is the only one to which I can look to protect American interests, redress wrongs or make reparation, yet I can hold no official relations with it and can do little to serve my Government or countrymen."

In regard to border complaints Foster felt that the Mexican Government "appears to be at last awakened to the pressing importance of giving attention to border troubles, a subject which I have omitted no opportunity to press upon its consideration." In line with his previous suggestion Diaz now seemed on the point of sending to the border "a prominent and prudent general with sufficient Federal force to compel obedience and cooperation on the part of local authorities."[41] This officer was to cooperate with General Ord. Foster also reported soon after Diaz' inauguration that he had been recognized by Germany, Spain, Salvador, and Guatemala.[42] Italy's recognition quickly followed. This gesture of good will on the part of the only other countries then accrediting diplomatic representatives to Mexico served to throw the American attitude into still bolder relief. Furthermore Diaz seemed to become progressively stronger instead of weaker, so that by midsummer his authority was recognized throughout Mexico including the state of Guerrero where Alvarez, former governor, had been in revolt. A general condition of peace existed in Mexico, administered by a firm hand backed by strong battalions, "with the exception of the occurrences on the Rio Grande frontier. . . ."[43]

Furthermore Diaz' growing strength and his apparent stability brought greater and greater impatience in Mexico with deferred recognition, an impatience which Foster shared.

---

[41] Foster to Fish, March 3, 1877, *ibid.*, LVIII. Foster to Evarts, May 28, 1877, *ibid.*, LIX.

[42] Foster to Evarts, June 1, 1877 (Telegram), *ibid*; Foster to Evarts, June 16, 1877, *ibid.*, See also Moore, *A Digest of International Law*, I, 148. England, France, and Austria had withdrawn their ministers as a protest against the execution of Maximilian and had not as yet in 1877 accredited new representatives.

[43] Foster to Evarts, July 30, 1877, *U. S. For. Rel. 1877*, p. 426.

" There is no concealment of the fact," he wrote late in the year, "that both with the public and in official circles there is growing restiveness and bitterness on account of this delay to obtain recognition." [44]   Meanwhile " satisfied that the Government at Washington misapprehended the situation in Mexico and the spirit of the Diaz Government," Foster was seeking leave to return to Washington and lay the case for recognition directly before the administration.[45]   He inferred from his instructions that recognition would not be extended until the questions between the two countries were settled. " In view of this phase of official matters and the present and prospective condition of this country I have, after mature consideration, concluded to suggest to you the propriety and desirability of directing me to visit Washington for a personal conference with you." [46]   This request was refused at first.   " While it might be desirable on some accounts," Secretary Evarts wrote, " that you should come to Washington in regard to Mexican matters, yet for reasons that will readily occur to you it is deemed to be inexpedient at present that you should leave your post.   Your action seems to have been in entire conformity with your instructions and it is not doubted that it will continue to be discreet, judicious, and energetic." [47]   A few months later at the request of the subcommittee of the House Foreign Affairs Committee this leave was finally granted as will be seen presently.

In spite of Foster's urgency, however, other forces and circumstances were at work which for more than a year after Hayes entered office and for eleven months of Diaz' constitutional tenure were to guide the American administration's hand away from recognition and toward a firmer policy on the border.   Most important, in all probability, was the feeling among many Americans, interested for various reasons,

[44] Foster to Evarts, November 13, 1877 (Unofficial), Despatches MSS, LX.

[45] Foster, I, 94.

[46] Foster to Evarts, September 10, 1877 (Personal), Despatches MSS, LX.

[47] Evarts to Foster, October 5, 1877 (Unofficial), Instructions MSS, XIX.

that the coincidence of a new administration in Washington and in Mexico City would be an opportune time for a thoroughgoing settlement of the old and troublesome question of the border by means of written guarantees as a prerequisite to recognition.

To that end Texan influence was especially strong with the Hayes Administration. Colonel Guy M. Bryan, prominent in the civil and military affairs of that state for many years, was a friend of long standing and a close adviser of President Hayes.[48] In his Autobiography he says:

> Shortly after President Hayes' inauguration he wrote me to come to Washington that I could "help him," which I did and was his guest at the White House for over three weeks—during the settlement of the Louisiana and South Carolina Legislative difficulties. When I left he told me that I had been of great service to him and that much of his kindly feeling toward the South was due to me.[49]

---

[48] The friendship between Hayes and Bryan began in Kenyon College in the late '30's and proved a lifelong attachment. E. W. Winkler (ed), "Bryan-Hayes Correspondence," *The Southwestern Historical Quarterly*, XXV, 99-102.

[49] Quoted in *ibid.*, pp. 101-102. Cited in Rippy, *The United States and Mexico*, p. 297, n. 3. As early as 1871 Bryan expressed himself as wanting "a free honest talk" with Hayes on conditions at the South, especially "the truth in regard to my own State." Bryan to Hayes, May 5, 1871, Hayes Papers MSS, Fremont, Ohio. Although a Democrat himself he expressed in 1876 the hope that Hayes would be nominated. ". . . he [Hayes] has of my own knowledge a personal interest in our State. He spent the winter and part of the spring of 1848 and '49 in Texas. Since then, he has kept up his interest in our state, and today has a better Texian library than many of our own educated citizens." Bryan to A. B. Norton, Galveston, Texas, April 18, 1876 (Copy), *ibid.* On the eve of Hayes' inauguration he urged Hayes to be "firm and true to your convictions (as expressed to me) and generous feelings in regard to these States. . . ." Bryan to Hayes, March 3, 1877, *ibid.* Bryan was evidently mentioned prominently for Minister to Mexico. The appointment was urged upon Hayes by Senator Maxey, of Texas, in a letter of April 1, 1877, *ibid.* Referring to this proposal Bryan said that he had been mentioned for several offices "without any agency of mine. . . . The last office named is that of Minister to Mexico. There is peculiar fitness in Texas having this appointment, could you properly tender this to me, permitting me to name the Secretary of the Legation, I would be strongly tempted to take it. I could not say this much to you however, had you not said I could 'aid you in public affairs.'" Bryan to Hayes, April 2, 1877, *ibid.* Bryan thus was being urged upon the administration as Minister to Mexico within a few weeks after it entered office. It is not clear from the Hayes' papers why the appointment did not take place. In a letter to Mrs. Hayes near the end of the

When he returned to Texas in an interview printed in the Galveston *News* Bryan said: " I believe that the interests of Texas will be more carefully looked after, better protected, and more summarily dealt with than heretofore." [50] It seems only reasonable to suppose, therefore, that the attitude of the Hayes Administration toward Diaz was partially molded at any rate by Bryan.

Also from many other Texans came demands for larger federal forces on the border and a firmer attitude toward Mexico in lieu of recognition. Governor Hubbard pictured the Diaz Government as weak and ineffective, questioned its good faith, and strenuously urged decisive action by the American Government on the border. In a ringing letter to President Hayes he said:

> The government and people of Texas have exhausted every means of communicating to the general government a correct knowledge of their grievances. They have forwarded individual petitions, memorials of the legislature and conventions, reports and depositions, and for years they have waited for action adequate to give the frontier of Western Texas protection. Up to the present there is insecurity to person and property on the Rio Grande. The only hope of protection and redress is in the general government. It would be folly to expect any change for the better, as far as the Mexican government is concerned.

He thought that the Mexican border population and officials were guilty of bad temper toward the United States and felt that Diaz' past record and present attitude afforded no indication of a desire " to enforce obedience to international laws and treaties from his border people." Even possible future peaceful relationships, he held, would not absolve the Diaz Government from reparations for the past.[51]

Hayes Administration Bryan wrote that he would support Hayes again for President. He thought in the main that the Hayes Administration had gained " the confidence of many good men in the South." He considered that Hayes had " much stronger claims " on the people of the Southern States than General Grant. Bryan to Mrs. Hayes, December 29, 1879, *ibid.* This last letter cited was written some time after the questions discussed in this chapter had been settled but is included as evidence of the close connection between Hayes and Bryan.

[50] *The Southwestern Historical Quarterly*, XXVII, 70.

[51] R. B. Hubbard (Governor of Texas), *Letter to President Hayes January 8, 1878,* p. 9. This letter was printed in Austin as a pamphlet. See also Hubbard to Evarts, October 10, 1877, 45th Cong., 1st sess., *H. Ex. Doc.* No. 13, p. 79.

At the same time members of both Houses of Congress from Texas were denouncing the Mexican Government for failure to protect the border, urging vigorous action on the administration, and using their votes on the pending army appropriation bill as a telling weapon. In an effective speech in the Senate in November 1877 Senator Maxey urged that a large part of the army, nominally 25,000 men, be sent to the border and that additional posts be added to the four already on the Rio Grande. Texas found herself almost helpless before the anarchy which had flared along the border for many years. The task called for permanent troops, not militia, who could not leave their civil pursuits for a great length of time without severe loss. The population of Texas was increasing at the rate of 300,000 persons a year, her wealth had doubled in three years. She did not want war but if it came it would be through no fault of hers.[52]

Further in a letter to General Sherman, Gustav Schleicher, representative from the 6th district of Texas including several border counties, pointed to the number of troops in and around Washington and in South Carolina and Louisiana when they were vitally needed on the Rio Grande and the Indian frontier.

If we say they are needed on the Indian frontier for the protection of our ever advancing and extending frontier and on the Rio Grande where we have a boundary in common with a turbulent and lawless country in which revolution is chronic and government powerless, we are answered that, however necessary they may be there, they are not used there but are where no troops are needed. The majority of Congress believe that it is the business of the States to protect life and property and preserve order in the States and not of the federal army.

We in Texas need the army, we have always found the great body of them as friends of our people and we are as proud of the achievements of some of the army officers as any class of men can be. General Mackenzie, General Ord and others are today the most popular and respected men in Texas. We are sincere in our wish to sustain the army and we feel the dilemma which makes us powerless and even makes our own support almost impossible. The only thing which would help us would be removal of the troops from those states.[53]

---

[52] S. B. Maxey, *Rio Grande Frontier* (Speech in the Senate November 14, 1877), pp. 15-17.

[53] Schleicher to Sherman, April 2, 1877, W. T. Sherman Papers MSS, XLVI.

That the administration, at least the War Department, felt this pressure of Texan representatives in Congress and realized their strategic position may be seen in an interesting letter from Sherman to Sheridan, commanding the Division of the Missouri of which the Department of Texas was a part. Sherman wrote:

> The Texas members [of the House] claim that we of the army owe them a debt of gratitude for saving the army bill this extra session, which is true, for the democrats had the power and were resolved to cut us down to 20,000 men this session, and to 17,000 in the regular term. There is some force in this claim, and unless we can reconcile the Texas democrats in the House, we will be slaughtered this winter. I. have called the attention of some democrats of the northwest to the danger of diminishing our force in Dakota, which will surely result in a renewal of the Sioux war and in checking the progress of settlements in that direction. Banning of Ohio and Bragg of Wisconsin (of the Committee) insist that we should strip Hancock's division (of the Atlantic) to strengthen the Rio Grande, but others agree with McCrary and the President that last summer's experience [54] demonstrates the absolute necessity of keeping the force, mostly artillery, where it is, nominally guarding the Lake, Atlantic and Gulf Coasts, but really for use in case of an organized resistance to the Revenue Laws, and labor mobs.

He added that there were eight regiments of cavalry in Sheridan's division—" four . . . north, four . . . south." " All I ask of you," he said, " is so to dispose of these four regiments as to fulfill the great purpose of preventing hostilities as well as to quiet the clamor of Texas people and Texas representatives." [55]

Meanwhile certain American business interests with a stake in Mexico seem to have girded themselves for the struggle over recognition and the vigorous use of United States troops on the border. Plumb apparently actively continued his opposition to recognition begun before the Grant Administration left office. Whether or not he approached the State Department as previously is not clear but a letter from Ord to Sherman in April 1877 would seem to indicate that his ideas were current among army men on the border. " I have a letter," Ord wrote, " from Mr. Plumb, copy enclosed—

---

[54] Sherman referred to the extensive railroad strikes and disorders in the United States during the summer of 1877.

[55] Sherman to Sheridan, November 29, 1877, W. T. Sherman Papers MSS, Letterbook.

while our officers on the frontier agree with him that Diaz partisans are likely to have a short career and a new revolution will probably soon unseat them, it is questionable if the Lerdo faction takes its place." [56]

Whatever Plumb's importance in the continuing recognition impasse, evidently the idea that he was exercising influence over the American Government unfavorable to the Diaz Administration gained considerable credence in Mexico. In June a startling article appeared in *El Diario Oficial* which claimed:

> Private advices from New York and Washington inform us that active labors have been commenced in the neighboring republic by Mr. Plumb representing railway companies and Mr. Lerdo de Tejada, to prevent the renewal of diplomatic relations between that government and our own, that by promises of grants of lands to railway construction companies, they have succeeded in interesting in their undertaking a group of adventurers and speculators; and that these combined labors have resulted in the American War Department (taking advantage of difficulties which both governments have always encountered in suppressing cattle stealing on the banks of the Bravo [Rio Grande] on account of the extent and unpopulated condition of the country) making hostile manifestations toward the Mexican republic in the order communicated to the Commander-in-Chief of the Army.[57]

Immediately Foster expressed the "surprise and deep regret" which such an article in the official government publication occasioned him. Vallarta replied that he did not know of such information having reached the Mexican Government and that he had not read the article. Foster thereupon left with the Foreign Office a copy of a memorandum outlining his conception of the negotiations on the question of crossing the boundary since Nelson's first proposal of January 4, 1871,[58] and asked to have it published in the *Diario Oficial* in order to clear up the position of the United States in regard to this crucial point. He also gave a copy to each

---

[56] Ord to Sherman, April 2, 1877, *ibid.*, XLVI. That Plumb also knew Sherman and had had "the pleasure of explaining" to him the affairs of his company in Mexico previously would appear from Plumb to Sherman, October 30, 1872, *ibid.*, XXXIV.

[57] Foster to Evarts, June 28, 1877, Despatches MSS, LIV, Enclosure No. 1, *El Diario Oficial*, June 21, 1877. The allusion to the War Department action has to do with the Order of June 1, 1877, to be considered later.

[58] For this memorandum see *ibid.*

member of the diplomatic corps for transmission to his home government. After a long cabinet discussion the Mexican Government decided to print a retraction and repudiation of the *Diario* article in the same journal. It was asserted: " We by no means think that Messrs. Lerdo and Plumb had a decisive influence in the determinations of the government of the United States no matter what efforts they may have made." No such supposition was thought to be warranted by the traditional attitude of the United States. As to the article itself there was declared to be " nothing in it which has an official origin." [59]

After some hesitation the Diaz Government sent Romero, Minister of the Treasury and especially friendly to the United States, to seek a compromise with Foster on the issue of publishing the memorandum. Romero pointed out the delicate position of the government in the matter before its own people. It could hardly afford to seem to be yielding to its much feared and in some quarters hated northern neighbor. He offered to print the substance of the memorandum without indicating its source. To this Foster agreed but the article did not appear. Romero called again the next day and said that Diaz had considered the matter from every side and now asked Foster to withdraw his request entirely. Foster finally yielded.[60] In explaining his action he wrote the Department that the Mexican Government was " chafing under the delay of recognition and smarting under what the public considers the hostile attitude of our government; and under the slightest pretext they may seek to make me the scapegoat of our government's supposed neglect and hostility. I therefore had to yield gracefully to the Diaz request." [61]

On the other side of the shield some American business interests seemed to favor recognition of Diaz. In a despatch of October 6, Foster noted the return to the United States of

---

[59] *Ibid.*, Enclosure No. 2.
[60] *Ibid.* See also Foster to Vallarta, July 23, 1877 (Unofficial), in answer to Memorandum Secretary of Foreign Relations, June 30, 1877, *Memo y notas*, pp. 17-18.
[61] Foster to Evarts, June 30, 1877 (Confidential), Despatches MSS, LIX.

General John B. Frisbie of California, described as "enthusiastic and . . . visionary" and actively interested in various railroad and colonization concessions in northern Mexico, "all of which will be materially promoted by recognition." Apparently he had made an impression on the State Department, for he had been commended to Foster's attention by the Department in a confidential letter of May 5 of which more will be said later.[62]

At all events no matter how great or small the influence of American business interests on the Mexican policy of the Hayes Administration their activities struck a responsive chord of suspicion in the Mexican breast. The period was a difficult one—an era of transition from the "old Mexico . . . pre-eminently a country of trails and primitive roads; . . . its transportation agencies . . . the Indian porter, the pack animal, and the two-wheeled cart," [63] to the new Mexico of modern railroad and mine. The old spirit gave way grudgingly, especially when faced by the prospect of railroads and mineral wealth exploited largely by American capital and of the weaker nation bound closely to its stronger neighbor by strategic links of steel penetrating to the heart of the home land.[64] Gradually the new forces triumphed [65] but

---

[62] Foster to Evarts, October 6, 1877 (Confidential), *ibid.*, LX.

[63] Powell, p. 91.

[64] *Ibid.*, pp. 103-104. For the slow progress of railroad development in Mexico against popular and governmental suspicion and inertia, disorder, lack of capital, difficult terrain, and other handicaps see *ibid.*, pp. 96-106. See also Foster, I, 26-27, 71. So strong were these forces that before 1874 only one railroad had been built, that from Mexico City to Vera Cruz, a distance with branches of about 292 miles. Even this distance required about 20 years in the building due to the disturbed state of the country and the poverty of its treasury. Powell, pp. 99 ff. It was then largely built with British capital. See also for Mexican difficulties in railroad building Foster to Evarts, August 3, 1877, *U S. For. Rel. 1877*, pp. 426-429; W. Hunter to Foster, December 20, 1873, John W. Foster Papers MSS.

[65] Plumb thought "it is truly astonishing to see the interest . . . that has been awakened in this country with regard to the subject of material improvements." Plumb to Barhyde, December 26, 1872, Plumb Papers MSS, XII. The new point of view was forcefully expressed in the *Revolución Económica*, August 24, 1876, one of "the most fair spoken and dignified" opposition papers under Lerdo, according to Richardson. "Politically we have nothing but mis-government. . . . We have no credit, we have no finances,

the first important concession to American railroad interests had not come until 1874 when Plumb secured his contract as previously noted. This concession was "bitterly opposed" in the Mexican Congress on the ground that it was unsafe to allow an American company to build a railroad in Mexico and dangerous to allow extensions of the railroad system of the United States into that country since it might very well be used for another invasion.[66]

To this infiltration of American capital were added many other causes for alarm in the Mexican mind. Hayes found his recognition and border policies regarded with all the cumulative force of years of distrust. This feeling, deeply rooted in the past and inflamed by every aggressive American action, real or fancied, crystallized in a fear of imminent American expansion into Mexico. Supposed Texan designs were a particular object of suspicion. In 1874 *El Diario Oficial* had warned that: "The Government should not be ignorant that the authorities of Texas are hostile to Mexico, as they represent the Democratic party of the South whose annexation tendencies are well known."[67] The Texan Congressman, Schleicher, was regarded even by the liberal Romero as one of the greatest forces for misunderstanding between the two countries from 1876-1878.[68] This seems also

---

and the country being disorganized, needs strong government; strong not only with bayonets, but with credit through its resources, through the integrity of its material and moral power. We need work, and we cannot obtain it so long as the government does not give absolute guarantee for the investment of capital . . .; we need easy and cheap means of communication and consequently money at a low rate, and illy can this be secured when, instead of procuring an influx of capital, an erroneous and heedless policy causes it to flee the country." Richardson to Fish, August 26, 1876, Enclosure No. 2, Despatches MSS, LVII.

[66] Foster, I, 110.

[67] Foster to Fish, September 19, 1874, Enclosure No. 1, *El Diario Oficial*, September 16, 1874, Despatches MSS, LII.

[68] Romero, *Mexico and the United States*, I, 467. Romero served successively as Secretary of the Mexican Legation in Washington, Chargé d'Affaires, and Minister from December 1859 to July 1868. He knew intimately Lincoln, Seward, Grant, and other leaders of the period in American politics, married an American, and when he returned to his own country he became a great force for liberalism and tolerance in the relations between the two countries. In 1882 he returned as Minister to the United States and served for many years. *Ibid.*, pp. iii-iv.

to have been somewhat the point of view of the Mexican Minister to the United States. In a memorandum of June 7, 1877, the Schleicher resolution on crossing was said to be "... *característico de las intrigas empleadas para agitar cuestiones respecto a la frontera y en contra de México."* [69]

Rumors had been rife in Mexico for years that various elements in the United States were pressing for expansion southward and they accounted for the sensitiveness and fear expressed in Mariscal's *"intrigas."* American newspapers and remarks of American public and business men were anxiously scanned, and the reaction to any hint of aggression, whether real or imagined, was violent. *El Diario Oficial* of September 30, 1874, had spoken indignantly of an article published some months previously in the San Francisco *Commercial Herald* in which the Mexican Government was alleged to have opened negotiations to cede territory to the United States. The article, according to *El Diario Oficial,* had been copied by British and European papers with variations on the theme of Mexican financial exhaustion.[70] The report was emphatically denied, as had been a previous rumor to the same effect in August. Such a cession had always been regarded with indignation by Mexico and "today the public man who should propose such a thing would not even be judged as a criminal: we should hand him over to the medical fraternity as a case of extreme lunacy." [71] Foster, in transmitting these comments to the State Department, thought them of great significance as appearing in an official publication.

Again early in 1876 *El Diario Oficial* had denied the "ridiculous reports disseminated by American speculators, and by certain enemies of the administration, in regard to secret treaties between the governments of Mexico and the United States, in order to cede to the latter nation some part of the

[69] Memorandum Mariscal, Mexican Minister to the United States, June 7, 1877. *Cuestión americana—negocios diplomáticos con los Estados Unidos—notas y documentos relativos* (edición oficial), p. 141.

[70] Foster to Fish, October 2, 1874, Enclosure No. 1, *El Diario Oficial,* September 30, 1874, Despatches MSS, LII.

[71] *Ibid., El Diario Oficial,* August 16, 1874.

national territory." Even if President Lerdo had power to do so, " never in any case, nor for any motive, would he cede one single jot of native soil in exchange for the greatest treasures of the world." The government, it was said, had been forced to telegraph a denial to the Mexican consul in San Francisco because the papers there had all published reports of such a proposed cession.[72] These reports, added to proposed American crossing of the border during the last year of the Grant Administration and aggressive efforts of American business interests, had wrought Mexican public opinion to a high pitch. Romero, however, had urged calmness, stating his belief that since the Civil War the United States had been opposed to expansion.[73] *La Revista Universal* also cited the defeat of the Santo Domingo annexation treaty and the pro- posed reciprocity treaty with the Sandwich Islands as evi- dences of a new non-expansionist policy on the part of the United States.[74]

Thus the Hayes Administration, troubled enough in all conscience at home, fell heir to dark and deep-seated suspi- cions of American designs in Mexico. Its failure to extend recognition and the firm military policy soon adopted fanned the embers into flame. *El Monitor Republicano* intimated that a war was desired to intrench the American adminis- tration at home. A war with Mexico would fit ideally into this purpose, it was feared. The South was said to favor annexation of all or part of Mexico for trade and commercial reasons but the North was thought to oppose. In any case Mexico would fight proudly, if war came, and with good effect for " a nation which struggles for its independence is invincible." [75] *El Siglo Diez y Nueve* gravely discussed reports of the attitude of the new American administration

---

[72] Foster to Fish, February 7, 1876, Enclosure No. 1, *El Diario Oficial*, February 6, 1876, *ibid.*, LV.
[73] Foster to Fish, May 4, 1876, Enclosure No. 4, statement by Matias Romero in *The Two Republics*, May 1, 1876, Despatches MSS, LVI.
[74] *Ibid.*, *La Revista Universal*, May 4, 1876, Enclosure No. 7, *ibid.*
[75] Foster to Evarts, March 19, 1877, Enclosure No. 2, *El Monitor Republicano*, March 17, 1877, *ibid.*, LVIII.

but felt sure that the good sense of the United States would prevent the attempt to establish a protectorate.[76]

So persistent were these rumors of American aggression, circulated in both countries, that Foster took cognizance of them in an "Unofficial and Confidential" despatch. He said:

I do not know whether the question often discussed in the American newspapers of a protectorate over this country has any support in the councils of President Hayes; but in the absence of all knowledge on this point, I venture the suggestion that the only pressure or influence we ought at present to exert in the internal affairs of this country is that which will secure the peace and good order of our frontier and the protection of American citizens and their interests in this Republic.[77]

However, the reports persisted, still further estranging unofficial relations between the two governments and weakening the forces toward official recognition. Apparently there seemed to be basis in fact for some of these stories. The American Legation came into possession of a letter from J. B. Bauman to one Antonio D. Richards in Mexico. It would seem that both men were interested in obtaining from Diaz railroad concessions in Mexico. Bauman said that he understood Lerdo was actively plotting in New York for a return to Mexico and to that end was making flattering offers to investors. Lerdo was to be thwarted if possible. He suggested that Richards or some other "reliable confidential agent" be sent to the United States. There he was to propose cession of a "certain portion of northern Mexico for the sum of $110,000,000," of which the United States was to hold back enough to settle American claims and was to "make a guarantee to Diaz of permanent government." Confidently he added: ". . . I have good reasons to believe that such a treaty could be effected in 90 days, and that perhaps I could receive the appointment as special agent or Minister Resident at Mexico to consummate matters." Richards was requested to "confer with President Diaz and let me hear from you immediately." [78]

[76] *Ibid., El Siglo Diez y Nueve*, March 22, 1877, *ibid.*
[77] Foster to Evarts, April 28, 1877 (Unofficial and Confidential), *ibid.*, LIX.
[78] J. B. Bauman to Antonio D. Richards, May 4, 1877, bound in Despatches MSS, LX, after No. 583.

In the same vein Foster reported in July that N. S. Reneau, another American business man, had approached Diaz and his Cabinet seeking a confirmation of an old Juárez railroad concession. Reneau informed the president and cabinet, grandiloquently, that he had special relations with the State Department and that recognition would be withheld until this old claim was revalidated. "It is hardly necessary," Foster added, "to say that most of the persons, who visit Mexico having private or corporate business [interests] view the existing government much from the standpoint of their interest or success." The situation was intensely unfortunate, Foster thought, as it prejudiced Mexican officials against the United States. He knew that the Department was not influenced in this way but Mexican officials did not.[79] In the same despatch Foster complained of articles appearing in the New York *Herald,* written by a Cincinnati correspondent. The United States, so the articles asserted, was negotiating with Mexico for the annexation of the upper five states of Mexico. The correspondent went so far as to give the names of the American and Mexican commissioners and a portion of the correspondence of the American Commissioners.[80] Later Foster observed quite rightly apparently: "There is no country in the world probably where political views are modified so much by business interests as in Mexico."[81]

To these reports of efforts of American business men to gain territory in northern Mexico must be added the pressure of a certain section of American opinion in favor of strategic expansion. For some time possible occupation of Mexican soil for the protection of the border had evidently been considered in American official circles. Such a step would naturally appear to Mexican eyes as the beginning of permanent expansion. Two years previously Fish had instructed Foster as follows:

I am aware of no purpose here of acquiring territory on that frontier. If, however, as has been suggested to us, that government

---

[79] Foster to Evarts, July 30, 1877 (Unofficial), *ibid.*
[80] *Ibid.*
[81] Foster to Evarts, October 6, 1877, *ibid.,* LXII.

is embarrassed by the risk of desertion in sending a regular force to that quarter it might not be indisposed to allow United States troops to cross and temporarily occupy territory whence the raiders are in the habit of coming. The tract for such occupation might be embraced in a line drawn from Matamoras to Laredo. You will consequently sound the Minister of Foreign Affairs on this point and report the result.[82]

It would seem that Ord came definitely to this point of view in his private correspondence with his old comrade-in-arms and commander, Sherman. In his official reports he dealt tactfully with the subject or maintained silence, but in his private letters to Sherman he unburdened his soul. That Ord was urging actively invasion of northern Mexico would appear from a letter written him by Sherman in November 1876, couched in the moderate terms in which the latter usually considered Ord's propositions. Sherman wrote:

I agree with you perfectly that we ought to declare with an emphasis that could not be questioned that the United States has no intention, now or in the future, to take any more Mexican Territory, and to encourage the Mexicans to cultivate anything, preferably sugar and coffee, on the other side of the Rio Grande. But there is no chance of our Government making any such promise. It would be a mere naked assertion of one executive to be denied by the next; or resolution of one Congress which cannot bind another. Now our business as soldiers is to take things as they are, to be sure of the facts, and to maintain peace. We must respect international law, and only hold communication with the Government of Mexico through our State Department. To invade Coahuila and hold it till relieved by Mexican troops would be war, and no amount of provocation or invitation could justify it. Mexico might well answer, "You now hold the state of Coahuila, keep it and pay us damages." Our Government would on your own theory of non-interference be compelled to disown your acts; and leave you personally and officially in a close place.[83]

As was to be expected, considering Ord's headstrong temperament, such advice fell on unheeding ears. In a letter written early in 1877 he insisted still more strongly on occupation of northern Mexico, and incidentally revealed the keen interest of high army officers in politics when a reduction in the size of the army is pending.

I must confess that I don't see anything except good to the army—that can result from the anarchy and demoralization among

[82] Fish to Foster, May 20, 1875, Instructions MSS, XIX.
[83] Sherman to Ord, November 2, 1876, W. T. Sherman Papers MSS, Letterbook.

the Mexican border states—this town has dozens of intelligent and gentlemanly foreigners—English, German, and Scotch,—who have been doing business in Mexico and have been driven away—and they *all* say that the country never was in such bad hands, so deplorable a condition—that all the best men are longing for Americans to take hold—that unless we do so soon there will hardly be the Trails left—this State and frontier has grown in importance wonderfully in the last two years. Bragg told me that the year I came in—250,000 people came into it—this year there will be an emigration of at least 300,000—and by the next presidential election the population will be nearly or quite two millions. . . . If the President showed a disposition to use the troops to protect and pacify the contiguous Mexican states which our interest calls for—he would secure a majority of the Southern democrats to vote *no reduction* of the army—just let him feel the public pulse on this question—there need be no war—there *was* no necessity for the last Mexican war—We *had* both Texas and California and Mexico couldn't and didn't attempt to invade either—Until our army showed itself on the Rio Grande and they feared invasion— they did not raise an army themselves—I have given up all hopes that there are loyal men of sense enough in Mexico to keep it together—or to keep its bandits from plundering wherever *stock are seen running at large*—now that being the case *what are we to do*. I make a plain, *honest* appeal to the Secretary of State in a letter today—*do* secure for its serious consideration.[84]

Rightly or wrongly the Hayes Administration was suspected of lending a ready ear to these annexation and expansion plans. In a Fourth of July speech at Woodstock, Connecticut, James G. Blaine, out of sympathy with many of the administration's policies, and feeling personally abused, adroitly disparaged its intentions toward Mexico. Speaking of the Order of June 1 to permit close pursuit across the border he said: " As a comforting and consolatory addendum to the whole scheme we are kindly assured that in no event shall any Mexican territory be acquired or annexed to the United States. As in many cases of similar design and movement, the most important feature may be that which is specially disavowed." [85]

Later in his *Memoirs* Foster recorded evidence of steadily growing Mexican distrust during this period and a widespread belief that the United States was again inflamed by a desire to absorb Mexico. He felt that " every positive act on our part was interpreted as a deliberate plan to provoke a con-

[84] Ord to Sherman, April 2, 1877, *ibid.*, XLVI.
[85] Charles R. Williams, *The Life of Rutherford Birchard Hayes*, II, 210.

flict and acquire territory." [86] A case in point involved General Frisbie already mentioned. Frisbie and his father-in-law, Vallejo, a Spanish landholder of prominence in California, went to Washington early in the Hayes Administration and laid before Evarts and others prominent in the administration a plan for putting pressure to bear on Mexico to force hostilities or the sale of some of the northern states of Mexico. Diaz was thought to be so hard pushed financially that he would consent rather than risk war with the United States and possible overthrow by the Lerdists. Thereupon the two audacious adventurers suggested their choice by the State Department as agents to bring about the purchase. Foster held that later they actually had been " empowered in a purely unofficial way to approach Diaz on the subject. There never was the remotest chance of success, but even the ghost of a chance was destroyed by their own conduct." Vallejo and Frisbie apparently were so elated by their new responsibility that they became garrulous. An ever watchful Washington correspondent eagerly published the main outline of their plan, the news sped to Mexico, and when they reached the latter country they found themselves confronted with a refusal by the Diaz Government to countenance their mission.[87] But the mischief was done so far as Mexican susceptibilities were concerned and the American Government was held responsible for encouraging such dubious, not to say dangerous, characters.

There is no doubt [Foster thought further] . . . that there had been a change of policy as to recognition after the inauguration of President Hayes, and there was some foundation for . . . [the] charge that a scheme had been formed to bring on a war through the Texas troubles. Some months later when I visited Washington I was informed on good authority that certain gentlemen, whose names were given me and who were specially interested in the success of the Administration of President Hayes, had conceived the idea that, in view of the tension in the public mind created by partisans of Mr. Tilden and of the disturbed condition of affairs in the Southern States, it would divert attention from pending issues and tend greatly to consolidate the new Administration, if a war could be brought on with Mexico and another slice of its territory added to the Union.

[86] Foster, I, 94.
[87] *Ibid.*, pp. 92-93.

The change of policy as to recognition of the Diaz Government
and the vigorous policy as to the Rio Grande frontier indicated in
the order of June 1, authorizing the crossing into Mexico of American
troops, may be explained by the existence of such a scheme.[88]

A summary of the evidence already presented would therefore seem to justify certain conclusions: (1) that Foster urged
on the State Department the recognition of Diaz before the
latter's inauguration as constitutional president in May 1877,
and continued his pleas for nearly a year; (2) that some
American business interests favored the recognition of Diaz;
(3) that others worked against recognition; (4) that some
of these interests were seeking annexation of parts of northern
Mexico; (5) that the Mexican Government suspected the

---

[88] *Ibid.*, p. 92.   Foster in his *Memoirs*, written years after the
event, seems much more sweeping in his criticism of the administration's Mexican policy than at the time.   Writing to President Hayes from Mexico City, December 24, 1877, he said: "I
cannot refrain from expressing to you the great pleasure I have
had in reading your Annual Message to Congress, which has just
reached us.   Your reference to the Mexican question is temperate and judicious, and cannot fail to have a favorable reception
here, where a more severe treatment of the matter was feared."
Hayes Papers MSS, Fremont, Ohio.   So far as Bryan's purported
pro-Texas influence is concerned, apparently so strong with Hayes,
it would seem to have been distinctly peaceful as regards Mexico.
He said: "Efforts will be made to drag you into a War with
Mexico *avoid it if you can*.   We want no more territory and semi-
barbarians *now*.   We have enough of both."   Bryan to Hayes,
October 26, 1877 (Confidential), Hayes Papers MSS.   A few months
later he wrote even more strongly in the same vein: "In consequence of representations said to have been made to the authorities
at Washington, I am induced to write you what I believe to be
the true feelings of nineteen-twentieths of the people of Texas in
regard to *war with Mexico*.   They do not want war with that
country.   Some persons who think the United States should acquire
more territory, and some who are exasperated or who have suffered
from raids of Mexicans and Indians from Mexico, may desire war.
What Texas does want is the establishment of friendly relations
with Mexico through railroads and steamboats, giving her citizens our products and receiving in return theirs.   This course will
do more to stop raids, and build up Mexico, and to make her what
we want her to be—*a good neighbor*, than any other.   Railroads
will always enable the government to protect the coast and Mexican
border of Texas promptly and effectually in all cases present and
future.   I think now as I did when in Washington that the best
course for our government to pursue to prevent raids, is to follow
raiders into Mexico, catch and punish them until Mexico can control her Mexican raiders, if war follows this course and it cannot be prevented, *then let it come*."   Bryan to Hayes, August
24, 1878 (Private, Executive Mansion Files folder), Hayes Papers
MSS.

annexationists of having influence in the counsels of the
Hayes Administration; (6) that Ord on the border was
urging in letters to Sherman and Evarts the necessity of
occupying strategic parts of northern Mexico; (7) that members of Congress from Texas and other Texans, in at least one
case close to President Hayes, by the weight of political pressure and personal advice sought to convince the administration of two alleged main factors in the situation: viz., (a)
that Diaz was weak and incapable of preserving order on the
border—hence not worthy of recognition, (b) that such
being the case the United States should adopt a firm military
policy on its own account; and finally (8) that political
gossip in Washington accused the Hayes Administration of
seeking to force Diaz into war to strengthen its own position
at home.

All of this evidence must be used with care when the causes
of the policy adopted by Hayes are sought. The period was
particularly stormy in both countries and extreme charges
are apt to be made at such a time. Furthermore Foster's
criticisms may have been due to the fact that his government differed with him on the question of recognition. It is
extremely difficult to determine just what were the moti-
vating forces in the minds of President Hayes and Secretaries
Evarts and McCrary. In an important memorandum for a
cabinet meeting which is undated, but which from the text
was evidently written during the summer of 1877, President
Hayes said: " Should Diaz be recognized as Prest of Mexico?
Shall we determine it now or let Mexico hang by her eyelids
during August. There is no good reason why we should not
recognize M. when we are ready. Lerdo has no force—
Escobedo is under bonds not to make war—this gives him a
moral reason for not going on." [89] This would seem to indicate that eight months before recognition Hayes was strongly
favorable personally toward this course. The delay is hard
to explain except in terms of the forces already cited. But
whatever the arguments brought to bear on the Hayes Administration and their effect two facts remain. The first of

[89] Cabinet Notes, *ibid.*

these is that the administration *did* adopt a vigorous new military policy on the border; the second is that recognition *was* delayed for many months.

Turning first of all to the Hayes military policy on the border it seems plain that a determination to deal vigorously with the situation developed within a few weeks after his inauguration.   Lawless conditions along the international line and Diaz' alleged failure to remedy them may have been the principal reasons for this new determination.   What seems more likely is that a combination of forces, first of all a sincere feeling of the seriousness of the situation and secondly pressure by Texans, American business interests, and army men led to the Order of June 1.   The immediately decisive factor, in all probability, was a series of strong statements by army officers concerning continued disorder.   Shafter reported early in March that not "the slightest attempt" was being made by Mexican authorities to prevent Indians who had raided in the United States from "finding a refuge in the towns when pursued, and a market for their stolen plunder at all times."   He asserted:

> To effectually put a stop to the Indian raids from Mexico, it will be necessary to do all scouting for Indians on the Mexican side of the Rio Grande. . . .   Full authority to operate in Mexico as we choose is the only way in which life and property can be made secure on this frontier.   It is an incontrovertible fact that all the raids are made from Mexico to this side, and none from this to Mexico, and the people who are being robbed and murdered are American citizens.

Sheridan forwarded this report to Washington with the recommendation that "the Mexican Government be compelled to prevent those hostile incursions." [90]

Marked influence of these reports upon the State Department may be seen in Evarts' instructions of March 31.   He wrote:

> . . . that the only way to check these atrocities is to follow the delinquents into Mexico and there attack them in their lairs, is probably well founded.   As the authorities of that country

---

[90] Shafter Commanding District of Nueces to Assistant Adjutant General Department of Texas March 9, 1877, 45th Cong., 1st sess., *H. Ex. Doc.* No. 13, p. 135.   See also endorsement by Sheridan, March 19, 1877, *ibid.*, p. 136.

seem to be unable or unwilling to check the depredations, the President may soon have to take into serious consideration the expedience of acting pursuant to Colonel Shafter's opinion. Undoubtedly it would be preferable to enter Mexican territory for the purpose indicated with the consent or with the acquiescence of the government of that Republic. If, however, these should be refused and the outrages persisted in, this government may deem itself warranted in punishing wrongdoers wherever they may be found.

It may not be amiss for you informally to intimate these views to persons important in the capital.[91]

In line with his instructions Foster, in reporting the murder of seventeen Americans in the previous months by Indians said to be from Mexico, called Vallarta's attention to Shafter's recommendation. This recommendation, Foster said, would have to be taken into consideration by the United States.[92] He also reiterated the need for an able general and a larger Mexican force on the border. General Blanco had been sent to Matamoras on a political mission but no force had accompanied him and Governor Canales of Tamaulipas refused to recognize Blanco's authority, as did many other Mexican local officials. Vallarta replied that it was important to have an agreement for joint action of troops but lack of official relations made this difficult. He " was quite earnest in impressing upon me the desirability in this connection of restoring official relations between the two countries " and as a prelude to the settlement of other questions not mentioned in the despatch.[93] Foster thought from the conversation that the Diaz Government when recognized might agree to some mutual arrangement for crossing the boundary in pursuit of raiders, probably not a treaty but an agreement between the commanders on the border with the approval of both governments. Foreign troops could come into Mexico according to the Mexican constitution only by permission of Congress. Mexican pride made such permission impossible but a military understanding between commanders with the approval of the two governments might possibly be concluded.[94]

---

[91] Evarts to Foster, March 31, 1877, Instructions MSS, XIX.

[92] Foster Memorandum to Minister of Foreign Affairs, June 23, 1877, *Memo y notas*, pp. 3-4.

[93] Foster to Evarts, April 24, 1877, Despatches MSS, LIX.

[94] *Ibid.* This part of the despatch is omitted in *U. S. For. Rel. 1877.*

Referring to his instructions of May 4, 1875, Foster said that they " contemplated such an arrangement." He went on :

Should the President and you consider it desirable to effect an arrangement of this character, I have respectfully to request specific instructions to be acted upon when the question of recognition is disposed of. Although the condition of affairs on the frontier and in different Mexican authorities may justify instructions to the military to cross the Rio Grande in pursuit of marauders I consider it as much more preferable *to save the national pride of this people by the understanding I suggest.*[95]

Soon thereafter more raids by Mexicans and Indians into Texas having taken place, one involving a theft of two hundred head of cattle,[96] Evarts again threatened official crossing if the Mexican Government did not aid in restraining the raiders.

It is apprehended that the Mexican Government is not well aware that although for a heavy pecuniary consideration,[97] it has released the United States from obligations in respect to predatory incursions of Indians from this country into Mexico, obligations . . . [of] that government in respect to similar marauders from that country into the United States are entire as provided for both by public law and by treaty. The duty of that government, therefore, at least to aid in restraining its savages from depredations upon us seems to be clear. If this duty shall continue to be neglected, we may be compelled in self-defense to disregard the boundary in seeking for and punishing those bandits.

Foster was ordered to make " unofficial representations to this effect." [98]

These instructions very evidently left the door open to further unofficial, diplomatic discussion of the question of raiding and proposed methods of prevention. But three days later, before Foster could possibly receive them, let alone take up the matter anew with the Mexican Foreign Office, the Secretary of War in Washington cut the Gordion knot by issuing the famous Order of June 1, to General Sherman.

[95] *Ibid.,* Despatches MSS, LIX.
[96] Evarts to Foster, May 28, 1877, 45th Cong., 1st sess., *H. Ex. Doc.* No. 13, p. 12.
[97] See Treaty of 1853, William M. Malloy (ed.), *Treaties, Conventions . . . between the United States and Other Powers,* I, 1122-1123.
[98] Evarts to Foster, May 28, 1877, Instructions MSS, XIX.

After referring to a report by Shafter on "recent raids" into Texas McCrary said:

The President desires that the utmost vigilance on the part of the military forces in Texas be exercised for the suppression of these raids. It is very desirable that efforts to this end, in so far at least as they necessarily involve operations on both sides of the border, be made with the cooperation of the Mexican authorities; and you will instruct General Ord, commanding in Texas, to invite such cooperation on the part of the local Mexican authorities, and to inform them that while the President is anxious to avoid giving offense to Mexico, he is nevertheless convinced that the invasion of our territory by armed and organized bodies of thieves and robbers to prey upon our citizens should not longer be endured.

General Ord will at once notify the Mexican authorities along the Texas border of the great desire of the President to unite with them in efforts to suppress this long continued lawlessness. At the same time he will inform those authorities that if the Government of Mexico shall continue to neglect the duty of suppressing these outrages, that duty will devolve upon this government, and will be performed, even if its performance should render necessary the occasional crossing of the border by our troops. You will, therefore, direct General Ord that in case the lawless incursions continue he will be at liberty, in the use of his own discretion, when in pursuit of a band of marauders and when his troops are either in sight of them or upon a fresh trail, to follow them across the Rio Grande, and to overtake and punish them, as well as retake stolen property taken from our citizens and found in their hands on the Mexican side of the line.[99]

This order, although couched in friendly phrases and inviting cooperation by the Mexican military in case the raids continued, caused an extraordinary outburst of rage in Mexico. As a matter of fact the order really represented a distinct departure in American policy, as the Mexicans were quick to see. Efforts had at various times been made to effect a crossing agreement and threats of such an order had been conveyed to Mexico through diplomatic channels on several occasions but it had never actually been given. Previously, crossings had been made under orders of local military commanders on the border. Late in 1875 Ord, as commander of the Department of Texas, had begun giving orders for crossing and assuming responsibility in specific instances. The War Department had extended tacit consent for such crossings by its silence but never before had it given official

[99] Evarts to Foster, June 4, 1877, Enclosure Secretary of War to General Sherman June 1, 1877, 45th Cong., 1st sess., *H. Ex. Doc.* No. 13, pp. 14-15.

permission for crossing. Another feature which seemed to hold important possibilities was the fact that the matter of crossing was left to the discretion of General Ord who has been shown to have been anxious to occupy portions of northern Mexico in an effort to cope with lawlessness on the border.

In any case Mexican anger reached white heat. Newspapers of various points of view united in a great cry of protest against what was regarded as potential invasion of Mexico. *La Epoca,* a Diaz paper, thought that "neither reason nor right" was on the side of the United States. The latter had not been able to prevent marauding into Mexico and it was hoped that the American sense of justice and dignity would prevent the United States' making similar requirements of Mexico. Diaz forces should "pursue to the death" marauders from Mexico into the United States but should "resist by force the aggression of force." [100]

El Federalista, Lerdo supporter, called the Order of June 1 "a serious offense to the national dignity and to the sovereignty and independence of Mexico." The Order was declared to be unlawful because "an armed invasion of foreign territory is equivalent to a declaration of war." Mexican "patriotism . . . and . . . love of country" have been awakened and if "fate should reserve new trials for the national patriotism . . . we would not be Diaz men, we would be Mexicans; and it would be sufficient to see Mexico raise the national banner in front of the foreigner, for us to rally round him in union with all those who form the Lerdist party. In the present danger to the country we would recognize no insignia but that of Mexico." [101]

El Pájaro Verde, a Conservative Catholic organ, thought the Mexican people undivided by party on this question, presenting "a spectacle at once grand, imposing, worthy in every way of praise, consideration, and respect." The question was considered as one involving "the integrity of Mexi-

---

[100] Foster to Evarts, June 22, 1877, Enclosure No. 1, Despatches MSS, LIX. No dates are given on Enclosures in this Despatch.
[101] *Ibid.,* Enclosure No. 2.

can territory, respect to its flag." The action of the United States was called "cowardly" and in violation of treaties. It was described as "a country of insatiable tradesmen" trying to be "the arbitrator of the destinies of the world." The gauntlet had been cast down to all Latin America, it was asserted, and although poor and without a navy and inadequately prepared in other directions Mexico would pursue, if need be, a guerilla warfare.[102] Another opposition paper, *El Monitor Republicano,* characterized the Order as "a formidable threat of the nation that not without reason had been called the American colossus." Now was the time for every Mexican loyal spirit to burn with "the holy passion called patriotism." President Hayes was thought to be seeking to distract American public opinion from the circumstances of his own election. All Mexico must rally, forgetting faction and party, in the face of "the wounded national dignity."[103]

El Colonia Española, a Spanish journal of Mexico City, thought that the question involved the fundamental clash between two races, not one of the "family quarrels" which had marred the relations between Mexico and Spain. Mexico could put two million men on the battlefield and the paper proposed to publish a series of articles on guerilla tactics "which will be very useful to the people."[104] Still another point of view was expressed by *El Siglo XIX,* independent politically. The situation might prove a blessing in disguise so far as Mexico was concerned. The "sacred fire of patriotism" lighted by the American action would be "a blessed virtue" if it suppressed "fratricidal struggle" within the country.[105] *El Monitor Constitucional,* another supporter of the Diaz régime, thought that the Order "deeply affects our sovereignty and international rights." It urged, however, that the press "act with prudence" and praised what it considered "the temperance and moderation" of the Mexican Government in the matter. In defense of this point of view it was thought doubtful if the Order would be carried out

---

[102] *Ibid.,* Enclosure No. 3.
[103] *Ibid.,* Enclosure No. 4.
[104] *Ibid.,* Enclosure No. 5.
[105] *Ibid.,* Enclosure No. 7.

" without previous and long consideration on the part of the government at Washington and we believe with reason that the orders to General Ord will be withdrawn." [106]   On the other hand *The Two Republics,* an American newspaper of Mexico City, asserted that the American Government was only performing an obvious duty to its citizens " after many years of forbearance." Ord was authorized to confer with the Mexican authorities on the best methods of suppressing the raids and to invite their cooperation in this effort. Only in case such cooperation were not forthcoming were American federal forces to cross in pursuit of raiders. In such case raiders alone were to be attacked and not innocent Mexican inhabitants.[107]

So far as official Mexico was concerned the protest seems to have been equally resentful. Mariscal, minister of the Lerdo Government in the United States, thought the Order adopted after border depredations had begun to decline. He repeated the old arguments that the depredations were mutual, the raids being carried out in both directions, often by persons of doubtful nationality.[108] Vallarta " inveighed bitterly against the military Order of June 1, declaring that it had disregarded all the rules of international law and the practice of civilized nations, and treated the Mexicans as Kaffirs of Africa." The Minister of Foreign Affairs asserted vehemently that a declaration of war would have been more considerate. No government in Mexico could survive against popular indignation, he asserted, if it did not repel invasion by force of arms.[109] In a memorandum of June 30, Vallarta said that the government of Mexico " has understood the significance and appreciates the consequences of the instructions given to General Ord." The fact that Ord's authorization for crossing was only conditional " does not alter its offensive character toward Mexico." For in the first place fulfillment

---

[106] *Ibid.,* Enclosure No. 8.

[107] *Ibid.,* Enclosure No. 6.

[108] Mariscal to Evarts, June 7, 1877, Notes from the Mexican Legation MSS, XXIV.

[109] Foster, I, 91; Foster to Evarts, June 20, 1877, *U. S. For. Rel. 1877,* p. 411.

of the order was left to the discretion of Ord. Furthermore Mexico could never authorize even conditional invasion of her territory. Thirdly it was held that the very wording of the Order carried recognition of an offense to Mexico in the phrase " while the President is anxious to avoid giving offense to Mexico he is nevertheless convinced that the invasions . . . should be no longer tolerated." [110] In another sharp note from the Mexican Legation De Cuellar claimed: " For some years past invasions of United States forces have been succeeding each other constantly assuming graver character." He held that silence of the United States gave assent to the claim of Governor Coke of Texas that Texas troops were justified in invading Mexico since they were doing the work which should be done by American federal troops.[111]

This excited state of the Mexican spirit, in Foster's opinion, illustrated " the volatile and childish character of this people." Romero possessed " equanimity " but for the most part the whole Mexican mind was filled with hatred of the United States. Most newspapers were outspoken in their bitterness against the Hayes Administration—" disaffected generals and dilapidated officials have been offering their services to the government for war against the rapacious northern giant "—and the impression was general with the people that conflict was inevitable. Diaz in a conference with the Spanish Minister " seemed to be rather pleased with the situation—told him he regarded war as quite certain—that the Mexican army was in good condition—that the United States would find a different reception than in 1846-'47 and that the government could make an honorable and successful resistance." Vallarta went so far as to tell the German Minister that he thought that war with the United States would " consolidate " the position of the Diaz Administration.[112]

[110] Memorandum Secretary of Foreign Relations, June 30, 1877, in reply to Memorandum Foster, June 23, 1877, *Memo y notas*, p. 14.

[111] José T. de Cuellar to Evarts, September 7, 1877, Notes from the Legation MSS, XXIV.

[112] Foster to Evarts, June 30, 1877 (Confidential), Despatches MSS, LIX.

Apparently then from a diplomatic point of view the Order was a mistake, embittering as it did unofficial relations between the two countries. Foster who was in a better position than any other American to estimate the diplomatic situation said:

The order of June 1st last, of the Secretary of War to General Ord, to cross into Mexico in pursuit of raiders has done more to create a hostile feeling and obstruct diplomatic adjustment of our difficulties than all the other events combined. That order I understand to be based upon the recommendation of military officers in command in Texas; at least not based upon my despatches to your Department.[113]

Even from a military point of view its wisdom at first seemed doubtful, especially since any action under it would almost inevitably, in the turbulent state of the Mexican mind, lead to counteraction by Mexican forces. The first indication of this came in the Order of June 18 by Pedro Ogazon, Minister of War, to General Gerónimo Treviño, commanding the division of the north of the Mexican army. Treviño was to station troops so as to intercept robbers passing either way across the border but he was not to cross himself. He was to invite the cooperation of American commanders and was to cooperate upon their invitation but— and here lay the crux of the question so far as the Order of June 1 was concerned—under no circumstances was he to permit American troops to cross the frontier without the authority of the Mexican Congress, the only body which under fraction 16, article 72 of the Mexican constitution might permit such crossing. He was ordered to transmit these instructions to General Ord or whoever commanded the United States troops as soon as possible and to inform him that if an invasion took place he was authorized to "repel force by force."[114] Foster in commenting on the Mexican order said: "In view of the extraordinary character of the inclosed order, I have protested to the minister of foreign affairs against its unwarranted assertions in regard to the

---

[113] Foster to Evarts, December 14, 1877 (Unofficial), *ibid.*, LXI.
[114] Foster to Evarts, June 21, 1877, Enclosure, *U. S. For. Rel. 1877*, pp. 416-418.

action and intention of our government, and have stated that I regard its spirit as unfriendly and calculated unduly to excite and prejudice the Mexican people against the United States." [115]

The reply of the Mexican Foreign Office to Foster's representations on this question was equally as vigorous as his charges. The Order of June 18 was declared to be "not the work of a moment nor of any . . . hastiness." It had been fully discussed in the cabinet "with the calmness and meditation such a serious subject required." [116] The Mexican Order was declared to be "based on International Law, and was but a fulfillment of an undeclinable duty on the part of the . . . Government." It was held that the Order of June 1 violated Article 34, fraction 3 of the Treaty of 1832, Article 21 of the Treaty of 1848, and Article 7 of the Treaty of May 31, 1854.[117] Furthermore it was claimed to be "an accepted maxim established by the best known writers on International Law, that no State can order its troops into a foreign territory without the permission of the latter's sovereign." Even with permission to enter a foreign country these troops could exercise no jurisdiction such as punishment of criminals or recovery of stolen property, and here again the Order of June 1 was considered to violate international law.[118] Further, Foster's charges that the Mexican Government was doing nothing to protect the border were declared to be absolutely groundless. The American Minister naturally could

---

[115] *Ibid.*

[116] Memorandum Secretary of Foreign Relations, June 30, 1877, in reply to Memorandum Foster, June 23, 1877, *Memo y notas*, pp. 15-16.

[117] See Malloy, I, 1096 for Treaty of 1832 Article XXXIV; p. 1117 for Treaty of 1848 Article XXI; and p. 1124 for Treaty of 1854 Article VII.

[118] Memorandum Secretary of Foreign Relations, June 30, 1877, *Memo y notas*, p. 15. The Mexican position was still further elaborated in *Correspondencia diplomática relativa a las invasiones del territorio mexicano por fuerzas de los Estados Unidos de 1873 a 1877*, pp. 5-11. The Mexican Government denied the American charges of ineffectiveness and lack of good intention in enforcing order on the border and the American claim that these "invasions" were not hostile to Mexico. It was held that the Order of June 1 was "offensive to Mexico and contrary to the international pacts between the republics."

not know in a majority of cases of " the orders which through various Departments have been issued by the Government for the pursuit, capture, and punishment of criminals, as well as of those addressed to different courts urging speedy adminis- tration of justice." [119]

Fortunately Ord and Treviño avoided the most warlike im- plications of both orders by an unexpected, and under the circumstances surprising, amount of cooperation. Ord was careful, for the most part, to avoid friction with Mexican regular forces by making his crossings in localities where they were not stationed. Also for the purpose of furthering good will and cooperation in the border region Ord and Treviño held a series of conferences. On June 30, Ord visited the Mexican commander in his quarters in Piedras Negras and shortly thereafter Treviño returned the call. The upshot of these amicable conversations seems to have been a new spirit of understanding and cooperation on the border. Although no definite plans were laid Treviño promised to guard the line against Mexican bandits seeking plunder in the United State and Ord promised wherever possible to prevent passage of bandits from the United States into Mexico.[120] For this understanding Treviño was severely criticized in the Mexican press, but some of this criticism apparently faded when Ord's orders were modified from Washington in the light of the border understanding, or perhaps to prevent a clash with Treviño's troops. These new orders stated that American troops were not to cross when there was a Mexican force ready to execute the duty of suppressing and punishing predatory incursions into American territory.[121]

---

[119] *Ibid.*, p. 21.

[120] For Treviño's report of this conference see Foster to Evarts, July 13, 1877, Enclosure No. 2, Despatches MSS, LIX. Ord claimed, according to Treviño, that troops of either country could pursue bandits into the other country reporting to the authorities of the latter for information and aid. Treviño insisted that crossing was a more formal matter than this, requiring consent of the respective Congresses. Ord telegraphed Sheridan June 19 before the interview referred to above: " There is a good understanding . . . on the basis of my instructions regarding prompt action to sup- press marauding and the cooperation of our troops on both sides of the river in necessary pursuit." *U. S. For. Rel. 1877*, p. 419.

[121] *Report of Secretary of War for 1877*, p. XIV.

Very soon events arose on the border to test this new spirit of cooperation. General Escobedo, Lerdo's Minister of War, was busy on the Texas side of the border plotting a counter-revolution. Early in June some of his Lerdistos crossed into Mexico and were shortly thereafter driven back onto American soil opposite the Mexican town of Paso del Norte. There they were attacked by their pursuers. The Diaz forces soon retreated into Mexico and Captain J. M. Kelley of the 10th cavalry telegraphed Ord for instructions as to whether or not he should cross the Rio Grande in pursuit. Ord ordered him not to do so fearing that an incursion into Mexico in the heated state of relations might " stir up the central authority," and the War Department approved.[122] At the same time the State Department was determined to gain a disavowal by the Diaz Government of the crossing into Texas. Therefore Foster was directed to call attention to this " grave violation of international law which cannot for a moment be overlooked." He was asked to urge the matter upon " the *de facto* Government with whom you are holding unofficial intercourse . . . and to say that the Government of the United States will confidently expect prompt disavowal of the act with reparation for its consequences and punishment of its perpetrators." [123] Vallarta expressed gratification at the new orders to Ord on crossing and promptly disavowed the action of the Mexican troops and ordered an investigation to fix punishment and reparation. He said Treviño had been ordered that in " obedience to article 72, section 16, of the federal constitution he should not consent to the troops of the United States entering into our territory and that in respect to the sovereignty of that Republic he should prevent Mexican [troops] from treading on foreign territory." [124] As a result of several more attempts to organize Lerdo forces on the American side of the border Escobedo, leader of the movement, and several of his aides were arrested in Texas for violation of American neutrality laws and with Diaz' growing

[122] Evarts to Foster, June 21, 1877, *U. S. For Rel. 1877*, p. 413.
[123] Evarts to Foster, June 21, 1877, Instructions MSS, XIX.
[124] Foster to Evarts, July 9, 1877, Despatches MSS, LIX.

strength these counter-revolutionary troubles gradually ceased to trouble the border.[125]

During the summer and fall of 1877 and the early winter months of 1878 cordial cooperation continued with a few minor exceptions. As an instance of this spirit late in July General T. Naranjo, second in chief of the Mexican Line of the North, reported the disposition of the troops under his command to Ord and wrote that he had issued orders to his troops on the river Salado to advance to cover those engaged in watching Escobedo and Winker. He promised to keep the American commander informed of the further disposition of his troops and scouts.[126] Also Diaz began to reinforce the border, as troops could be safely released from duty in other parts of the country. *El Diario Oficial* reported, November 12, that the two divisions of federal troops already on the border under Generals Treviño and Canales numbered 4,792 men and that a third division of approximately 2,000 men had been ordered to reinforce them.[127] One report of 1,500 troops sent from Vera Cruz to the border proved false,[128] but about a month later Foster had information which he deemed reliable that 3,000 troops in Mexico City were under orders to march overland to the border. In the same despatch he noted that Diaz had an army of 40,000, more than double the number under arms when Lerdo was in power.[129]

In fact so cordial was the cooperation between Ord and

---

[125] Foster to Evarts, July 20, 1877 (Telegram), *ibid.*; Major William R. Price, 8th Cavalry, commanding Ringgold Barracks to 1st Lieutenant R. A. Williams, Acting Assistant Adjutant General District of the Rio Grande, July 21, 1877, 45th Cong., 2d sess., *H. Rept.* No. 701, pp. 269-270; *Report of the Secretary of War for 1877*, p. 81; Foster to Evarts, July 27, 1877, Despatches MSS, LIX.

[126] Ord to Adjutant General, Washington, D. C., Telegram, July 21, 1877, Enclosure Naranjo to Ord, July 19, 1877, 45th Cong., 2d sess., *H. Rept.* No. 701, Appendix B, pp. 267-268.

[127] Foster to Evarts, November 14, 1877, Despatches MSS, LX. On this despatch Hunter noted that a copy was to be sent to the War Department for its information. "The number of troops as stated is nearly a match of the whole army of the United States," he commented pointedly. Although the army nominally numbered 25,000 men, many of the regiments were greatly depleted.

[128] Foster to Evarts, October 6, 1877, Despatches MSS, LX.

[129] Foster to Evarts, November 10, 1877 (Confidential), *ibid.*

Treviño that the former, so eager earlier for official permission to cross, within a few months sought modification or complete repeal of the Order of June 1. Belief in Treviño's sincerity, his apparently effective efforts to remove border Indians to the interior of Mexico, and a feeling that the Order of June 1 constituted a threat to the commercial development of the border probably tempered Ord's judgment in the matter.

I've been conciliatory to General Treviño as could be [Ord wrote Sherman] and think he deserves it—as he is earnest and one of the few Mexican Gen'ls that leaves the impression that you can build on him—it is our interest to try to back him with his people and keep him in office—he . . . [is] removing the raiding Indians to the interior and it would be good policy for us to have the Mexicans on the border and in the interior to think that through his exertions and influence the directions to cross troops under the June '77 order has been modified,—publicly—as from the tone of the President's message I am led to believe it is his intention to do at the first opportunity. I am officially advised of the capture of the San Carlos Apaches—and have so reported and Gen'l. Treviño informs me that he has commenced to move the Kickapoos to an interior state—too far to annoy or raid and that the Kickapoos and Lipans that are left will be sent to an interior state also—so that—based on this removal—the President could direct when he receives proof of the fact that marauding savages have been removed from the borders of Texas to such a distance that they could no longer be a terror to our people and a sufficient force of Mexican troops have been placed on that border to prevent their return—the order authorized by his letter of the—of June 1877 was no longer necessary and that I could be so advised—that would leave the Department at liberty to cross in pursuit of such Indians should they return—or he might add that—the Department commander would be advised to consider the order to cross—rescinded—unless these Indians again returned to the Texas borders—in any event—the prospects for a better commercial communication must begin on this border—and I think they have commenced and it is advisable to relieve the border people of anything that savors of a threat—and see how far such action on our part will invite a confidence from them—

I'd invite them to send a few cadets to Annapolis and West Point and suggest a cooperation in the matter of bimetallic currency—so as to have a dollar good on both sides, and if possible all through South America—it would promote trade.

P. S. Treviño and staff are pleased at their reception and have been wherever they went—each town through committees offering them and giving them a military turnout. I think they feel very much relieved.[180]

---

[180] Ord to Sherman, January 3, 1878, W. T. Sherman Papers MSS, XLIX. Sherman pencilled a notation on the back of this letter as follows: " To the Secretary. Please read this as private. Do you think it wise or proper to suggest to General Ord to ask officially

While American troops crossed a dozen or more times during the two years or more that the Order was in force only on one occasion did open hostilities threaten. Rippy rightly says that " it is perhaps a high compliment to the tact and restraint of the military officials of both countries that they were able to avoid a brush between their respective troops." [131] The one approach to open conflict occurred late in September 1877. Lieutenant Bullis crossed with about 90 regulars and attacked the Indian village of Zaragoza, Mexico. Lieutenant Colonel Shafter fearing that he might be attacked in turn moved to his support with 300 men. Bullis' forces were found to be retreating toward the border before a superior Mexican body, but when the American cavalry, now some 400 strong, formed a line of battle, the Mexican regular troops under Colonel Inocente Rodriguez retired.[132] This movement of American troops into Mexico on a " cold trail " was " very severely criticized " by " the Mexican press and public men." It was held that the expedition constituted a violation of the Order of June 1 since neither Bullis' nor Shafter's troops were in sight of raiders nor on a fresh trail. Bullis' object was declared to have been to attack an established Indian camp by order of his superior, Lieutenant Colonel Shafter, who had thus, according to this point of view, deliberately invaded and insulted the Mexican nation.[133] Foster himself wondered if the Mexican criticism of Shafter were not " in some respects . . . well taken." He feared that incursions into Mexico against established villages would lead to conflict rather than to the

for a modification of existing orders to cross on the frontier in pursuit of ' fresh trails,' etc. W. T. Sherman."

[131] J. F. Rippy, " Some Precedents of the Pershing Expedition into Mexico," *The Southwestern Historical Quarterly*, XXIV, 313.

[132] *Ibid.* For details of this affair see 45th Cong., 1st sess., *H. Ex. Doc.* No. 13, pp. 53-54; Foster to Evarts, October 27, 1877, *U. S. For. Rel. 1877*, p. 531 (includes report Colonel Rodriguez to General A. R. Falcon, Chief of the Line, Piedras Negras, September 29, 1877) ; Foster to Evarts, October 16, 1877, Enclosure telegraphic report General F. F. Naranjo, October 9, 1877, to Mexican Minister of War, Despatches MSS, LX.

[133] Foster to Evarts, October 31, 1877, *ibid.* See also De Cuellar to Evarts, December 14, 1877, *U. S. For. Rel. 1877*, p. 665.

" peace of the frontier." [134] Vallarta insisted that the Mexican Government expected the government of the United States to disavow the act and punish Shafter as the former had done in the case of the Mexican troops who had pursued the Lerdistos into Texas.[135] Although Shafter was considered " as an officer of discretion and ability " he was ordered before a court martial as a result of this Mexican criticism and the uncertainties in the case.[136]

Despite the dangerous possibilities of this incident the American and Mexican troops again cooperated later in the year in the attempted recovery of horses stolen from Texas ranches and said to be in Mexico. In the words of Ord's report to Sheridan:

Lieutenant Ward was sent to the Rio Grande to find trail of horses stolen and driven into Mexico on 15th instant. Has just come in. The Mexican troops got to the river on the morning of 20th. Ward showed the Mexican lieutenant the trail, and at his invitation crossed the river and joined the Mexican troops. They followed the trail together all day, going about 25 miles. As it had rained heavily the trail was hard to follow, and another hard rain setting in they found it impossible to follow it farther. The trail was left about three miles from Newtown and only six or eight miles below where it crossed the river. Ward says that there was perfectly good feeling among Mexican soldiers and our own, and that the lieutenant offered to go with him anywhere he thought the horses could be found.[137]

Ord's report was " very bitterly commented upon " in the Mexican press and the punishment of the Mexican officers who had permitted the crossing was demanded. So great was the clamor that Secretary of War Ogazon felt called upon to remind Treviño of the Order of June 18 in regard to resistance to American crossing. He was further ordered to discover the officer who had aided the crossing and report him to the War Department.[138]

---

[134] Foster to Evarts October 31, 1877 (Confidential), Despatches MSS, LX.

[135] Foster to Evarts, November 28, 1877, ibid., LXI.

[136] Secretary of War George W. McCrary before House Committee on Military Affairs, December 10, 1877, 45th Cong., 2d sess., H. Misc. Doc. No. 64, p. 11.

[137] Evarts to Foster, January 2, 1878, Enclosure Sheridan to Townshend incorporating Ord's telegram to Sheridan, U. S. For. Rel. 1878, pp. 536-537.

[138] Foster to Evarts, January 17, 1878, ibid., p. 542.

In short the Order of June 1 by no means snuffed out disorder on the border, but it aided greatly in checking it.[139] Mexican pride was aroused. The Diaz Government had already planned to reinforce the border and send an able commander there. These plans were precipitated by the American order and to prevent American crossing, if for no other motive, Mexican federal forces were quick to cooperate on all important occasions. In all fairness it must be admitted that Diaz' growing strength, his evident desire to obtain American recognition, the rapid settlement of the frontier, and the coming of the railroad would probably eventually have brought comparative peace to the border in any case. But such admission is not to say that the Order of June 1 and the cooperation growing out of it did not play an important part in reducing border lawlessness.

From a military point of view therefore the Order seems to have proven desirable and, under the circumstances and

---

[139] Several other acts of lawlessness were recorded during the year. On August 12 a party of Mexicans from Tamaulipas crossed to Rio Grande City, county seat of Starr county, Texas, and released two prisoners and returned to Mexico following a fight in which the State Attorney and three jailers were wounded. The Mexicans were pursued by United States troops to the river. After a long diplomatic interchange the Mexican Government waived its exemption from extraditing its own citizens and extradited three of the assailants of the jail. See for this case Governor Hubbard to President Hayes, August 13, 1877, 45th Cong., 1st sess., *H. Ex. Doc.* No. 13, p. 43; Foster to Evarts, August 23-30, September 11, October 12, 1877, Despatches MSS, LX; Foster to Evarts, January 10, 1878, *ibid.*, LXI; Foster to Evarts, October 18, 1877, *ibid.* An uprising of Mexicans in El Paso county in the winter of 1877-1878 grew out of attempts of a company of Austin, Texas, to "locate" certain salt lakes of that county previously considered for generations to be reserved for the common use of inhabitants of western Texas and northern Chihuahua. After considerable rioting and the death of several Americans and Mexicans, United States troops restored order. See for this incident G. L. Andrews, commanding Fort Davis, Texas, to Adjutant General Department of Texas, Sheridan to Townshend, October 15, 1877 (p. 120), 1st Lieutenant L. H. Rucker, 9th Cavalry to Acting Assistant Adjutant General District of New Mexico, October 4, 1877 (pp. 125-127), 45th Cong., 1st sess., *H. Ex. Doc.* No. 13; *Report of the Secretary of War for 1878*, pp. 50-55; William Ray Lewis, "The Hayes Administration in Mexico," *The Southwestern Historical Quarterly*, XXIV, 141-142. Also newspaper reports of Apache raids into Sonora, probably from the Chiricahua Agency in Arizona, were confirmed by members of the Mexican Congress from Sonora. Foster to Evarts, December 21, 1877, Despatches MSS, LXI.

difficulties of the border, surprisingly effective. McCrary ardently defended the Order in his Annual Report of 1877. After noting the continuance of lawless incursions into Texas over a period of years he said that it " has long been evident that these incursions cannot be stopped so long as the Government of Mexico is either unable or unwilling to punish the marauders, and the United States is prevented from crossing the Rio Grande in their pursuit." Since Mexico was unwilling or unable to maintain a force sufficient to protect the border, the United States found it necessary to direct General Ord ". . . in the exercise of his own discretion when in pursuit of a band of marauders, to follow them, either when the troops are in sight of them or upon a fresh trail, across the Rio Grande, and until they are overtaken and punished, and the stolen property recovered." [140] Later he defended the order on the ground of necessity. " The ground upon which it was issued was . . . that it was considered a necessity and [I] think that, because a necessity, it was a right." [141]

Sheridan also was strongly of the opinion that pursuit into Mexico on a fresh trail was " the only means we could resort to " in defending the border, lacking sufficient troops or a satisfactory understanding with Mexico.[142] Texans during the Civil War and Reconstruction, Ord asserted, had submitted to " murdering of frontier inhabitants and plundering of the border settlements, because they did not see any way of relief; but now that they are reconstructed and about as good citizens as if they had been born in Maine (some of them were) they feel that something should be done to make life and property more secure on the border." He went on to say that if Mexico were " unable to . . . enforce its orders

---

[140] *Report of Secretary of War for 1877*, p. XIV.

[141] McCrary before House Committee on Military Affairs, December 10, 1877, 45th Cong., 2d sess., *H. Misc. Doc.* No. 64, pp. 6-7. President Hayes, presumably referring to this order in an undated Cabinet memorandum said: " The Mexican question—peace preserved. Border raids prevented for the first time since Texas was annexed." Cabinet Notes, Hayes Papers MSS.

[142] Sheridan before House Committee on Military Affairs, December 12, 1877, 45th Cong., 2d sess., *H. Misc. Doc.* No. 64, p. 68.

the remedy devolves upon us and I believe that the instructions already received (allowing our troops to follow the
trails of these marauders to their homes in the mountains
south of the Rio Grande, if necessary) are sufficient." During the last two full moons no raids had been reported below
the mouth of the Devilo river. Such a state of affairs, Ord
said, had not been known for years.[143] Thus the best military
experience seemed to point to the Order as sound. From the
diplomatic point of view, of which more will be said later,
another conclusion might be reached.

The second great question, that of recognition, was approached from the beginning with cautious step by the new
Hayes Administration. Soon after Diaz' letter was received,
which Foster had once suggested as sufficient to warrant
recognition, Evarts wrote: " It is deemed advisable . . . in
view of the present condition of affairs in Mexico to await
the progress of events and the action of the Congress of that
country at its coming session, before taking any further steps
in the direction of formal and official recognition of General
Diaz as the lawful President of the Mexican Republic." [144]
Early in May Diaz was duly installed as constitutional President of Mexico but still the administration in Washington
hesitated. Beset on all sides by advisers it apparently determined to follow the more conservative of these and demand
certain guarantees of Diaz, in regard to border questions particularly, as prerequisites of recognition. About the middle
of May the State Department outlined the viewpoint of the
Hayes Administration in a despatch which must be quoted
at length because of its importance.

> The Government of the United States in its dealings with the
> Mexican Republic has aimed to pursue not merely a just but a gener-
> ous and friendly course. While earnest to guard and protect the
> rights of its own citizens and the safety of its own territory, it does
> not seek to intervene in political contests or changes of administra-
> tion. It is accustomed to accept and recognize the results of a popu-

---

[143] *Report of the Secretary of War for 1877*, p. 80.

[144] Evarts to Foster, March 27, 1877, Instructions MSS, XIX. See
also Evarts to Foster (another instruction of same date), *ibid.*, for
approval of Foster's policy in deferring recognition of Diaz until his
constitutional inauguration.

lar choice in Mexico, and not to scrutinize closely the regularity or irregularity of the methods by which presidents are inaugurated. In the present case it waits before recognizing General Diaz as the President of Mexico until it shall be assured that his election is approved by the Mexican people, and that his administration is possessed of stability to endure and of disposition to comply with the rules of international comity and the obligations of treaties.

Such recognition, if accorded, would imply something more than a mere formal assent. It would imply a belief that the government so recognized will faithfully execute its duties and observe the spirit of its treaties. The recognition of a president in Mexico by the United States has an important moral influence which, as you explain, is appreciated at the capital of that republic. It aids to strengthen the power and lengthen the tenure of the incumbent, and if, as you say, the example of the United States in that regard is one that other nations are disposed to follow, such recognition would not be without effect, both upon the internal and external peace of Mexico. You justly remark that in fifty years there have been about sixty changes of administration in Mexico, and it may be added that those administrations have been longest lived that were most faithful and friendly in the discharge of their treaty obligations to the United States.

After noting with pleasure Diaz' willingness to meet the Mexican claims obligations, the despatch continued:

But it is a subject of grave regret that in other respects the customs of friendly intercourse and the obligations of treaties have been neglected, disregarded, or violated. Doubtless, in many cases, the central government was powerless to prevent these infractions. But they are such as this government cannot allow to pass without remonstrance, nor without insisting that it is the duty of a friendly power to use the means at its disposal to check or repress them. There have been raids and depredations upon the Texan frontier; theft, murder, arson and plunder; violation of post-offices and custom houses; incursions by armed men to destroy life or property; cattle stealing has become a profitable occupation; military officials posted to protect the frontier are said to have protected the robbers; forced loans have been demanded, and American citizens have been compelled to submit to unjust and unequal exactions. Within the past few weeks the guides of an American commander have been seized and carried into the interior, with threats of summary execution; and a consul of the United States, in gross violation of international comity, has been imprisoned. For each and all of these acts, many of them committed, if not with the sanction at least in the name of the Government of Mexico, not one single man, so far as is known to this government, has been punished.

It is not difficult to believe that General Diaz and his minister of foreign affairs earnestly desire friendly relations and recognition on the part of the United States, and it is gratifying to receive the assurances unofficially made through you that they are disposed to adjust and rectify these complaints and grievances, and are not unwilling to consent to some arrangement for concerted action between the military commanders of the two countries on the frontier for the preservation of peace and order and the protection of life and property. It is natural that Mexican statesmen should urge upon you the argument that the restoration of official relations between the two governments would open the way toward such an adjustment. But it is natural, on the other hand, that the Government of the United States should be disposed to believe that some guarantee of such an arrangement should be made the condition precedent to any recognition, rather than to trust to the possibility that it may ultimately follow.[145]

Evidently believing himself empowered by these instructions to negotiate an agreement with the Diaz Government precedent to recognition, Foster proceeded to suggest certain proposals. These arrangements, according to a memorandum which he soon drew up, should cover (1) border problems, (2) adjustment of outstanding claims, (3) protection of American citizens from forced loans and revolutionary actions, (4) establishment of a better basis for commercial intercourse.[146] As this study is concerned entirely with border problems, we shall consider the recognition controversy only in relation to those problems. Suffice it to say that the relative space given in the diplomatic correspondence to border and to other questions at issue between the two countries during these months shows clearly that border problems were of greatest importance in the recognition struggle.

First of all under his instructions of May 16 stating the recognition policy of the Hayes Administration Foster very evidently determined to make abolition of the Free Zone,[147]

---

[145] F. W. Seward to Foster, May 16, 1877, *ibid.* The question as to whether or not the Hayes Administration departed from traditional American policy on recognition by requiring protection of American life and property and observance of international obligations as tests of recognition in addition to stability and approval of the Mexican people is outside the scope of this study. For an able defense of the claim that Hayes was merely making explicit a requirement implicit since the time of Washington see C. C. Tansill, "War Powers of the President of the United States with Special Reference to the Beginning of Hostilities," *Political Science Quarterly*, XLV, pp. 26, 30, and Taylor Cole, *The Recognition Policy of the United States since 1901*, pp. 19 ff. For the opposing point of view see Charles W. Hackett, "The Recognition of the Diaz Government by the United States," *Southwestern Historical Quarterly*, XXVIII, 35 ff., and Julius Goebel, *The Recognition Policy of the United States*, "Columbia University Studies in History, Economics, and Public Law," LXVI, No. 1, p. 203.

[146] Foster to Evarts, June 18, 1877, Despatches MSS, LIX; Foster, I, 94.

[147] Referring to his instructions of February 12 in which the desirability of repeal of the Free Zone was emphasized Foster had

understandings as to pursuit and capture of border raiders, and provision for removal of certain Indians from the vicinity of the international line to American reservations essential forerunners of recognition. Vallarta, however, strenuously maintained that no guarantee should be required before recognition since the Diaz Government already possessed " all the conditions of recognition required by international law and the practice of nations." He held that the Mexican Government was ready to settle the question of claims of American citizens and give " reasonable guarantees for the preservation of peace on the frontier and for the protection of American interests in Mexico," but it was expected that such guarantees would follow recognition.[148] Further Vallarta expressed deep resentment at what he considered the unfriendly spirit of the Hayes Administration. He charged that its attitude toward Mexico signalized a change in American recognition policy, in his opinion brought about by former President Lerdo and certain Americans " who had personal and sinister purposes to accomplish," and that the American Government " had yielded too readily to the repre-

previously said that he would make the proposition known to President Diaz and his cabinet and try to get their reaction. The whole matter was a " troublesome question in Mexican politics." Attempted repeal would raise a storm and it was a question whether Diaz would " care to meet the opposition and trouble " such a move would stir up. Some three weeks later Vallarta came to the legation, Foster reported, and told him that the " Zona Libre " had been considered by the cabinet " in connection with my suggestion made to him." He stated that while his government recognized the force of the objections to its existence on the part of the United States, it was convinced that it was even a source of greater evil to Mexico; that it gave to a small portion of territory special privileges and exemptions not enjoyed by the rest of the Republic; that it was a far greater injury to Mexican revenue, that it was the occasion of constant trouble, lawlessness, and bloodshed; and that the Executive was clearly of the opinion that at least important modification, if not its absolute repeal, were necessary. He said however that it was sanctioned by an act of Congress, and that the subject would, therefore, have to be referred to that body. It had been committed to the Minister of Finance for thorough examination with a view " . . . to remedy the existing evils " by presenting the question to Congress for solution. Foster to Fish, March 3, 1877, Despatches MSS, LVIII; Foster to Evarts, March 24, 1877, ibid.

[148] Foster to Evarts, June 20, 1877, *U. S. For. Rel. 1877*, p. 410. The quotations are from Foster's despatch, hence are not Vallarta's exact words but Foster's interpretation of his remarks.

sentations of General Ord, who was an annexationist and seeking to precipitate a war between the two countries." He complained bitterly that the Order of June 1, far from stretching out the hand of friendship, treated the people of Mexico " as savages, as Kaffirs of Africa." He said that Treviño had been ordered to the border and if the Order of June 1 were carried out " the consequences might be of the gravest character." [149]

In reply Foster pointed out that the United States must proceed more circumspectly than European governments in regard to Mexican recognition because it was more deeply interested in Mexican stability than they. The problems of a long border, an adjacent coast line, complex common interests, and numerous treaties made the United States look with particular anxiety on any new government in Mexico. He denied that American recognition policy had changed and insisted that Ord's orders had been gravely misunderstood by the Mexican Government.[150] Since Mexico had shown inability to prevent border lawlessness the United States must adopt a more vigorous policy. Such measures as had been taken were essentially defensive and were not contrary to international law, treaties, and civilized practice as claimed by the Mexican Minister of War.[151]

In this atmosphere of suspicion and anger, growing out of deferred recognition and the Order of June 1, Foster now was forced to attempt written agreements as remedies for border conditions. Faced by popular wrath and anti-American feel-

---

[149] *Ibid.*, pp. 410-411. See also Memorandum Secretary of Foreign Relations, June 30, 1877, in reply to Foster Memorandum of June 23, *Memo y notas*, pp. 8-9, 13.

[150] A comparison of this statement with Foster's confidential despatches during this period and with his *Memoirs* will show that personally he thought the American recognition policy had changed and that the United States should recognize Diaz without further delay. But as representative of his government he had no choice but to carry out his instructions.

[151] Foster to Evarts, June 20, 1877, *U. S. For. Rel. 1877*, pp. 411-412. See also Memorandum of Foster to Minister of Foreign Relations, June 23, 1877, *Memo y notas*, pp. 4-6. Foster was also as already noted doubtful of the expediency of the Order of June 1 but of course this personal point of view did not find a place in his interviews with representatives of the Mexican Government.

ing the Diaz Government denied responsibility for border conditions and set itself firmly against any important concession prior to recognition. At first the Mexican Government had seemed willing to discuss proposed border arrangements but as the feeling in Mexico over the prolonged delay in recognition and over the American attitude on border crossings became more bitter, the Diaz Administration refused to make concessions until recognition were granted. The issue was thus clearly joined, the American Government holding that treaty guarantees as to the border must precede recognition, the Mexican Government holding that recognition was the first step toward discussion of border questions. Foster therefore found increasing opposition to his proposals for treaty settlement of the moot border questions. Soon after receiving his instructions of May 16 he embodied his interpretation of them in a series of memoranda [152] to the Mexican Foreign Office providing for return of certain raiding Indians from northern Mexico to American reservations, abolition of the Free Zone, capture and punishment of border raiders, and reestablishment of the Rio Grande boundary in line with the shifts in the main channel.

Many of the Indians raiding the American border from Coahuila and Chihuahua apparently had previously escaped from American reservations. Foster now proposed a treaty arrangement for delivery of these Indians by Mexican military authorities to American military authorities or Indian agents. These Indians included Lipans, Kickapoos, Mescaleros, Seminoles, and remnants of other tribes.[153] In regard to abolition of the Free Zone, Vallarta had previously explained that President Diaz and his cabinet could do nothing without the action of the Mexican Congress. Foster now asked assurance that a proposition for abolition would be presented to Congress in September and that the president would exert his influence to secure its passage.[154] The memorandum

---

[152] These memoranda are enclosed or described in three despatches, numbers 555, 556, and 557, all of the same date.

[153] Foster to Evarts, June 23, 1877, Enclosure, Despatches MSS, LIX.

[154] Foster to Evarts, June 23, 1877, Enclosure No. 1, ibid.

on border raiding and the boundary was longer, comprising
as it did a number of disputed points. It proposed the following articles for a treaty between the two nations: (a)
establishment of a zone—miles on each side of the Rio Grande
from the mouth to the point where it joins the New Mexican
boundary; [155] (b) permission for regular federal troops of
either nation to cross into this zone in pursuit of marauders
sought under Article III of the Extradition Treaty of
1861: [156] (c) provision that if citizens of the United States
or of any country other than Mexico were captured in close
pursuit within ——— hours by United States troops operating in Mexico they might be returned to the United States;
(d) the same provision to apply to capture of citizens of
Mexico or of any country other than the United States by
Mexican troops in the United States; (e) provision for return by the troops of stolen property to the country from
which it was stolen; (f) a stipulation that when Mexican
citizens suspected of raiding were captured by United States
forces in Mexico they should be delivered to the nearest
Mexican force and that similarly American citizens should be
delivered to the nearest American force; (g) trial by mixed
military courts; (h) each government to keep a high officer
and not less than ——————— troops in the part of the
above zone within its own territory; (i) the commanders of
these forces to cooperate; (j) the headquarters of the two
forces to be kept in telegraphic communication with each
other; (k) these provisions to be extended if necessary to
other portions of the border by agreement between the two
governments; (l) the boundary line along the Rio Grande to
be reestablished in line with the shifts in the main channel
of the river; (m) citizens of the United States to enjoy the
same rights of purchase, ownership, and sale of real estate and
other property in Mexico "on or adjacent to the boundary
line as permitted by the existing laws . . . by foreigners in
the interior states of the Mexican Republic;" (n) similar

---

[155] The number of miles was left blank as this was a mere pros-
pectus subject to future decision.
[156] See Malloy, I, 1126.

privileges to be extended to Mexican citizens in the United States; (o) this Treaty to be in force for ————— years and for one year after notice by one of the signatory governments.[157]

On its side the Mexican Government seemed ready to negotiate for modification of the Extradition Treaty of 1861 to the end that both governments bind themselves to surrender their respective citizens for crimes committed in the territory of the other. Foster expressed himself as considering this proposal harmless for certain crimes if joined to the suggested border zone.[158] In regard to border protection the Mexican Government was very careful not to commit itself to any proposal on the dangerous question of border crossing. It proposed as formerly that each country keep a sufficient force on the border under an able commander. These commanders (*jefes*) were to consult as to the best means of pursuing robbers.[159] While admitting that the American Government had repeatedly sought a reciprocal agreement on crossing the Mexican Foreign Minister asserted that the Mexican Government " has replied on all occasions that it is not

---

[157] Foster to Evarts, June 23, 1877, Despatches MSS, LIX. On this despatch Hunter noted that many of Foster's suggestions were in his opinion desirable but that he thought the " Senate and public of this country loath to sanction trials of offenders " in time of peace otherwise than by civilian courts and juries.

[158] Foster to Evarts, July 5, 1877, *ibid.* Hunter noted on this despatch that the whole matter " involves a grave question." Probably Mexicans, he thought, would receive justice in American courts, but Americans would probably not fare so well in Mexican courts. The systems of jurisprudence were different in the two countries. Mexican jurisprudence " even when most honestly administered may be said to be oppressive in its results particularly towards foreigners, and of these most of all citizens of the United States."

[159] J. M. Mata to Evarts, July 20, 1877, Enclosure entitled *Proyecto de convenio para establecer la seguridaden–la frontera entre México y los Estados Unidos de América*, Notes from the Legation MSS, XXIV. José M. Mata arrived in the United States in July with a commission as Minister from the Diaz Government and with instructions embodying the terms under which he might negotiate a treaty. The refusal of the Hayes Administration to receive him officially, however, continued Mariscal, Minister of the Lerdo Government, and all the Lerdist consuls as the official representatives of Mexico so far as the United States Government was concerned. Evarts to Foster, August 2, 1877, Instructions MSS, XIX; Foster, I, 88.

within its power to grant such a permission to foreign troops, and when it has been sought to obtain it of the Congress of the Union it has been seen that such a measure would not be approved." [160]

Apparently Mexican opposition to any sort of reciprocal border arrangement stiffened as the summer advanced without the extension of recognition and with American troops occasionally crossing under the Order of June 1. Foster wrote in rather gloomy key on August 19, that Vallarta had gradually changed from a position seemingly in favor of a reciprocal crossing agreement to one of suspicion and opposition. He asserted further: ". . . in the past month the suspicion has grown into a firm conviction here that we are only using the Rio Grande question as a pretext to force Mexico into a war for annexation and the sentiment is strongly against any reciprocal agreement for crossing the frontier or any stipulation having the appearance of a concession to the United States." He thought that Mexican labor and many other groups in the country considered the railroad riots of July in the United States as a pronunciamento against the Hayes Administration. He promised in case his negotiations with Vallarta failed to appeal directly to Diaz. [161]

Here the question stood while Foster pressed the American point of view upon Diaz, Romero, and Vallarta. During these conferences the Mexican Government according to Foster "resisted step by step the proposition for reciprocal crossing" but he was sure that it "will eventually agree to it." He considered such an agreement a *sine qua non* to a treaty on border disturbances and a treaty on border and

---

[160] Foster to Evarts, July 24, 1877, Enclosure No. 1, Memorandum Vallarta to Foster, June 30, 1877, Despatches MSS, LIX.

[161] Foster to Evarts, August 19, 1877 (Unofficial), Despatches MSS, LX. In spite of lack of recognition Diaz became very friendly with Mr. and Mrs. Foster personally. A few years later Diaz, attending one of Foster's "informal Tuesday night receptions" met the "beautiful and charming daughter of his implacable foe, the former Senator and Cabinet Minister" under Lerdo, Romero Rubio. "This acquaintance later ripened into a matrimonial engagement, and the winsome daughter of the Lerdist chief became 'the first lady' of the land." Foster, I, 99.

other questions as a necessary forerunner of recognition. Finally Vallarta agreed to compromise on an agreement providing for the pursuit of Indians in desert and unpopulated regions on the upper Rio Grande. In the more thickly populated lower Rio Grande valley he suggested a clause in the proposed treaty empowering the Presidents of the two countries to agree later on crossing in case the Mata project in operation failed to stop the depredations. Vallarta, however, wished to confine the proposal to certain sections of the lower Rio Grande and for a limited time to be fixed in the agreement. He also wished to hedge about the agreement with limitations on the distance the troops might go after crossing, provision for arrest and delivery of raiders to local authorities, and others. So far as the Free Zone was concerned, Vallarta declared the Mexican Government unable to consider its abolition. To these propositions Foster declined to agree. He asserted that the lower Rio Grande was the most often raided part of the whole border, therefore its status should be settled at once and not left to some future provision by the Presidents of the two countries.[162]

So embittered was a great section of Mexican public opinion that Diaz and Vallarta were condemned for even entertaining Foster's proposals. *El Federalista* condemned Diaz as begging recognition "even with humiliation." It claimed that he was selling Mexican "dignity as a nation" for a mess of pottage, "a sterile and useless recognition."[163] *El Diario Oficial* retorted that *El Federalista's* "information was false" and its attack "unjust and arbitrary."[164] Apparently this feeling of anger rose to new heights as the months passed and was reflected in a new firmness by Mexican officials against American demands. Foster, in November, reported a hostile feeling toward the United States and "a general belief that war between the two countries is almost inevitable." It was unanimously believed, he asserted, that the United States by its prolonged delay of recognition and

---

[162] Foster to Evarts, August 31, 1877 (Unofficial and Confidential), Despatches MSS, LX. Foster to Evarts, September 4, 1877, *ibid.*
[163] Foster to Evarts, September 13, 1877, Enclosure No. 1, *ibid.*
[164] *Ibid.*, Enclosure No. 2.

its attitude on border and other questions at issue, was deliberately trying to provoke a conflict. Even members of the government in some cases held this view, he said.[165]

Meanwhile, although Vallarta steadily refused to yield the contested point of reciprocal crossing,[166] Zamacona was sent to the United States with instructions, according to *El Diario Oficial*, to seek recognition as a right under international law not as a " courtesy or favor " on the part of the United States. He was also empowered to open negotiations for the settlement of border problems. But above all he was not to add force, by word or deed, to the " erroneous " American belief that recognition was a life and death matter to Mexico. He was to give the American Government to understand that his mission did not have for " an object solicitation of . . . recognition." [167] However, Foster was far from encouraging as to the success of the mission, knowing as he did the attitude of the American Government. He told Zamacona that for the time being at least he saw no prospect of recognition " as my government was unwilling to enter into diplomatic relations with a government in Mexico which did not have the ability and the disposition to discharge its international obligations." Zamacona thereupon disavowed any intention of seeking official recognition and asserted that he was to act only as the " private agent of the Mexican government." [168] But whatever his status and in spite of the indifference, real or assumed, of the government toward recognition in its official journal the very fact of his being sent on such a mission would seem to indicate a strong desire on the part of the Diaz Government to settle the recognition controversy.

During the following weeks the Foreign Office continued willing to cooperate in matters involving extradition [169] but

---

[165] Foster to Evarts, November 12, 1877 (Confidential), Despatches MSS, LX.

[166] Foster to Evarts, November 8, 1877, *ibid.*

[167] Foster to Evarts, November 16, 1877, *ibid.*

[168] Foster to Evarts, November 12, 1877, *ibid.*

[169] Foster to Evarts, November 21, 1877, Enclosure No. 2, *ibid.* This circular, addressed by the Department of Foreign Relations to

it remained adamant in the face of Foster's border proposals. Late in the month he advanced a new plan for curbing lawlessness on the border, the outstanding feature of which was reciprocal crossing. Each country was to agree to keep an adequate force of regulars on the border, although numbers were not specified. These forces were to be allowed to cross reciprocally in close pursuit and were to return as soon as they had apprehended the raiders or in case they lost the trail. They were to exercise no other jurisdiction than arrest and were to deliver their prisoners to the properly constituted civil or military authorities of the state where the arrest took place. No passage of the border was to take place where there was a sufficient force on the other side or opposite a large town, this question being left to the discretion of the respective commanders. Each country was to permit extradition of its own citizens charged with crimes under Article III of the Treaty of Extradition. Military commanders were to designate fords for the live stock trade and the authorities of the frontier states were to furnish facilities for the recovery of stolen property. The chief executives of the two countries were to have power to extend the treaty without ratification of such extension beyond the five-year period for which the treaty was to run with its additional year after notice of termination.[170]

This proposal was rejected and the whole question of arrangements on border questions prior to recognition was definitely put aside by Vallarta. The Mexican Government had decided, Foster wrote, that any " agreement to or signing of any one of the memoranda submitted by me previous to recognition, would signify a humiliation for Mexico which would not be tolerated on the part of its citizens in any administration." Foster now for the first time showed that the American position on guarantees before recognition was beginning to waver by his reply to this brusque stand by Vallarta. He asserted significantly that even if Diaz were recog-

the Governors of the Frontier States, requested them to inform the Department quickly of all cases involving questions of extradition. They were to conform exactly to the Treaty of 1861.

[170] Foster to Evarts, November 28, 1877, *ibid.*, LXI.

nized his attitude toward the Free Zone, border marauding, ownership of real estate by Americans in northern Mexico near the border, and many other disputed points would still be subjects for treaty negotiations.[171]

Probably this partial change of front on the part of the administration in Washington reflected, in part at least, a lively barrage from the floor of the House and Senate directed at its Mexican policy. On November 1, the House adopted unanimously a resolution introduced by Schleicher calling on the President to transmit to the House information, if not incompatible with the public interest, as " to the condition of the Mexican border in Texas, and to any recent violation of the territory of the United States, by incursions from Mexico." [172] On November 12, these papers were duly sent to the House and the next day were referred to the Foreign Affairs Committee.[173] Various interests in the House becoming restless however as the Committee's research did not bear immediate fruit, a resolution was passed referring to the Committee part of President Hayes' Message relating, in the words of the Resolution, to the " recognition of President Diaz, of Mexico, and the difficulties on the Rio Grande border." The Committee was also instructed to find the " best means of removing the existing and impending causes of difficulty between Mexico and the United States." [174]

While the Foreign Affairs Committee was considering these data still more pressure was being brought to bear on the administration to recognize Diaz on the floor of the House itself. Representative Cox, of New York, introduced on January 11, 1878, a resolution calling on President Hayes to give his reasons, if not incompatible with the public interest, " for refusing to recognize the present Government of Mexico under General Diaz." [175] A month earlier the Senate

---

[171] *Ibid.*

[172] 45th Cong., 2d sess., *H. Rept.* No. 701, p. I; *Cong. Record*, 45th Cong., 1st sess., p. 211.

[173] 45th Cong., 1st sess., *H. Ex. Doc.* No. 13, p. 1. See also Hackett, *The Southwestern Historical Quarterly*, XXVIII, 51-52.

[174] 45th Cong., 2d sess., *H. Rept.* No. 701, p. I.

[175] *Ibid.*; *Cong. Record*, 45th Cong., 1st sess., p. 290.

had shown its active interest in the question of recognition. Senator Conkling, of New York, had introduced a resolution calling for appointment of a committee of seven from the Senate to study the best means of promoting commercial intercourse with Mexico and of establishing " a just and peaceful condition of affairs " along the border. In particular the Committee was " to ascertain and report the facts touching the present government of Mexico." The resolution was speedily passed and three days after its introduction the members had been appointed.[176]

The reports of these Committees did not influence recognition, since it was extended before they were made. But the testimony brought out, particularly that of Foster before the sub-committee of the House Foreign Affairs Committee probably had marked influence on the administration.[177] As indicated earlier in the chapter Evarts. had at first refused Foster's request for a leave of absence to present the Mexican situation to the Department in person. However, under the spur of congressional resolutions the administration was forced to relent and order Foster home for a flying visit, " paramount reasons " of policy requiring his return to his post as quickly as possible.[178] Almost immediately on receiving his instructions Foster left for the United States.[179] Apparently the President and Secretary Evarts were satisfied from Foster's testimony before the House sub-committee and his conferences with State Department officials that recognition should be extended without delay.[180] Furthermore Cox introduced another resolution in the House March

---

[176] The members were Conkling, of New York, Hamlin, of Maine, Howe, of Wisconsin, Jones, of Nevada, Cameron, of Pennsylvania, Eaton, of Connecticut, Maxey, of Texas, Hackett, p. 53; *Cong. Record*, 45th Cong., 1st sess., p. 120.

[177] Hackett, pp. 52-53; Foster, I, 95.

[178] Evarts to Foster, December 31, 1877, Instructions MSS, XIX.

[179] Foster to Evarts, January 30, 1878, Despatches MSS, LXI. No railroad yet connected Mexico City with the United States and the telegraph lines stretching across the uninhabited wastes of northern Mexico and southern Texas were often disrupted by storms or raiders. Therefore most official communications were sent to Vera Cruz by rail, thence to the United States by ship. Official communications were thus two weeks or more in arriving. Foster, I, 26.

[180] *Ibid.*, p. 95.

11 inviting President Hayes to recognize the Diaz Government, which was described as having fulfilled " the requirements of international comity and law for the purpose of recognition by our government." [181]

At all events the long deferred recognition was almost immediately extended after Foster's visit. Evarts argued that Diaz had apparently fulfilled the conditions of recognition required by the American Government. Mexico was relatively peaceful, its government relatively stable. Apparently the Diaz Government intended to fulfill its treaty obligations, as evidenced by prompt payment of two successive installments under the claims award and the increasing vigor of its measures on the border. If Diaz really found his government embarrassed in discussion of the pending matters the American Government was willing to " waive its own preferences as to the fittest manner and time of adjusting the difficulties " between the two countries. Therefore Foster was " authorized to say to Mr. Vallarta that henceforth your communications will be official and in the usual form with recognized powers." [182]   On April 8, Foster resumed charge of the legation and the next day he formally recognized the Diaz Government.[188]

Thus sixteen months of controversy over recognition were brought to a close. The period had been a troublous one and relations had at times been strained to the point where war was discussed as a possibility. Happily one of the great questions at issue between the two countries had been settled but several years were to pass before satisfactory agreements could be arrived at on the border. Meanwhile the American Government, having failed to make good its contention for border guarantees as a prerequisite to recognition, now lost no time in urging such guarantees after recognition should be extended.[184]

---

[181] *House Journal*, 45th Cong., 2d sess., pp. 636-637. Both this and Cox's former resolution were referred to the Foreign Affairs Committee.

[182] Evarts to Foster, March 23, 1878, Instructions MSS, XIX.

[188] Foster to Evarts, April 8, 1878, Despatches MSS, LXI; Foster to Evarts, April 9, 1878 (Telegram Cipher), *ibid.*

[184] Evarts to Foster, March 23, 1878, Instructions MSS, XIX.

CHAPTER III

Border Lawlessness, 1878-1881

In the first flush of enthusiasm after *de jure* recognition relations between the two countries greatly improved and the general atmosphere in Mexico City partook of the nature of a love feast. Diaz gave Foster a great official dinner and the American minister reciprocated at the legation in honor of President Diaz and his cabinet.[1] Soon, however, ominous war clouds began once again to bank along the horizon. Most important in all probability, in rechilling the atmosphere, was the failure permanently to solve the situation on the border. A new Escobedo revolutionary movement in Texas in the spring and summer of 1878 caused American troops to cross into Mexico repeatedly and kept the Mexican press in a turmoil of excitement while the Mexican Government and Mexican public opinion stubbornly resisted treaty arrangements on the border until the Order of June 1 be withdrawn. So serious was the border situation that by October war was again considered as probable by the majority of informed Mexicans.[2] At the National Independence Day celebration in Mexico City September 15, 1878, the annual patriotic poem when read proved to be bitterly anti-American. Foster and his family finally felt the only dignified course to be withdrawal from the festival and as they left the great gathering they were assailed by shouts of "War!" and "Death to the Yankees!"[3]

At the same time official opinion in the United States was deeply dissatisfied with the early fruits of recognition. Evarts wrote in August that in spite of recognition "the condition of affairs upon the Rio Grande frontier remains substantially the same. . . . The United States instead of receiving re-

[1] Foster to Evarts, May 2, 1878 (Unofficial), Despatches MSS, LXII.

[2] Foster, *Memoirs*, I, 99-101.

[3] Foster to Evarts, September 21, 1878, Despatches MSS, LXIV; Foster, I, 101.

dress encounters delays, denials, and postponements at the capital while in the disturbed localities its officers meet with active opposition." [4]   Similarly Foster, on the ground in Mexico City, was forced to the conclusion, after nearly seven months, " that the flattering promises held out by the Mexican Foreign Office of the good effects of recognition have all been disappointed." [5]

Thus the border situation and with it the future of cordial relations between the two countries seemed dark indeed in the closing months of 1878. Apparently little permanent progress was being made against the forces of lawlessness. But considered fifty years after the event and in the light of difficulties already enumerated and others now to be considered, it seems little wonder that disorder yielded slowly. First of all the smallness of the force available, American and Mexican, was a prime consideration. As early as 1871 General Sherman had written to his brother, John Sherman: " The people here [in Texas] do not appreciate the necessity for the constant reduction of the forces and the increased economy and parsimony which necessarily must go on till the army simply becomes utterly powerless." [6]   This condition still held good in the late '70's, as may be seen from the letters and testimony of military men who were most closely in touch with the situation. Army men generally deplored the smallness of the force stationed on the border. " I send you by mail, today," Sheridan wrote to Sherman, " an application of Gen'l Ord for an additional regiment of cavalry. There ought to be more troops on the Rio Grande but it troubles me greatly where to get a regiment even. The 3rd Cavalry can go if we are willing to take the risk to the Nebraska and Wyoming frontier." [7]   At the same time the fact must be constantly borne in mind that this testimony, while expert as to the problem of policing the border, was

---

[4] Evarts to Foster, August 13, 1878, Instructions MSS, XIX.
[5] Foster to Evarts, October 30, 1878 (Confidential and Unofficial), Despatches MSS, LXV.
[6] W. T. Sherman to John Sherman, May 18, 1871, W. T. Sherman Papers MSS, XXX.
[7] Sheridan to Sherman, November 24, 1877, ibid., XLVII.

undoubtedly prejudiced by the desire of the army officers to have a large army.

Testifying before the House Military Affairs Committee on December 8, 1877, Ord reported 2,941 troops under his command. These consisted of a staff of 48, cavalry forces numbering 1,723, infantry 1,125, and Indian scouts 45. These forces, according to Ord, fell short of even a minimum requirement. He asked for 5,000 troops, of whom 3,000 were to be cavalry.[8] About the same time Sherman testified before the same committee that Mexico was said to have about 4,000 regulars on the border while the United States had only about 1,900. He thought that 4,000 regulars on the American side would be " amply sufficient," with infantry and cavalry in about the same proportions. The infantry should be stationed in posts and used for operations in the mesquite, while the cavalry should be used in the open prairie.[9] Sherman, writing privately to Sheridan a few days later, said:

I was three days before the military committee of the House last week, submitted to a miserable cross questioning by a parcel of men utterly hostile to us, professionally and practically, but I stuck to my points closely, and am glad to find that your opinions and mine coincide absolutely. I admitted that the Rio Grande border needed 4000 effective men, half infantry and half cavalry, but that taking the demands of the whole country and the seemingly hostile action of Congress, I did not see how we could do more than has been done, that the quantity of raiding was less now than formerly and that the present clamor was only a repetition of what had arisen almost every year since 1846, that to withdraw cavalry from the Sioux region would result in the murder of twenty good men to save the bare chance of one ranchman in Texas a few hundred dollars worth of cattle or head of mustang ponies.[10]

Furthermore to garrison seventy-three permanent posts in the Division of the Missouri extending from Canada to the Rio Grande, Sheridan in 1878 reported only 4 companies of artillery averaging 53 men each; 8 regiments of cavalry,

---

[8] 45th Cong., 2d sess., *H. Misc. Doc.* No. 64, p. 77.

[9] Sherman before the House Committee on Military Affairs, November 21, 1877, *ibid.*, p. 19. The seeming inconsistency between Sherman's and Ord's figures may be explained by the fact that Sherman referred to the border while Ord referred to the whole department of Texas.

[10] Sherman to Sheridan, November 29, 1877, W. T. Sherman Letterbook 1872-1878 MSS.

averaging 765 men each; 18 regiments of infantry, averaging 452 men each. Thus in this great area of about 1,000,000 square miles, almost one-third of the United States proper, only 14,168 men patrolled the lonely reaches of the western Mississippi valley and fought the fierce Sioux and Apache in desert, mountain, and plain. This force, scattered in small garrisons of a company or two each through the Departments of Dakota, the Platte, and Missouri, averaged about one man for each seventy-five square miles; in the Department of Texas one man for éach one hundred and twenty square miles.[11] In short, in every area along the border as large as Rhode Island ten men on the average had to maintain posts, open up roads, protect mail coaches and railroad construction crews, and pursue bandits, usually far from their base of supplies and in a country much of which was indescribably wild, bewildering, and inhospitable. With great armies the task would have been difficult enough; with the pitifully small forces available it seemed almost hopeless.

Here centered the essential factor in the problem. For not only was the force totally inadequate but its elements were so widely scattered as to render effective support almost out of the question. Of course only by spreading thinly forces at its command could the War Department even make a weak attempt to cover the vast region, but this did not obviate the necessity for more posts and troops. Secretary of War McCrary urged the expenditure of " a few millions of dollars," if necessary, to provide more forts along the Rio Grande so that a chain might be forged, made up of properly manned posts at average intervals of forty miles. He would garrison these posts with infantry and patrol the intervening distances with cavalry.[12]   Sherman, writing to Maxey on the same subject, said: " I certainly will favor any proposal to build suitable posts along the Rio Grande frontier because it

---

[11] Annual Report Lieut. Gen. P. H. Sheridan, Commanding the Division of the Missouri, October 25, 1878, in *Report of Secretary of War for 1878*, p. 33.   See also to same effect report of Ord, October 2, 1878, *ibid.*, p. 81.

[12] McCrary before the House Military Affairs Committee, November 23, 1877, 45th Cong., 2d sess., *H. Misc. Doc.* No. 64, p. 4.

forms a national boundary, and is likely to be permanent."
He thought it desirable to build a new fort between Ringgold
Barracks and Fort McIntosh and another between the latter
and Fort Duncan. If others could be added he " should
prefer small blockhouses, connected with the larger posts by
telegraph, which would give prompt notice of the crossing of
any raiding party." [13] Raids, as previously noted, occurred
mostly in the territory between Fort Brown on the south and
Eagle Pass or Fort Duncan on the north, a distance of 402
miles. Sherman urged that two additional posts in this
harassed region would be as valuable as 25,000 more men.[14]
Farther north Fort Davis, nearest permanent garrison to the
Rio Grande in northwestern Texas, was 140 miles from Fort
Quitman and 100 miles from Paso del Norte.[15] Thus huge
gaps between permanent posts often of a hundred miles or
more enabled raiders to slip through easily.

Side by side with small and scattered numbers border conditions themselves fought against adequate control. Tre-
mendous distances, great hardships of climate and topogra-
phy, and the galling activity of the border banditry, often
brought men and horses to the point of exhaustion. Sheridan
reported late in 1877 that outbreaks during the year had
kept the troops on the border busy night and day. Some
cavalry regiments during the spring and summer had marched
as many as 4,000 weary miles under the blazing sun and
under the stars. He added that the year's gruelling campaigns were a substantial repetition of those for the past ten
years. Many of the men had died from sickness or exposure
or were on the hospital list. Some companies had dwindled
to thirty or forty effectives and should be recruited without
delay to a hundred men each.[16] Some of the regiments,
Sherman reported later, had been in the border country for

---

[13] Sherman to Maxey, March 31, 1879, W. T. Sherman Letterbook
MSS.

[14] Sherman before House Military Affairs Committee, November
21, 1877, 45th Cong., 2d sess., *H. Misc. Doc.* No. 64, p. 20.

[15] Special Report of Col. Edward Hatch to Headquarters of the
Department of Missouri, September 6, 1879, in *Report of Secretary
of War for 1879*, pp. 87-88.

[16] *Ibid., 1877*, p. 58.

ten years and he urged the necessity of replacing them as soon as possible with fresh troops.[17]

The posts themselves were often necessarily situated in the dreariest country and the men suffered greatly from droughts, germ-laden drinking water, sandstorms, great heat, and other discomforts of a wild rugged frontier in a semi-arid region. Lack of green foodstuffs in some of the posts, due to poor soil and slow transportation by the lumbering army wagons, caused sickness and emphasized their isolation from the outside world.[18] In many cases only the telegraph and an occasional wagon train linked the troops in their squat brick, wooden, and adobe barracks with life outside. Almost intolerable boredom was the result. Officers and men on the frontiers of Arizona, New Mexico, and Texas felt themselves neglected and yearned for families, schools, churches, and other features of "refined society," Sherman wrote.[19]

In addition to isolation and unhealthful surroundings the little scattered posts were often inadequate to accommodate even the company or two which usually occupied each of them. Senator Maxey early in 1879 quoted Ord as estimating that sixteen companies in the Department of Texas were without quarters. Ord claimed, according to Maxey, that while the military frontier had extended 150 to 200 miles in recent years, practically nothing had been spent for new troop quarters in his Department. If the present force were to be maintained, Ord urged that the government "should make provision to house them." [20]

It seems small wonder in the face of these hardships year

---

[17] Sherman to Senator Maxey of Texas, March 31, 1879, W. T. Sherman Letterbook MSS. Maxey was a member of the Senate Military Affairs Committee. In his Annual Report November 6, 1882, Sherman said from 10 to 15 years. *Report of Secretary of War for 1882*, p. 8.

[18] James L. Rock and W. I. Smith, *Southern and Western Texas Guide for 1878*, pp. 28-36. The facts were by courtesy of Major General Ord and Dr. M. K. Taylor, Assistant Surgeon, U. S. A.

[19] *Report of Secretary of War for 1882*, p. 8.

[20] Maxey to Sherman, May 29, 1879, W. T. Sherman Papers MSS, XLIX. Maxey had introduced a bill calling for $200,000 for such troop housing and sought Sherman's views to "lay before the Committee and the Senate."

after year that the troops should have failed in some cases to keep their morale at its highest. Writing to Sherman in 1876 Ord said:

> . . . but what I want to say Gen'l is that I have again asked to have the 24th taken away from this Dep't—I can get along much better without them—one half the officers are under charges by the other half, the six companies at Brown and Ringgold have only about thirty men for duty—and their officers except Potter, Shafter, Bullis and one or two others are of little or no use—except to breed courts martial—they need discipline and the change would be of service to them.[21]

Officers sometimes reported sick [22] or allowed their friends, especially members of Congress, to use influence to have them given other assignments, with " the most damaging influence on the army." [23]   In the same vein Ord wrote to Sherman earlier in 1876: " My principle business now is trying the department—about one half the officers at some posts have preferred charges " against the other half. Ord expected the latter half to prefer counter charges soon.[24] The colored troops seem to have been a particular source of trouble: " The 10th Cavalry," Ord wrote, " are all fighting each other—haven't so far done much—wish I could get leave to mount an Infantry Reg't . . . it might shame the colored cavalry to do something." [25]

With all due allowances for Ord's excitability and apparent penchant for exaggeration the situation must have been serious enough. Colonel A. V. Kautz, commanding the Department of Arizona, had much the same point of view as Ord. " I must remind you again," he wrote Sherman in 1878, " of the heavy weights I am obliged to carry in running this Department." Two of his officers whom he mentioned by name he described as " habitually soaked with whiskey in a manner . . . that incapacitates them more or less." Another he referred to as having " a treacherous hand all the time stab-

---

[21] Ord to Sherman, August 8, 1876, ibid., XLIV.
[22] Sheridan to Sherman, October 25, 1876, ibid.
[23] Report of Secretary of War for 1882, p. 8.
[24] Ord to Sherman, June 2, 1876, W. T. Sherman Papers MSS, XLIII.
[25] Ord to Sherman, January 16, 1876, ibid., XLII.

bing me in the dark." He spoke of the "utter worthless-
ness" of still another officer. "There is no use preferring
charges," he added, "if the accused has any friends he
always gets off, and the effect is worse than it would be if he
had not been tried." [26] Probably such charges did not apply
to the army as a whole in the border country. Sherman felt
that by and large the troops had done "all that that number
of men could do." [27] However, the evidence submitted would
seem to indicate that at least some of the officers and men
were below the pitch of efficiency required for successful
bandit hunting in such a difficult country.

Another factor which must have detracted from the efficiency of the troops and thus have prolonged disorders on the
border was friction between Ord and his immediate superior,
Sheridan, with relations apparently becoming progressively
more and more strained until Ord's retirement in 1881.
Sheridan charged Ord with inefficiency, with exaggerating
border disorder under the influence of interests anxious to
involve the United States in war with Mexico, and with vio-
lating military regulations in writing to his old friend Sherman over his [Sheridan's] head. He wrote in 1877:

> The Division Commander knows too well the confusion which
> existed in the Department of the Platte, while under the command
> of Gen'l Ord to not fully realize what may exist in the Department
> of Texas.[28]

A few weeks later he wrote again:

> If you will permit me I will say confidently that it is my belief
> that we cannot have any quiet or peace on the Rio Grande as long
> as Ord is in command of Texas. I have lost confidence in his mo-
> tives, and his management of his Department is a confusion.
> If he could be sent somewhere else—and a good man put in his
> place he could soon bring peace and quiet to that frontier. I am
> sorry to say that it is my belief that Ord is the trouble down there.[29]

---

[26] Kautz to Sherman, February 13, 1878, ibid., XLVII.

[27] Sherman before House Military Affairs Committee, November
21, 1877, 45th Cong., 2d sess., H. Misc. Doc. No. 64, p. 20.

[28] Sheridan's endorsement on an anonymous letter dated September
13, 1877, and signed "Reliable Citizen" of Eagle Pass, Texas, com-
plaining to the Secretary of War of alleged bad treatment of soldiers
at Fort Duncan, Texas. W. T. Sherman Records, Endorsements and
Memoranda, 1876-1882, MSS, I.

[29] Sheridan to Sherman, November 24, 1877, W. T. Sherman Papers
MSS, XLVII.

After two years of further irritation and friction Sheridan expressed himself even more emphatically.

General Ord's eccentricity of character and the devious methods which he employs to accomplish his ends, some time since forced me to doubt his motives in some of his official actions and so much had this impression gained on me that for a long time I have reluctantly avoided any personal correspondence with him. I have doubted his motives in some of his recommendations for expenditure of public money and even in his calls for and disposition of troops: and the facility with which revolutions, raids, murders and thefts are generated on the Rio Grande border whenever an emergency demands even the temporary withdrawal of a few troops or even a special officer from the Department is somewhat remarkable. . . . I distrust his management of affairs in Texas and I feel that we want there an officer free from schemes and with such an officer I believe the constant irritation represented as existing on that frontier would be to a great extent if not wholly allayed.[30]

Apparently the quarrel involved Major General John Pope, commanding the Department of Missouri,[31] over the question of transfer of certain important territory from his Department to Ord's. At any rate Pope wrote to Sherman early in 1880: " Ord wanted the El Paso region retransferred to his people but Sheridan objected for very conclusive reasons—our means of supplying communications with that region are far better than from San Antonio. . . . These are my opinions and I am sure that they are those of Sheridan also and I trust that you will *not* yield to the wishes of those who beyond doubt have some other than the public interest in view." [32] Apparently also the story of friction between San Antonio and Chicago, Headquarters of the Division of the Missouri, was known in other army circles. Major General Nelson A. Miles even went so far as to intimate, rather untactfully it would seem, that he might be considered an available successor to Ord. He wrote John Sherman, Secretary of the Treasury, in 1877:

General Sheridan informs me that he has got to send a reg't of infantry and one of cavalry to the Rio Grande at once and that

---

[30] Sheridan to Sherman, December 12, 1879, *ibid.*, LI.

[31] The Department of Missouri under Pope was a subdivision of the Division of the Missouri under Sheridan and should not be confused with the latter.

[32] Pope to Sherman, February 18, 1880, W. T. Sherman Papers MSS, LI.

General Ord seems to be in the hands of those who are getting up a war with Mexico. General Sheridan seems to be opposed to it and not satisfied with the course the military have been taking there. In fact unless there is a decided change we will be involved in a war with Mexico very soon. Now I neither presume the Government, nor the people, desire a war at this time, and I believe there is no necessity for any trouble on that line. If there is a chance of any change I could be assigned to command of that Department and I believe it would be for my interests. Please do what you can for me.[33]

Placed in a difficult position by this serious rift between his old comrades-in-arms Sherman sought to mollify Sheridan so far as possible, at the same time recognizing Ord's weaknesses. " General Sheridan's reflection on General Ord is a little hard. I do not believe General Ord would tolerate for a moment any act of injustice . . . ," he stoutly asserted.[34] Questioned by the House Military Affairs Committee as to Ord's qualities of command on the border Sherman tactfully avoided the full implications of the question. The subject, he said, was delicate. It was sufficient that the President had sent him there. Officers had to be used according to the necessities of the country. " General Ord has both rank and experience, and generally speaking he has, I think, given satisfaction not only to the government but to the people of Texas." [35] On the other hand he wrote to Sheridan:

I have been conscious for some time that you attribute much of the clamor on the Texas border to General Ord. You of course know that Ord was sent there without my assent by President Grant, but the immediate motive was of course to make a place for Crook, and also to have Auger at New Orleans. To change Ord *now* under pressure might damage him, but I am more convinced that a cool and less spasmodic man in Texas would do more to compose matters on that border than mere increase of Cavalry, for which now is the cry.

I would not object if Terry should go to Texas or Auger, leaving Crook to handle all the Sioux. . . . If Crook were in command in Texas, and Mackenzie had his own and the Eighth Cavalry with a couple of Regiments of Infantry on the Rio Grande I believe raiding would cease, and what is equally desirable all the clamor would cease with the Texas representatives and they would be our fast friends in Congress.[36]

---

[33] Miles to John Sherman, November 25, 1877, John Sherman Papers MSS, CL.

[34] Sherman's Endorsement on Reliable Citizen's letter (see n. 28), W. T. Sherman Records, Endorsements, and Memoranda MSS, 1876-1882, I.

[35] Sherman before House Military Affairs Committee, November 21, 1877, 45th Cong., 2d sess., *H. Misc. Doc.* No. 64, pp. 25-26.

[36] Sherman to Sheridan, November 29, 1877, W. T. Sherman MSS,

These sentiments of Sherman privately expressed to Sheridan would seem to show that as early as 1877, no matter what might be his personal feeling, he agreed substantially with the latter as to Ord's temperamental unfitness for the Texas command, involving as it did long stretches of an important international boundary. At the same time Senator Maxey, representing at least a portion of Texan opinion, found Ord's work good and recommended his retirement as a major general, the rank which he held brevet. Usually, Maxey said, he opposed " retiring an officer on any other than his actual rank . . . yet there are special and exceptional cases, which move out of the general rule. This is one of them.

" When he [Ord] took command of the Department of Texas, life and property on the frontier were very insecure. He has brought order out of chaos, and leaves life and property on the border fairly secure and the Department in splendid condition." [37] But all question of the merits of this controversy aside, a controversy with ramifications in Washington and various departmental headquarters, the fact remains that so great was the uproar and so disturbed were army " politics " that the efficiency of the border patrol could scarcely fail to suffer.

In still another direction Ord seems to have had great trouble, perhaps through no fault of his own. He was placed in the doubly difficult position of having to stand between Texans who sought use of volunteer Texas troops in border

---

Letterbook, 1872-1878. Sherman and Ord had campaigned together as young lieutenants against Seminoles in Florida and in the gold country on the American River in California. Later still they fought together in the Civil War. Sherman, *Memoirs*, I, 22, 38, 40, 48, 49, 57, 85, 87, 89, 102, 103, 109, 110, 288, 289, 291, 355, 359, 372; II, 26, 413. Their correspondence as contained in Sherman's Papers shows a deep attachment. Sherman therefore tried to advise Ord. "Thanks for your letter—and yet other thanks for your good will . . . ," Ord wrote to Sherman, July 31, 1879. W. T. Sherman Papers MSS, L. A few months later Ord spoke of Sherman's " rebukeful letter about private letters on O. B." [official business]. He also urged that Sherman give him " credit for the best intentions—and at the same time you can bet that if any other fellow can do it [manage the Department of Texas] I have no objections." Ord to Sherman, February 23, 1880, *ibid.*, LI.

[37] Maxey to Sherman, December 17, 1881, *ibid.*, LIV.

work and War Department circles which were usually opposed
to their use. Raising volunteer companies in time of emergency had been the practice in Texas from the early days
when there were no regulars on whom to rely. As Reconstruction waned and the Democratic party came back into
power in Texas a battalion was organized in 1874 for the general defense of the frontier and the suppression of lawlessness and a special force of frontier or police troops was
created for service in particular localities.[38]   With such
bodies of men already in service and nearly all the men of
the frontier trained in riding and the use of arms and ready
to form more companies almost at a moment's notice, great
pressure was brought to bear on the regular army officers to
accept volunteers. This is evidenced by a letter of Ord to
Sherman in the fall of 1877 enclosing a copy of a letter
which he had received from " Delegate Schleicher." Ord
wrote:

> You perceive he has taken umbrage at my not wanting Texas
> volunteers—and providing thereby for his and the governor's friends.
> I am trying to carry out the whole orders of the President, and no
> more—If the President wants war he can get it by calling out the
> Texas Volunteers. I am of the opinion that neither the President,
> or the Secretary of State is disposed to encourage a war until other
> means fail to obtain the desired end—but I am advised from good
> sources that the governor has ordered the state troops to concentrate
> at Laredo *and that they have* intimations from the governor that
> if a chance occurs to go into Mexico they should do so . . . it is
> probable if they go into Mexico they will be driven back—and then—
> what next! I have notified Colonel Shafter to send one of his com-
> panies of cavalry to Laredo—and have sent a detachment to Carizo,
> opposite Guerero—the last moon (just over) passed without a raid
> from Mexico—and this is the third without a raid—in my opinion
> the frontier authorities will try and restrain the Lipans and Kicka-
> poos from coming over, so long as my present orders [the Order of
> June 1, 1877] are in force, or a treaty provides for similar action—
> Schleicher insinuates that I have the *permission* of the Mexican
> Gen'ls to cross regulars—in pursuit of raiders—the facts are that
> when I interviewed for one day or two Treviño (by directions from
> Washington) he took advantage of our being alone, to ask me (as
> a sort of favor) and *privately* not to send others than regular troops
> into Mexico—and hoped I would send those under discreet com-
> manders—and this I promised should be done—and I am now sorry
> I communicated this information to Mr. Schleicher, as he does not
> seem inclined to receive it in the spirit it was given, but maybe he

[38] Dudley G. Wooten, *A Comprehensive History of Texas, 1685-
1897*, II, 329.

looked forward to big results politically *and is* mad at my not working in his interest. I hope General you will have a talk with the President on this matter—and advise me if my course is approved. I am quite sure that it harmonizes with your views, and the true interests of the country—these Texas frontier men would (to make money) plunge the country in a war with all Europe, of course since my report and positive declination to have Texas volunteers—unless in the case of offensive movements—my Texas popularity is over—except with those who fought in the rebellion—who all say that they have had all the war they want.[39]

On the other hand Sherman, more conservative in most of his border judgments than Ord, seemed to feel that under certain circumstances use of state forces might be necessary to a limited extent and for a limited time. He wrote an endorsement on the copy of a letter from Ord to the Governor of Texas, dated July 19, 1878, in which he suggested the use of state troops in connection with United States troops for pursuit and arrest of white American raiders and thieves, since the state troops had power of arrest while the regulars did not. " I fear," Sherman said, " that the desperadoes of our frontier will soon learn that our troops cannot attack them, and that the mail routes and horse ranches will have enemies more dangerous than Indians or Mexicans." [40]

About two years later Sherman seemed even more definitely convinced of the advisability of limited use of state forces against raiders in cooperation with regulars. " It is manifest," he said, " that we have not soldiers enough to protect hundreds and thousands of new settlements growing up in the vast region inland, infested by bands of hostile Indians." He recommended reference of the question to the military commanders on the border " with the request that authority be granted [to these commanders] to call out local volunteers for a limited period and in limited numbers." [41]

---

[39] Ord to Sherman, October 25, 1877, W. T. Sherman Papers MSS, XLVI.

[40] Endorsement of July 30, 1878, W. T. Sherman Records, Endorsements, and Memoranda, 1876-1882 MSS, I.

[41] Endorsement, June 8, 1880, on a communication of June 1, 1880, from W. G. Rich, Acting Governor of New Mexico, to Sherman, enclosing a letter to the Governor from W. J. Crosby and other citizens of Shakespeare, N. M., stating that the town's supplies had been cut off by raiding Indians and asking, if regular troops could not be sent, authority for calling out volunteers. *Ibid.*

By such expressions, however, Sherman did not intend incorporation of these volunteers into regular units, even as scouts. This is clearly shown in an endorsement of November 1880. " The pressure on officers to accept the services of -volunteers on the frontier is very great and must be resisted. Else every officer in pursuit of Indians will accept the services of these bodies which profess to understand so much of the Indian character. No matter what may be the fact, we are restricted by the plain requirements of the law to restrict the army to the organization and numbers fixed by law." [42] Thus it would seem that employment of state troops against raiders and, in case of their employment, the degree of that employment, led to endless controversy between state and army officials and to differences of opinion among army men themselves.

Perhaps in the light of the foregoing factors the troops would have found difficulty enough in the ordinary course of policing an international frontier against smugglers, immigration law violators, and fugitives from justice. In the case of the Mexican border, however, too much emphasis cannot be placed on the special problems of Mexican revolutionary movements organized on American soil, filibustering, the flight of deserters, the Free Zone, forced loans on Americans, and raiders.

All of these points of friction continued in greater or less degree for some time after formal relations were established. In a note written a few days after recognition was extended by the Hayes Administration, De Cuellar in the Washington legation complained to the State Department of alleged Mexican revolutionary organizations on American soil. He quoted the Mexican commercial agent at Brownsville as reporting in a telegram to the legation that seditious persons were organizing at La Noria and San Isidro. They were only awaiting the arrival of Escobedo, according to the telegram, to cross to the Mexican side and begin active armed operations

---

[42] Endorsement, November 10, 1880, on papers relative to employment of Captain Fontain and six men as scouts by Col. Geo. P. Buell, 15th U. S. Infantry, *ibid.*

against the Diaz Government. He urgently requested the
State Department to take any means it might see fit to cope
with the situation.[43] Within two weeks Zamacona also left a
memorandum at the State Department claiming that arms
were being collected in Texas by revolutionists for a sudden
movement into Mexico. Some of these purchased by Escobedo, according to the memorandum, had been deposited in
the house of Wulfing H. Labaht, a merchant of San Antonio,
subject to the order of Daniel Wuste of Eagle Pass. More
arms were expected soon at San Antonio from Austin under
the care of a revolutionist named Enrique Mexia.[44] Furthermore Vallarta reported word from the Mexican consul at San
Antonio of a band of alleged revolutionists at Laredo.[45] The
consul charged that they were really ordinary raiders instead
of Lerdo partisans as they claimed to be. He also reported
word a week later from the military commanders at Matamoras and Camargo that one band of alleged revolutionists
had left Brownsville two days before supposedly for Reynosa,
Mexico.[46] Early in May De Cuellar again brought to the
attention of the State Department persistent reports in Texas
newspapers and from Mexican confidential and commercial
agents at San Antonio of revolutionary bands armed in
Texas, some of which were reported to have crossed.[47] In
response to the Mexican Government's urgent requests the
State Department reported various measures taken to pre-

[43] De Cuellar to Evarts, April 13, 1878, Notes from the Mexican
Legation MSS, XXV.

[44] Zamacona Memorandum, *ibid.* See also Zamacona to Evarts,
July 31, 1878, *U. S. For. Rel. 1878*, p. 679, for extract from the
Report of the Mexican consul at San Antonio. Three wagons drawn
by four mules each and loaded with carbines arrived at Laredo,
Texas, May 1 from San Antonio. They were addressed to Santos
Benavides (father-in-law of Garza Ayala) and contained about 400
carbines. Twenty-five cases of carbines (with 10 guns in each case)
arrived at Laredo May 30 from San Antonio. They were also con-
signed to Benavides. Memorandum of the Mexican Legation left at
the State Department, June 17, 1878, Notes from the Legation MSS,
XXV.

[45] Foster to Evarts, April 22, 1878, Despatches MSS, LXII.

[46] Foster to Evarts, April 29, 1878, *ibid.*

[47] De Cuellar to Evarts, May 3, 1878, *U. S. For. Rel. 1878*, p. 674.

vent and, if a case arose, to punish any violations of the neutrality laws.[48]

Despite these precautions Zamacona wrote shortly thereafter: " During the past two weeks various parties of men, enlisted and armed in Texas, have crossed from that State to the territory of Mexico, creating local disorders which will not extend to the interior of the country, but which may exert a pernicious influence in the frontier districts." [49] In the early morning hours of May 27 Lerdist forces crossed from Texas near Brownsville, with a detachment of the garrison of Matamoras giving battle to one body of revolutionists. Another body stopped to plunder Mexican ranches and the wagon train of Indalecio Garcia on their way to Reynosa. Zamacona, who reported this action to the State Department, asserted that several Americans, of whom he named five, were engaged in the attack on the wagon train.[50] Some of these revolutionists were soon dispersed and their leader, Escobedo, captured by Diaz forces. " The Revolutionary movement which began on the Rio Grande frontier in the month of May and continued through June has been successfully suppressed so far as any large bands are concerned," Foster wrote late in July. " Up to the present time the authority of General Diaz continues to be generally obeyed throughout the Republic." [51]

The extent of this revolutionary activity is hard to gauge. As in so many questions of border disorder reports from north and south of the international boundary were conflicting. Over against the Mexican reports already cited may be set that of Captain Sellers, Commanding Fort McIntosh, Texas. He denied any knowledge of revolutionary bands at Laredo but he admitted that Isadore Salinas with forty men

---

[48] See Zamacona to Evarts, June 8, 1878, Notes from the Legation MSS, XXV.

[49] Ibid. In a later note Zamacona asked that by " civil or military measures, the aforesaid Garza Ayala and Salinas at least be removed from the districts bordering on Mexico where they continue to plot against the peace of that Republic." Zamacona to Evarts, June 21, 1878, ibid.

[50] Zamacona to Evarts, June 8, 1878, ibid.

[51] Foster to Evarts, July 27, 1878, Despatches MSS, LXII.

had crossed to the Mexican side below Piedras Negras and that Mexican troops in the towns of Nuevo Laredo and Piedras Negras had advised Captain Kennedy to be on the watch for Salinas' return. He also claimed to have crossed the river and held an interview with Colonel Aleguria during which he invited the latter to cross to the American side and show him any rebel body. Aleguria refused and also refused to send an officer on the same mission, although later he did so, according to Sellers. The American officer thereupon accused the Mexican of being lukewarm in his desire to catch the rebels.[52]

Fortunately for the relations between the United States and Mexico these revolutionary activities ceased to be a major diplomatic and military problem for thirty years after the defeat and capture of Escobedo. Not until the first decade of the twentieth century when the reins of power fell from the aging hands of Diaz did they again constitute such a problem. A few sporadic Mexican expeditions, bent on marauding or revolution or both, were recruited on the frontier but were scattered without diplomatic consequences. Colonel Willcox, commanding the Department of Arizona, reported in 1880, for instance, an expedition raised by one Marquez on or near the Sonora line close to the Gulf of California. There was no proof that the expedition had been organized on American soil, according to Willcox. After Marquez' defeat and expulsion from Sonora, however, he attempted to raise another force in the region of Tubac and Tucson, Arizona, clearly in violation of American neutrality laws. When pursued by Captain W. A. Rafferty and a portion of the 6th Cavalry the conspirators were soon scattered.

Similarly the filibustering expeditions which had marked the period before recognition seem from a study of the records to have diminished greatly as Diaz made his position strong and thus made filibustering a relatively unprofitable proceeding. It was charged by the Mexican consul, C. Castro, at Brownsville, July 29, 1877, that the " *orden imprudente* " of

---

[52] Evarts to Zamacona, October 30, 1878, *U. S. For. Rel. 1878*, pp. 682-684.

June 1 *"animó a los filibusteros y anexionistas"* but he brought forward no proof.[53]   About the same time Vallarta, writing to Mariscal, Mexican Minister to the United States, asserted that the Mexican Government had information of filibustering expeditions fitting out in San Francisco against Lower California. Mariscal was to ask the United States Government to prevent these attempts.[54] It was thought that this filibustering was caused by a desire on the part of certain Americans for Mexican frontier mineral wealth, especially of a group of agriculturists in California.[55] Not until 1880 does another hint of such expeditions appear. In his Instructions of September 1, 1880, John Hay reported that the general commanding the Department of the Pacific had arrested eight persons suspected of attempting to organize an expedition against Mexico.[56] Then the issue shaded off until the disorders incident to Diaz' decline.

Another series of continuing problems on the border involved the attempted apprehension of Mexican army deserters, shots fired across the international boundary, and the alleged crossing of local police officers from the United States into Mexico to capture criminals sought on the American side of the line. A group of alleged deserters from the Mexican army escaped to the American side early in 1880, and were said to have been fired upon from the Mexican side. Several were thought to have been wounded and a few weeks later another deserter making a similar dash was said to have been killed. Mr. Morgan, the American minister, asked for a disavowal of the firing under international law and the Treaty of Guadalupe Hidalgo and requested that orders be

[53] *Organización de expediciones filibusteras en Estados Unidos para invadir territorio nacional May 15, 1877–January 1, 1878*, the Mexican Legation to Ministry of Foreign Relations, Library of Congress Photostats of the Mexican Archives MSS.

[54] *Correspondencia relativa a expediciones filibusteras organizadas en California contra México 1876-1877*, Vallarta to Mariscal, March 31, 1877, *ibid.*

[55] *Ibid.* Secretario de Gobernación to Secretario de Relaciones (no date given but evidently from the date of the whole correspondence early in 1877), *ibid.*

[56] John Hay, Acting Secretary of State, to Morgan, September 1, 1880, Instructions MSS, XX.

issued to prevent a recurrence of the incident.[57]   The Mexican Government promptly ordered an inquiry and issued "peremptory orders" against repetition, if the inquiry showed that Mexican forces were at fault.[58] However, almost a year later Morgan reported that the Mexican Government had still not disavowed the shots fired after the Mexican deserters "although it would seem that sufficient time had elapsed to enable [them] to obtain information which Mr. Ruelas informed me, had been asked for." [59]   The Mexican Government finally replied that a disavowal had been implicit in the note from the Legation of November 16, 1880.[60]

On the other hand, complaints were registered by the Mexican Government against alleged firing across the boundary from the United States in an attempt to halt escaped prisoners. On one occasion it was claimed that twelve or fourteen prisoners escaped from the Laredo, Texas jail and that shots were fired after them as they fled into Mexico. This was held by the Mexican Government to be a graver question than the Mexican fire after deserters.[61]   Morgan disagreed, pointing out that in the former matter the shots took effect, causing one fatality, while in the latter they ricocheted off the water of the Rio Grande without causing injury.[62] A little later, it was claimed that the inhabitants' of Laredo fired "a great many shots toward the Mexican bank of the Rio Grande" after groups of escaping prisoners. The hope was expressed that the United States would adopt the same "most positive orders" which the Mexican War Department had issued in the case of the Mexican shots fired after the deserters.[63]

---

[57] Morgan to Evarts, July 27, 1880, Despatches MSS, LXIX.
[58] Morgan to Evarts, August 3, 1880, Enclosure Ruelas to Morgan, August 2, 1880, ibid.
[59] Morgan to Blaine, May 30, 1881, ibid., LXXII. On this despatch Hunter, apparently had noted: "It is high time, it seems to me, that another application should be made to that Government."
[60] Morgan to Blaine, August 6, 1881, ibid., LXXIII.
[61] Morgan to Evarts, October 27, 1880, Enclosure No. 1, Fernandez to Morgan, October 19, 1880, ibid., LXXI.
[62] Ibid., Enclosure No. 2, Morgan to Fernandez, October 27, 1880.
[63] Navarro to Evarts, November 16, 1880, Notes from the Legation MSS, XXVI.

More serious than firing across the border was the crossing of police officers from the United States into Mexico without permission in order to apprehend fugitives from justice. Zamacona reported in the spring of 1881 that the Mexican consul at El Paso had informed the Mexican legation that a Texan "gendarme," named James Gillett, had crossed with a companion from the village of La Isleta to Zaragoza, Mexico, and there arrested an American citizen sought in Texas. On his return to the American side of the line the fugitive, either with or without the consent of the constable, was strung up to the crossbeams of the gate in the courthouse yard by the vigilantes of Socorro.[64] Shortly thereafter Zamacona wrote that it was reported from the customs house at Palominas, Mexico, and from the Mexican consul at Tucson that a sheriff, accompanied by three men, had crossed the boundary from Tombstone, Arizona, without formalities under the Extradition Treaty of 1861, had captured his man, and returned to Arizona. Punishment of the persons involved was requested as well as provision against future difficulties of the kind.[65] Secretary Blaine communicated this request to the secretary of the interior and in turn requested that the territorial authorities of Arizona punish the guilty persons and in the future maintain the law and treaties involved.[66]

In the next place the Free Zone continued to be one of the important elements in the disturbed border situation during the period under discussion in this chapter. Romero even went so far as to hold that there was a "close connection" between border marauding and the Free Zone question.[67] Evidently the State Department had much the same opinion, as indicated by a series of despatches continuing for some time after recognition. In August 1878 Evarts expressed again the regret of the United States at the failure of the Mexican Government to abolish the Free Zone. The occasion was the consideration of a despatch from Foster trans-

---

[64] Zamacona to Blaine, April 19, 1881, *U. S. For. Rel. 1881-1882*, pp. 827-828.
[65] Zamacona to Blaine, July 25, 1881, *ibid.*, pp. 837-838.
[66] Blaine to Zamacona, August 2, 1881, *ibid.*, p. 838.
[67] Romero, *Mexico and the United States*, I, 465.

mitting a copy of the new Mexican Treasury regulations.[68] Foster writing a few days later said that smuggling from Texas to the Mexican border, thence inland in Mexico was reported " to be carried on upon so large a scale as to seriously interfere with receipts of the Customs House at Vera Cruz [the chief source of revenue of the Federal Treasury] and to greatly unsettle commercial values and trade." [69] But a month or so later he was forced to write that reports in the United States that the Free Zone was to be abolished or changed were untrue.[70]

Repeatedly Foster pressed upon the Mexican Government the urgent necessity of abolishing the Free Zone. He held it to be a base for smuggling and a source of much disorder on the frontier. He reminded the Mexican Government of Vallarta's statement that the Mexican cabinet had considered the advisability of repeal. Vallarta had at the time admitted, according to Foster, that the Mexican Government was convinced that the Zone was a greater source of evil to Mexico even than to the United States. It had led to a depleted Mexican revenue, to bloodshed and disorder, and had given special treatment to a small territory. President Diaz was of the opinion, Foster quoted Vallarta as saying, that the Zone must be modified or possibly repealed.[71] The executive branch of the Mexican Government, however, reported that it had no authority to act without the permission of the Mexican Congress.[72]

As a matter of fact strong pressure was being brought to bear by certain Mexican towns and interests for an extension of the Zone, rather than for restricting or abolishing it. Blaine enclosed to Morgan for reference to the Mexican Government a petition of some of the citizens of El Paso, Texas, against proposed extension by the Mexican Government of the Free Zone to include El Paso, Mexico.[73] In reply to

---

[68] Evarts to Foster, August 10, 1878, Instructions MSS, XIX.
[69] Foster to Evarts, August 17, 1878, Despatches MSS, LXIII.
[70] Foster to Evarts, September 23, 1878, *ibid.*, LXIV.
[71] Foster to Evarts, October 14, 1878, Enclosure No. 3, Foster to Avila, September 26, 1878, *U. S. For. Rel. 1878*, p. 657.
[72] Foster to Evarts, October 14, 1878, *ibid.*, p. 654.
[73] Blaine to Morgan, August 5, 1881, *ibid.*, *1881-1882*, pp. 782-783.

Morgan's query Mariscal, the Secretary of Foreign Relations, indicated that the petition of a group of Mexican citizens for the above extension had not yet been acted upon. Extension as well as abolition could only be brought about by an act of the Mexican Congress. The present Zone had been established by executive action without previous congressional sanction but Congress had soon made the Zone legal by granting its formal approval. In the present instance Diaz would not recommend the extension and there was no "likelihood of its passing." [74] The United States Government was evidently gratified by this attitude of the Diaz Administration toward the Free Zone. "Without manifesting too great an interest in the subject," Foster was instructed that he might say in "informal conversation" that "the assurances . . . relative to 'zona libre' had been received with evident satisfaction by your government." [75]

Meanwhile opposition to the Zone was rekindling on the American side of the line. Senator Richard Coke, of Texas, wrote to Secretary Blaine:

> The subject [of the Free Zone] is an important one not only to Texas but to the whole country. The creation of the "zona libre" on the west bank of the Rio Grande has had the effect to destroy local American commerce on that river, to diminish greatly customs revenues, to promote smuggling, and, by attracting there large numbers of bad men who engage in that unlawful business, to add greatly to the lawlessness of that border. Heretofore the "zona libre" has been confined to the Lower Rio Grande. Its extension will surely subject the country on the Upper Rio Grande to the same evils which for years have afflicted the lower country, and which for a time were so grave as seriously to threaten a rupture between the United States and the Republic of Mexico. [76]

Thus the Free Zone continued a permanent source of friction during the period under discussion and thereafter without an agreement between the two governments for its abolition being brought about.

At the other extreme high Mexican and American duties on animals and food products worked a hardship on both

---

[74] Morgan to Blaine, August 25, 1881, Despatches MSS, LXXIII.

[75] Robert R. Hitt, Acting Secretary of State, to Morgan, September 15, 1881, U. S. For. Rel. 1881-1882, p. 805.

[76] Blaine to Morgan, August 18, 1881, Enclosure, Coke to Blaine, August 8, 1881, ibid., pp. 797-798.

sides of the border, according to Ord. In 1875, he asserted, corn was cheap in Mexico and high in Texas. Much corn was smuggled into Texas to escape the high duties and there sold in the high market. In 1877 and 1878 a drought produced almost a famine in northern Coahuila and Chihuahua and Mexican troops and horses had to be supplied with food from the United States. Much of this food for men and mounts was smuggled into Mexico, Ord charged, to escape high Mexican duties. In 1879 a drought in Texas made the process work again in the other direction. These high food duties worked an especial hardship on poor people, Ord claimed, who could not get smuggled articles. Also herds on one side of the line might starve for food because they could not be driven to the other side without paying duty.[77]

The foregoing problems then remained troublesome but the most vexed of all questions on the border during this period, as previously, continued to be that of raiding. As already remarked, Indians and white border ruffians crossed the boundary frequently from one country into the other with the Indians particularly fighting fiercely for this last frontier, the Southwest. They complained that the whites killed or drove the buffaloes into the Rockies and as the buffaloes faded into the distance their sole means of support, except for government annuities, faded with them and they perforce must turn to raiding the cattle of their white conquerors.[78] With their hardy, frugal, outdoor existence, their strong tribal feeling, their knowledge of the country, and frequently their modern fighting equipment, the raiding Indians were most formidable adversaries. Furthermore, attempts to concentrate these nomadic warriors of the vast frontier country within relatively constricted reservations led to chafing, restlessness, and occasional dashes for freedom. On the other hand, some of the Indian raiders never had been on the reservations.

Thus Indians escaping from reservations or refusing to go upon them subjected both sides of the border to trial by

[77] *Report of Secretary of War for 1879*, pp. 91-92.
[78] Carl C. Rister, *The Southwestern Frontier 1865-1881*, pp. 77-78.

fire. Foster wrote the State Department in August 1878 that the Mexican Government was protesting against a recent raid into Mexico probably by Apaches from the Chiricahua reservation.[79] In the same month Mata claimed that Indians from the United States reservations "in the brief space of five days sacrificed 68 human lives and stole one hundred and some head of cattle " in Mexico.[80] Foster circumstantially confirmed the latter point of view on Indian raiding from reservations when he reported in September 1879 that Indians from Fort Stanton reservation were said to be raiding practically at will into Texas.[81]

Part of this trouble may have come from the fact that agents in charge of reservations were said to be empowered to give leaves of absence to a portion of the Indians for hunting outside the reservation. In this connection a protest was made by the Mexican Government in the fall of 1879 accompanied by affidavits of citizens of the town of Janos, in the canton of Galeana, Sonora. According to reliable reports reaching Mexican officials the agent in charge of the San Carlos reservation in Arizona was planning to give leave of absence to 2,000 Indians for forty days and the Mexican Government feared that they would raid Sonora.[82] These charges were flatly contradicted by the United States Government, the Commissioner of Indian Affairs denying that Indians were allowed to leave the reservation. Evarts in his instructions said further that the report that " Indians on certain reservations are in the habit of quitting those tracts, on leave of absence and foraging or depredating in Mexican territory " was untrue so far as the leaves of absence were concerned. " The reply of the Interior Department seems

[79] Foster to Evarts, August 29, 1878, Despatches MSS, LXIII.
[80] El gobernador de Chihuahua dice que los norte americanos son los que incitan a territorio de México para asesinar y robar November 4, 1877–January 20, 1879, Enclosure Mata, Secretary of Foreign Relations to the Governor of Chihuahua, August 8, 1878, Library of Congress Photostats of the Mexican Archives MSS.
[81] Foster to Evarts, September 12, 1879, Despatches MSS, LXVIII.
[82] Foster to Evarts, September 11, 1879, ibid. See for the same charge Zamacona to Hunter, September 15, 1879, Notes from the Legation MSS, XXV.

conclusive as to the non-existence of the practice complained of." [83]

Under what circumstances the Indians left the reservations seems after all immaterial. The main question is did they escape and, if so, did they raid the border? Foster evidently felt the evidence clear that some at least of the raiding Indians had escaped from United States reservations. " It appears to be a well authenticated fact," he wrote, " both from Mexican sources and the reports of our army officials in Texas and New Mexico, that a large number of Indians have escaped from our reservations and are now hiding in the mountains of Chihuahua." [84]   The governor of the state of Chihuahua claimed that the testimony of officers at Fort Bliss showed that forty Indians and thirty squaws had escaped from the San Carlos reservation into Mexico where they had " committed innumerable murders and robberies in that State." [85] Apparently also the Indians who escaped from United States reservations often raided on the American side of the boundary. Ord asked Sherman if he could not do something "through the President or Mr. Schurz to have the Indians of Stanton Reservation removed to the other side of the Bravo—they are now so situated as to be a continued threat to Texas and I could dispense with three or four companies of cavalry and the same number of infantry and at least two posts—but for these Reservations and the raids of [their] Indians into this state." [86]

On the other hand, it is probable that some at least of the Indian raiders were made up of different Apache, Comanche, Lipan, and Kickapoo bands which had never been on a reservation. In other words, the evidence furnished by military observation would seem to show that many of the Indian

[83] Evarts to Foster, October 14, 1879, Instructions MSS, XX; Zamacona to Evarts, October 14, 1879, Notes from the Legation MSS, XXVI.

[84] Foster to Evarts, December 27, 1879, *U. S. For. Rel. 1880-1881*, p. 727.

[85] Zamacona to Blaine, August 18, 1881, *ibid. 1881*, p. 844.

[86] Ord to Sherman, July 31, 1879, W. T. Sherman Papers MSS, L. See also De Cuellar to Evarts, May 1, 1880, Notes from the Legation MSS, XXVI.

raiders were " wild " Indians,[87] with the United States Commissioner of Indian Affairs expressing very much the same
judgment. He thought the raids carried out by desperate
whites and Indians "belonging to no particular reservation." [88] In addition Mackenzie, commanding Fort Clark,
Texas, spoke of a band of about 107 Lipan Indians in northern Coahuila who left the United States " many years ago
and took refuge in Mexico," [89] thus before the concentration
policy of the late '70's.

As to the reservations themselves some observers felt that
the administration would be more efficient and Indians prevented from escaping if they were put under military control. " To the Indian," Hamlin Garland said, " it was the
soldier—the man in blue uniform—not the civil agent sent
out from Washington to dole out bad and insufficient rations
to a conquered race, that represented courage, justice and
truth." [90] Military men complained that the Indians were
administered from Washington rather than by military forces
on the ground.   Sherman wrote to J. Q. Smith, after the
latter's retirement as head of the Bureau of Indian Affairs:

As I have often explained to you the difficulty of administration
in the Indian Bureau arose from the fact that each tribe needed
special treatment according to its past history and existing preju-

[87] Special Report of Col. Edward Hatch to Headquarters Department of the Missouri, September 6, 1879, in *Report of Secretary of
War for 1879*, p. 88.

[88] *Report of Commissioner of Indian Affairs for 1881*, p. 3.

[89] *Se niega a los Indios Lipanes el permiso que piden para establecerse en Santa Rosa, Coahuila (February to September 27, 1878)*
Library of Congress Photostats of the Mexican Archives MSS, Bvt.
Brigadier Gen. R. L. Mackenzie to General R. Falcon commanding
the Mexican line of the North April 26, 1878, Enclosure. Pope
thought that: "Nine-tenths of the reports concerning this reservation" had little foundation and that many of the reported raids
were really from Mexico. Hunter, Acting Secretary of State, to
Foster, October 1, 1879, Enclosure Pope to Col. W. D. Whipple,
Assistant Adjutant General, September 4, 1879, *U. S. For. Rel. 1880-
1881*, p. 709.

[90] Hamlin Garland, *The Book of the American Indian*, below illus-
tration opposite p. 200. Francis E. Leupp, former commissioner of
Indian Affairs, in his work, *The Indian and His Problem*, pp. 26-27,
also thinks that destruction of wild game by settlers and the government substitution of food allowances had debauched the Indian
and led him into a life of idleness, drinking, and finally depredation.

dices and the absolute impossibility of controlling these from Washington. The Commissioner also restricted by specific appropriations, could not make issues of provisions and stores to meet the clamor of the day, and the consequence was that disorder resulted from starvation and distress, which the Commissioner could not relieve." [91]

Pope felt that the fact that the military authorities did not have control of the Indians on the reservations added greatly to border confusion and disorder. He thought, however, that the Indians on the Mescalero Apache reservation thirty or forty miles from Fort Stanton were the only Indians in his department (Department of the Missouri) of whom complaint could be made. The garrison of Fort Stanton ". . . under the orders of the President, has been occupied for many months in aiding the governor of the Territory to suppress disorders" among some of these Indians. "If the Army be given control of this reservation, security against raids of any kind may be safely guaranteed." [92] Sheridan also thought that Indian troubles on the border might be improved by placing the Fort Stanton reservation under military control.[93] On the other hand, F. E. Leupp, representing the civil authority, lauded control of backward tribes by the military but thought such control too rigid for more advanced tribesmen.[94]

Furthermore, Pope thought that the reservations ought to be removed from the neighborhood of the border where escaping Indians caused international complications by raiding. He felt that the agents were unable or unwilling to tell when the Indians had left the reservations.[95] With this the Indian Commissioner partly agreed. While asserting that many of the Indian raiders were not from reservations and that in many cases they were enticed into raids by whites, or raids were charged to Indians when really carried out by whites, he thought that the Mescalero Apaches and "eventually all

---

[91] Sherman to J. Q. Smith, January 23, 1878, W. T. Sherman Letterbook 1872-1878, MSS.

[92] Hunter to Foster, October 1, 1879, Enclosure Pope to Whipple, September 4, 1879, *U. S. For. Rel. 1880-1881*, p. 709.

[93] Sheridan to Sherman, December 12, 1879, W. T. Sherman Papers MSS, LI.

[94] Leupp, p. 105.

[95] *Report of Secretary of War for 1881*, p. 118.

other Indians " should be removed north of the mid line of Arizona and New Mexico.[96] A suggestion that Lower California be utilized as a reservation for marauding border Apache Indians failed to gain the assent of the Mexican Government.[97]

Faced by the many difficulties thus caused by reservation and " wild " Indians the troops were hard pressed in their attempts to overcome Indian raiding, and international complications continued to arise. One of the worst problems, but a typical one, was furnished by the desperate Apache chieftain, Victorio. About 1870 the Chiricahua Apaches under Cochise, Victorio's predecessor, together with 500 Mimbrenos, Mogollones, and Mescaleros had been assigned to the Ojo Caliente reservation in western New Mexico. Cochise soon fled the reservation but returned in 1871. Complaints of Indian marauders by neighboring white settlers caused removal of the troublesome Indian band to Tularosa, sixty miles to the northwest, but the Indians were restless and about 1,000 of them fled to the Mescalero reservation on the Pecos river and Cochise again went on the war path with about 300 of his dusky followers.

When Cochise died, Victorio became leader and the band was allowed to settle on the Mescalero reservation. But local authorities inflamed by Victorio's previous raids, found indictments against him and some of his followers for murder and robbery. Thereupon Victorio and part of his band again fled the white man's law and for more than two years wrote their names in letters of fire along the border.[98] In September, 1879, Victorio with about sixty warriors attacked the herders of Company E, 9th Cavalry while they were herding their horses at Ojo Caliente, New Mexico. In the ensuing fight all of the herders, eight in number, were killed or

---

[96] *Report of Commissioner of Indian Affairs for 1881*, pp. 3-4.

[97] For the suggestion see Blaine to Morgan, August 31, 1881, Enclosure copy of letter Gov. John C. Fremont of Arizona Territory to Secretary of the Interior Kirkwood, August 20, 1881, *U. S. For. Rel. 1881*, pp. 803-804.

[98] Smithsonian Institution, *U. S. Bureau of American Ethnology Bulletin No. 30*, pp. 64-66.

wounded and about forty-five horses were driven off by the Indians. Probably Captain Hooker had been careless in his dispositions, according to Pope, but the horses were within sight of the post and the Indian raid was wholly unexpected.[99]

All of the troopers who could be collected were soon in the saddle in pursuit under Major Morrow of the 9th Cavalry, commanding in southern New Mexico and closely pressed by the troops, the Indians raced for the mountains north and west of Ojo Caliente. A series of running fights scattered the warriors into small bands after they had killed a number of Mexican herders, but due to the difficulties of the rugged country Morrow could not force a decisive action. The following March, however, Colonel Hatch moved with a large force to dislodge Victorio from his mountain stronghold and relentlessly drove him across the Rio Grande into the San Andrez mountains where in a severe clash Captain Carroll of the 9th Cavalry and seven of his men were badly wounded. Thereupon Hatch returned to American soil, but later recrossed the river and pursued Victorio from mountain range to mountain range, late in June and during July and August the troops engaging in desperate running fights with Victorio's band of 150 to 200 warriors.[100] Finally Victorio was forced deep into Chihuahua where Hatch was forbidden to go by orders from Washington, after an application of the United States Government to follow the Indians had been refused by the Mexican Government.[101]

Following these severe actions a special force was stationed on the frontier between Quitman and the Guadalupe mountains to watch for the possible return of Victorio. In the summer of 1880 he did recross the Rio Grande near Eagle Springs about 100 miles below the town of El Paso, captured a stage on the El Paso–San Antonio route, killed several persons, and tore down the telegraph wires for some distance. Again he was pursued, attacked, and forced back into Mexico. A second time the Indians crossed the border

---

[99] *Report of Secretary of War for 1880*, p. 86.
[100] *Ibid.*, p. 87.
[101] *Ibid.*

above Eagle Springs and again were driven back into Mexico.[102] Pope felt that the outbreaks were due to government efforts to remove Victorio and his band to the San Carlos Agency in Arizona for he had given no trouble while at Ojo Caliente. His present outbreak was his fourth within five years; three times he had been brought in and turned over to Indian Bureau authorities and each time had escaped. Pope thought his capture for the fourth time was unlikely, although he might eventually be killed. Since he was under indictment for murder in New Mexico, he probably would prefer death in battle to being hung.[103]

Whether or not Pope's judgment of the responsibility of the Indian Bureau was just, his prediction as to Victorio's manner of death was accurate. The Indians extended their depredations into Mexico even as far south as the vicinity of Chihuahua City but after several indecisive skirmishes Mexican forces in October 1880 succeeded in surrounding Victorio with his force of 100 warriors and 400 squaws and children at Tres Castillos, Chihuahua. In a desperate fight lasting several hours the Indians' ammunition was exhausted and many of the warriors were killed, Victorio himself falling dead of wounds. His successor, Nana, collected the remnants of the scattered band and, reinforced by Indians from the Mescalero and San Carlos Agencies, continued to harry the border from July 1881 to April 1882, finally being forced back into Chihuahua by American troops.[104] Seventy-three persons were officially reported as " killed by hostile Apaches during Victorio's outbreak " . . . twenty Americans, fifty-three Mexicans,[105] but the loss of life was probably much greater, one authority estimated the number as high as four hundred.[106] At times as many as 2,000 cavalry and hundreds of Indian scouts had sought Vic-

---

[102] *Ibid.*
[103] *Ibid.*, p. 88.
[104] *U. S. Bureau American Ethnology Bulletin No. 30*, pp. 64-65.
[105] Report J. J. Coppinger, Acting Assistant Inspector General, July 26, 1880, in *Report of the Secretary of War for 1880*, pp. 105-106.
[106] *U. S. Bureau American Ethnology Bulletin No. 30*, p. 64.

torio, lack of water and the superior Indian knowledge of the country handicapping the troops. In addition some of the Indians on the American side were charged with furnishing food to the marauding Indians. Nearly all of the water holes and springs were said to be in the hands of these sympathizers and the troops often had to pay exorbitant prices for grain and water.[107]

Fortunately for Arizona Territory Victorio's raiding was practically confined to the long reaches of the New Mexican border. " By a judicious and timely disposition of troops, attempts by Victorio's band to enter this Territory have been frustrated," Major Biddle reported in the autumn of 1880.[108] At the same time, however, that Victorio was ravaging the border of New Mexico some of the Chiricahuas of the San Carlos Agency were raiding the Arizona frontier. In 1880 Juh and Geronimo with 108 followers, who had previously escaped, were captured and returned to San Carlos but in September 1881 Juh and Nahdi again fled the reservation with a band of Chiricahuas. Forced by the troops into Mexico they were joined in April 1882 by Geronimo and the rest of the hostile Chiricahuas of San Carlos together with Loco and a fugitive group from Ojo Caliente.[109] Their activities will be considered more at length in the following chapter.

Trouble also developed in 1881 among the White Mountain Coyoteros on Cibicu creek in southern Arizona owing to a medicine man named Nakaidoklini who claimed the power to raise the dead. Several Indians, mourning their dead, paid the prophet liberally to bring back their departed loved ones and when he failed he blamed the powerlessness of his charms upon the presence of the white man in the vicinity. At this juncture the troops attempted to arrest " Nockay " upon the formal request of the Indian agent at the White Mountain reservation. At first it was hoped to seize him

---

[107] Report Colonel Edward Hatch, August 5, 1880, in *Report of Secretary of War for 1880*, p. 97.
[108] Report Major James Biddle, Acting Assistant Inspector General Department of Arizona, September 10, 1880, *ibid.*, p. 213.
[109] *U. S. Bureau American Ethnology Bulletin No. 30*, pp. 64-65.

when he came among the Indians to hold dances and incantations, but he did not keep his appointment. Consequently more direct methods were adopted, but the forces which were sent out to bring him in were attacked after accomplishing their mission with the resulting death of a captain and ten privates. In the mêlée the medicine man was also killed. The upshot of this affair was that Chiefs George and Bonito and seventy-four White Mountain Apaches fled to Victorio in Mexico, thus bringing new cause for international irritation.[110]

Efforts to catch these Indian raiders were rendered more difficult, according to American army men, by the assistance given them in their raids by certain elements on both sides of the border. Ord wrote Sherman early in 1877: ". . . the Indians are on the watch all the time—they are in league with intelligent Mexicans—and have Americans or foreigners claiming to be such—on this side to warn them and help to dispose of the plunder—in short the raiding business is becoming the paying commerce of some of the interior towns and the coming in and going for bands of horses—to supply the Mexican market is known in advance."[111] Americans of Santa Rosa in northern Coahuila reported the sale by Lipans and Kickapoos of many American horses. Their brands scarcely obliterated, these horses were said to be sold in the town's public square in broad daylight for five to ten dollars a head or for a few bottles of mescal. Making a pretense of farming and stock raising their chief returns, at least in the case of the Lipans, came from raiding into Texas.[112] Ord claimed "undoubted evidence," according to Foster, that these Indians were partly Kickapoos sheltered by the Mexican Government. This the Mexican Gov-

---

[110] *Ibid.* Annual Report Major General Irvin McDowell, Commanding Division of the Pacific and Department of California, October 14, 1881, Enclosure 5a Report Col. E. A. Carr, 6th Cavalry, Fort Apache, September 2, 1881, in *Report of Secretary of War for 1881*, p. 143.
[111] Ord to Sherman, January 15, 1877, W. T. Sherman MSS, XLV.
[112] *Report of Secretary of War for 1878*, Enclosure 4b Judge Thos. M. Paschal Castroville, Medina Co., Texas, to Ord, August 26, 1878, pp. 83-84.

ernment denied.[113] On the contrary it was asserted that the raids were by Lipans and that General Treviño was actively organizing a campaign against the Lipans and Mescaleros of northern Coahuila.[114] It would seem further that the officials of Coahuila were alive to the menace of these Lipan raiders. "*Los Lipanes,*" Governor Charles of Coahuila wrote, "*se han distinguido, por su carácter rapaz, por la infidelidad en el cumplimiento de sus compromisos, y por la sanguinaria y cruel.*"[115]

At the same time Mexican civilians were accused of being among the raiders with the cognizance and aid of a Mexican officer. Evarts in September 1878 reported information "of a most reliable character" of "continued depredations of the Mexican citizens of Ximenos and the neighborhood, under the head of one Areola, upon the Texas border. It is reported on the best authority that the officer in command of the Mexican troops at Piedras Negras is not merely cognizant of the repeated thefts of American cattle, but that he positively protects the raiders, furnishing them with arms on occasion, and is moreover a receiver to a large extent of the stolen property, feeding his troops, even, upon the beef."[116] Areola was at last arrested by Mexican authorities but reports that he was to be sent to Coahuila for trial seem not to have been based on fact. Schuchardt, the United States Vice Consul at Piedras Negras, reported in 1880 that Areola appeared from "time to time in this town" and that he and his followers "are as free since their return as ever before."[117]

An excellent summary of the American position on purported raids from Mexico, Indian and white, is contained in Foster's note to Avila of November 22, 1878:

---

[113] Foster to Evarts, September 7, 1878, *U. S. For. Rel. 1878,* p. 593.

[114] Foster to Evarts, September 13, 1878, Despatches MSS, LXIV.

[115] *Se niega a los Indios Lipanes el permiso que piden para establecerse en Santo Rosa, Coahuila, February–September 27, 1878,* Library of Congress Photostats of the Mexican Archives MSS.

[116] Evarts to Foster, September 20, 1878, *U. S. For. Rel. 1878,* p. 612.

[117] Morgan to Evarts, September 21, 1880, Enclosure Schuchardt to Morgan, August 18, 1880, Despatches MSS, LXXI. Philip H. Morgan succeeded Foster as American Minister to Mexico in 1880.

The main complaint of my government for years past has been, and now is, that Mexican territory is made the base of operations for armed bands of raiders to prey upon the people of Texas; that expeditions are there organized and raiding companies continually cross the frontier to murder American citizens and rob them of their property; and that they bring the stolen property over into Mexican territory and openly dispose of it in public market or private sale. These acts, committed on Mexican territory, constitute offenses punishable by the local law of all civilized nations. It is on account of the failure of the Mexican Government to inflict any punishment, so far as I am advised, in a single case in the course of a long series of years of disorder and plundering, that the Government of the United States complains. . . .[118]

On their side Mexican officials and citizens charged that Mexican border states suffered severely from raids of Indians and outlaws from north of the boundary. Governor Charles of Chihuahua early in 1878 reported word from the authorities of the District of Monclovia that "*varias partidas pequeñas de Indios bárbaros han entrado al territorio del Estado causando robos y depredaciones.*" These Indian raiders were supposedly from across the Rio Grande.[119] During the same summer the municipal president of Rosales, Coahuila, reported to the Mexican Department of Foreign Relations that his district was losing cattle and horses through raids "to such an extent that most of them are now unable to sow their grain." The stolen stock largely found its way into Texas, he charged. Near Buena Vista on the old San Antonio Road in Texas eighty yoke of oxen belonging to the citizens of his district were said to be impounded.[120] Farther west the commander of Mexican federal troops in Sonora late the same fall reported bands in Arizona formed for depredations into Mexico. The United States Government was asked by the Mexican Government to punish these alleged raiders.[121] About the same time the governor of Coahuila reported that Antonio Vargas, a rancher of Texas, had stolen a herd of

---

[118] Foster to Evarts, November 4, 1878, Enclosure No. 2 Foster to Avila, October 22, 1878, *U. S. For. Rel. 1879*, p. 732.

[119] *H. Charles, Gobernador de Chihuahua, comunica que indios bárbaros procedentes de Estados Unidos han invadido el territorio mexicano haciendo depredaciones,* Enclosure Guerra to Vallarta, January 4, 1878, Photostats of Mexican Archives MSS.

[120] Zamacona to Evarts, July 25, 1878, Notes from the Legation MSS, XXV.

[121] Foster to Evarts, November 2, 1878, Despatches MSS, LXV.

cattle from the citizens of Guerrero, Coahuila. They were
said to have been sold to Antonio Perales, residing near San
Antonio, Texas.[122] A few months later the governor of
Chihuahua reported word from the Gefe Politico of the Canton of Bravos that a herd of beef cattle had been stolen from
residents of that canton and delivered to a Mr. Contreras,
then sold to a butcher. The thieves were said to be two
United States citizens.[123]

Mexican officials also complained in 1880 of the " scan-
dalous deeds " of the Texan outlaw Robert E. Martin in the
Ascension Valley, Chihuahua.[124] His band was said to be
made up of Mexicans and Texans who met, swooped down
upon herds of cattle, drove away their booty, disposed of
them, separated, and vanished until another secret rendezvous
brought them together again.[125] It was reported from Chihuahua that in one raid eighteen horses and eighty-five
head of cattle had been taken and that in a desperate fight
with three American outlaws, thought to be members of the
Martin band, two horses had been recovered.[126] In November
Navarro reported continued sufferings of the inhabitants " of
the infant colony " of Ascension from Americans " led by the
notorious outlaw Robert E. Martin." It was urged that the
United States " arrest and punish " these raiders.[127] A
petition from Juan M. Zuloaga representing the citizens of
Ascension protested " the unheard of and premeditated outrages [which have been committed] . . . with entire impu-
nity [by] Texas outlaws." It was claimed that the citizens " have already lost all their horses, and the greater part
of their meat cattle." They feared that they might be forced

---

[122] Foster to Evarts, April 30, 1879, Enclosure copy of report by
the Governor of Coahuila, September 4, 1878, ibid., LXVII.

[123] Enclosure copy of report by Governor of Chihuahua, February
7, 1879, ibid.

[124] Navarro to Evarts, November 15, 1880, Subenclosure Juan M.
Zuloaga to Governor of Chihuahua, August 30, 1880, U. S. For. Rel.
1881-1882, pp. 818-819.

[125] Navarro to Evarts, August 28, 1880, Notes from the Legation
MSS, XXVI.

[126] Navarro to Evarts, October 18, 1880, Enclosure Governor Chihuahua, August 18, 1880, subenclosure copies letters Municipal President Janos, August 1 and August 11, 1880, ibid.

[127] Navarro to Evarts, November 15, 1880, ibid.

to abandon their homes founded after "many weary labors ...
hardships and privations." Seven Mexicans had been killed
in the district by raiders and Martin, when charged with
some of these depredations and tried in the Quitos District
Court of Texas, had been acquitted, unjustly it was thought.[128]

In June 1881 the Mexican minister again called attention
to the "frequency and magnitude of the thefts committed in
the frontier State of Chihuahua by outlaws from Texas."
He thought that the United States Government "realizes
the situation . . . and is disposed to use all means at its
command" to end the trouble but apparently for some reason
was unsuccessful.[129] Several sworn statements accompanied
this note. Inocencio Ochoa and Juan José Sanchez in the
Criminal Court of the District of the Bravos swore to "positive information" that their cattle, after being stolen had
been driven to the Rancho de Santa Teresa in Texas and there
killed or rebranded.[130] Herrera S. Gonzalez swore that
"trustworthy persons" had seen 400 head of cattle from his
ranch "Providencia" scattered through the nearby border
regions of Texas.[131]

In the light of these disturbances on both sides of the
boundary leaders in Washington and Mexico City were constantly casting about for solutions to the serious problems presented by raiding along the border. As previously noted
the Mexican Government protested vigorously the Order of
June 1, 1877. Nevertheless, crossings by American troops continued and in July 1878 the Mexican Government expressed
its "profound displeasure" at such action by Mackenzie
and Shafter in the previous month.[132] The Mexican Government held for some time that any negotiation on the
subject of reciprocal crossing must come after, not before,

[128] Enclosure petition from Juan M. Zuloaga to the Governor of
Chihuahua, August 30, 1880, *ibid.*
[129] Zamacona to Blaine, June 6, 1881, *ibid.*, XXVII.
[130] Enclosure Governor of Chihuahua to Mexican Minister of Foreign Relations, April 28, 1881, *ibid.*
[131] Enclosure Gonzalez to Governor of Chihuahua, May 21, 1881,
ibid.
[132] Foster to Evarts, July 15, 1878, Enclosure No. 1 Mata to Foster, July 12, 1878, *U. S. For. Rel. 1878*, pp. 555-557.

withdrawal of the Order of June 1, 1877, as Vallarta informed Foster a few weeks after recognition. In reply Foster assured him that the United States Government would withdraw the Order of June 1 as soon as the Mexican Government agreed to measures which would make the Order unnecessary. A few days later Vallarta came to Foster with the hopeful word that Diaz had determined to ask permission of the Mexican Senate for an agreement as to reciprocal crossing in unpopulated districts of the border. Foster answered that he hoped the measure would be enacted, at the same time fully appreciating the difficulties the Diaz Administration faced in making such an agreement, due to the sensitiveness of the Senate to Mexican public opinion, and the sensitiveness of public opinion to any act which countenanced the possible presence of American troops in Mexico.[133]

As a matter of fact the opposition press aroused itself when Diaz' " initiation " on the subject of reciprocal crossing in unpopulated areas passed the Mexican Senate even with the reservation that such an agreement should not be made until the Order of June 1 were repealed.[134] *El Diario Oficial* denied the charge that a border crossing treaty had been entered into with the United States but carefully concealed from the public what the Mexican Senate had actually done.[135] In spite of this assurance *El Monitor Republicano* sniffed the air suspiciously, serving notice upon José M. Mata, new Secretary of Foreign Relations, that he must make no arrangement with the United States which did not provide for reciprocity. A guarantee of Mexican boundaries, it was felt, should precede any negotiation on border difficulties and a specific declaration to that effect must be forthcoming from the United States Government as a forerunner to negotiations on crossing. " The faith of treaties is suggested to us. What are treaties worth to the colossus of the north? Did they not exist in 1836, when it favored the

---

[133] Foster to Evarts, May 23, 1878, Despatches MSS, LXII.
[134] Foster to Evarts, May 30, 1878, *ibid.* See also Foster to Evarts, June 27, 1878, *ibid.*
[135] Foster to Evarts, June 26, 1878, *U. S. For. Rel. 1878*, p. 553.

independence of Texas? Did they not exist in 1848, when it despoiled us of the half our territory?" [136]

Due ostensibly to the crossing of American troops but really, in all probability, to this sharp reaction of Mexican public opinion, the attitude of the Diaz Administration again changed markedly. If the incursions into Mexico of American forces were to continue they might make the Mexican Government " unable to. realize its purposes of arriving at a pacific solution in harmony with the dignity and interests of both countries. . . ." [137] · In reply Foster said that he could not regard the change of course by the Mexican Government as justified by the recent crossing of American troops. He now reiterated what he had told the former Secretary of Foreign Relations—that the Order of June 1 could not be withdrawn until the negotiation of " some reciprocal agreement which should make existing instructions unnecessary." No such agreement was as yet forthcoming due to the attitude of the Mexican Government. [138]

Correspondence over the Mackenzie and Shafter crossings continued to excite the Mexican press and public during the summer of 1878. Foster wrote early in August that for two weeks relations with the United States had " almost exclusively occupied . . . the attention of this City." Ord's reported visit to Washington had led to a rumor that the Order of June 1 was " to be more vigorously enforced," and other rumors were current of an " early rupture of diplomatic relations " because of the Mata-Foster correspondence on Mackenzie. [139] *El Diario Oficial,* however, urged continued dignity and calmness in the face of difficult border problems. [140] Although a week later the question of peace or war between the two countries was still the vital topic in Mexico City, *El Diario Oficial* of August 15 reported that a con-

[136] *Ibid.,* Enclosure *El Monitor Republicano,* June 25, 1878, pp. 553-554.
[137] Foster to Evarts, July 15, 1878, Enclosure No. 1 Mata to Foster, July 12, 1878, *ibid.,* p. 556.
[138] Enclosure No. 2 Foster to Mata, July 15, 1878, *ibid.,* p. 558.
[139] Foster to Evarts, August 6, 1878, Despatches MSS, LXIII.
[140] *Ibid.,* Enclosure *El Diario Oficial,* August 5, 1878.

ference between Secretary Evarts and the Mexican Minister in Washington had been held and that relations between the two countries might be expected to " be preserved in a satisfactory state." [141]

Soon also the old charges of undue influence on the border policy of the American Government by " wily speculators," desirous of additional Mexican soil and the treasures beneath it, reappeared in the Mexican papers. *El Monitor Republicano* claimed that American public opinion was spurred on against her neighbor to the south by speculators operating in the press and urging war and the invasion of Mexico. War, if it came, would not be forced by the action of a handful of Indians and conspirators—from whom Mexico suffered as did the United States—but by nefarious American interests. Raids into the United States were given more publicity in the American press than those from the United States into Mexico, it was charged.[142]

While " wily speculators " were said to be working upon American opinion, a charge for which the *Monitor* did not offer proof, it would appear that the Diaz Administration was making considerable effort to influence American opinion on its own account. To this end Foster claimed that Frisbie and an Englishman named Pritchard, an old friend of Diaz but an " unprincipled scamp," were serving as secret agents of the Mexican administration.[143] Documents purporting to commission Pritchard to seek influence over the American cabinet and press were soon thereafter published by various New York papers. Their authenticity was not denied by *El Diario Oficial,* according to Foster, and they were " accepted by the [Mexican] public as genuine." [144]

---

[141] Foster to Evarts, August 15, 1878, *ibid.*

[142] Foster to Evarts, September 7, 1878, Enclosure No. 1 *El Monitor Republicano*, September 5, 1878, *ibid.*

[143] Foster to Seward, September 9, 1878 (Personal), *ibid.*

[144] Foster to Evarts, October 26, 1878, *ibid.*, LXIV. In this same despatch Foster speaks of another alleged Mexican agent, C. Edwards Lester, a resident of New York. Mata, while minister to the United States, was said to have employed him to write an historical pamphlet on Mexico. This he was said to have done under the title " The Mexican Republic, An Historical Essay. C. Edwards Lester." For this work Foster said that the Mexican Government had paid him $3,000.

Another one of the documents "discovered" was an alleged letter from Diaz to Pritchard, dated December 27, 1877, in which Diaz spoke of his gratification at Pritchard's work in the American press. This work should be "systematized and organized" and for that purpose Pritchard must cooperate with "others equally animated by the same praiseworthy intentions." He was to keep in touch with Zamacona, Mexican Minister to the United States, and for his work he was to receive $400 per month.[145]

Thus by October the Mexican press and people were so deeply stirred by the controversy over border crossing, and charges and counter charges as to the forces behind each government's position, that a successful issue of the whole matter seemed hopeless. *El Monitor* urged that the Mexican Constitution did not confer on Congress the power to consent to reciprocal crossing and with this *El Federalista,* a Lerdo organ, agreed. *El Libertad* took a gloomy view of the whole situation, fearing that the next presidential election would result in civil war and this in turn would inevitably lead to the invasion of Mexico by the United States. The only ray of hope lay in the probability that such action on the part of the United States would unite all Mexico.[146] Foster was scarcely less pessimistic in a despatch late in the same month in which he summarized relations between the two countries. As to border controversies, Mexicans had been punished for aiding American troops in pursuit of bandits while Mexican citizens who organized raids on Mexican soil against the United States had not been punished. Furthermore, instead of referring the Free Zone question to the Mexican Congress for repeal or modification, the Diaz Administration had republished the original decree. The laws prohibiting American ownership of real estate in the border states were still in force and forced loans were still levied on Americans although declared unconstitutional by the Mexican Supreme Court.[147]

So matters drifted with relations in an unsatisfactory condition. The Mexican opposition to the Order of June 1 con-

[145] Enclosure No. 2, *ibid.*
[146] Foster to Evarts, October 10, 1878, *ibid.*
[147] Foster to Evarts, October 29, 1878, *ibid.,* LXV.

tinued as strong as ever and formed an impasse in the negotiations over reciprocal crossing. In February 1879, even
the usually moderate Romero paid his respects to the Order
in no uncertain terms. He claimed that the attitude of the
Hayes Administration previously on recognition and its continued attitude on border questions ranked among the greatest
obstacles to the strengthening of commercial relations between the two countries. He asserted, further, that the delay
in recognition from 1877 to 1878 was contrary to past practice and based on no well-founded motive and he considered
the Order of June 1 a flagrant violation of Mexican sovereignty claiming " that the government of the United States
entertained sentiments of hostility towards Mexico, and was
looking for motives or pretexts for creating difficulties between the two countries." [148]

Persistently, however, American military men and diplomatic officials continued to urge Mexican official cooperation
with American forces on the border. Foster told Ruelas at
the Mexican Ministry of Foreign Relations in July 1879 that
the United States could do nothing concerning the Apaches
in the neighborhood of Janos, Chihuahua, so long as the
Mexican Government did not officially permit American
troops to cross.[149] In reporting occasional raids of Indians
from Chihuahua and Sonora into the United States, and·
from the United States into Chihuahua, Hunter wrote Foster
in part as follows in October 1879: " You are instructed to
take an early opportunity to urge upon the Government of
Mexico the propriety of cooperating with the military forces
of the United States in suppressing Indian raids upon the
border and returning to their proper jurisdiction Indians who
may have strayed from the territory of one nation into that
of the other." [150] About the same time Colonel Hatch, com-

---

[148] Foster to Evarts, February 15, 1879, Extract from " *Exposition* " by Romero, *ibid.,* LXVI.

[149] *Se ordena a la autoridades de los estados fronterizos del norte
que remitan informes mensuales sobre las incursiones de los indios
salvajes October 28, 1878–July 27, 1880,* Enclosure Foster to Ruelas
July 11, 1879, Photostats Mexican Archives MSS.

[150] W. Hunter, Acting Secretary of State, to Foster, October 1,
1879, Instructions MSS, XX.

manding the District of New Mexico, and Brigadier General Willcox, commanding the Department of Arizona, joined in requesting that Indians "now on Mexican soil be returned to commanding officer of the post most easily reached by Mexican authorities, or delivered to United States troops at some point the Mexican Government may designate on the frontier of New Mexico." They were described by Hatch as "renegade Indians from the Warm Spring, Chiriquis, and White Mountain Indians" who had been in Chihuahua and Sonora for some years raiding back into New Mexico, Arizona, and Texas. When pursued by American troops they were said to flee into Mexico. "If the troops were allowed to follow them their capture or destruction would follow. Concert of action with the Mexican troops at the time they are committing depredations in New Mexico and escaping to the mountains of the State of Chihuahua, would end in their destruction." [151]

No such permission was granted until 1882 and in the meantime another moot question continued to disturb border relations—that of ownership of property by foreigners on the Mexican side of the border. Of these foreigners Americans were the most numerous and in April 1879 Foster protested to Ruelas concerning alleged invidious discrimination against Americans in ownership of property in the frontier states as an infringement of Article 3 of the Treaty of 1831.[152] In reply Ruelas claimed the right of a sovereign state "to concede or refuse to foreigners the privilege of acquiring real estate" as being indisputably and universally recognized. Moreover most-favored-nation treatment under Article 3 of the Treaty of 1831 referred to navigation and commerce. This question of acquisition of territory by foreigners on the Mexican borders was not aimed primarily at Americans, Ruelas asserted, since it applied equally to Guatamala. How-

---

[151] Hunter to Foster, October 1, 1879, Enclosure No. 3 Hatch to Pope, Commanding Department of Missouri, August 14, 1879, including copy of telegram to same effect from Willcox, August 9, 1879, *U. S. For. Rel. 1880-1881*, p. 710.

[152] Foster to Evarts, May 27, 1879, *ibid. 1879*, pp. 810-811. See Malloy, *Treaties, Conventions, . . .* , I, 1086.

ever a moment later he seems to have qualified his own words, perhaps unconsciously. His country acted, he said, on experience gained in the " not very remote events recorded in its own history." The lesson of Texas, he thought, had made Mexico "more cautious and far-seeing in the future " in allowing foreigners to colonize in the mother country.[153]

The whole matter was further reviewed by Evarts in the instructions he now sent Foster. Mexico, he said, "prohibited . . . citizens of the United States, belonging to States coterminous with that country from acquiring real estate in the Mexican border states. The discrimination in this respect between those citizens and other foreigners, is still believed to be invidious, unnecessary, at variance with treaty and quite incompatible with those friendly relations which the obvious interest of both countries requires should be maintained between them." The Mexican Government apparently thought it necessary to make such discrimination to avoid the situation " by which they imagine they lost Texas." The cases were very different, Evarts thought. The United States did not expect that Mexico " will again make extensive grants of land within its jurisdiction to be colonized by citizens of the United States. Mexico has a perfect right to exercise its discretion upon that point. This however should not extend so far as to exclude the citizens of the United States in general or the citizens of Texas, New Mexico, Arizona, and California from acquiring real estate in the border states of that Republic. This exclusion is believed to be both impolitic and unjust, for it cannot fail to cause an irritation which sooner or later, might lead to other than peaceable causes to make such acquisitions." The Mexican law of 1863 practically discriminated against the American border states by name. United States citizens must be thought of as a whole not as residents of a particular state. Articles 2 and 3 of the Treaty of 1831, while limited by their wording to commerce and navigation, might be construed to include property within their purview.[154] Far from yielding to this

---

[153] Foster to Evarts, May 27, 1879, *U. S. For. Rel. 1879*, pp. 810-811.
[154] Evarts to Foster, June 23, 1879, Instructions MSS, XX.

argument the Mexican Government proposed late in the year, in connection with the dispute over an international railroad charter, to embody in the charter the Decree of February 1, 1856, which prohibited the acquisition of real estate by foreigners within twenty leagues of the American frontier.[155] Thus the matter remained unsettled.

In spite of these points of friction a more hopeful side of the whole matter of border relations began gradually to appear. The Mexican Government showed increasingly active evidences of a new spirit of military cooperation. George W. McCrary, Secretary of War, in his Annual Report for 1878 stated that border raids were "fewer in number than during any year for a long period." He attributed this falling off in disorder to vigorous action by United States troops under the Order of June 1, 1877. In addition he reported that: "A considerable Mexican force has been sent to the vicinity of the border to operate against the bands of Indians infesting that region, and the avowed purpose of the Mexican Government is to put a stop to raids upon our people and territory." [156] "Mata . . . agreed with me that the Indians in Coahuila [were] . . . the chief source of the present troubles on the frontier," Foster wrote in August 1878, "and that it was the earnest desire of his government to repress their raids and, if necessary, to secure their removal or that of the part of them guilty of the raids." The raiding, Mata said, was an evil common to both sides of the border. In a later interview with Diaz, the latter had given him to understand that so long as the Order of June 1 were in force American troops could not be allowed to cross the border for any purpose. Diaz promised, however, to order the Mexican military commander in Coahuila to remove the offending Indians in that state to the interior.[157] Ord also watched with hope the campaign of Treviño against the hostile Indians in northern Mexico late in 1878, saying " . . . it will

---

[155] Foster to Evarts, December 24, 1879, *U. S. For. Rel. 1880-1881*, pp. 719.
[156] *Report of Secretary of War for 1878*, p. VI.
[157] Foster to Evarts, August 24, 1878, Despatches MSS, LXIII.

be a great satisfaction if the campaigns of General Treviño are successful, and we can be relieved of the necessity of hunting savages who do not belong to us but to Mexico; and it will be a pleasure as well as a duty for us to contribute to his success by every means in our power." [158]

After the Areola outbreak near Piedras Negras Diaz issued orders to the commander at the latter place to watch the "persons designated as raiders," according to Foster. The Mexican Government promised to take still further steps in an effort to prevent cattle stealing in Texas but felt that it might not be able to cope with the situation, just as the United States had not been able.[159] In March 1879 Foster wrote that the arrest of Areola and a number of outlaws (fourteen in all) was reported by the United States Consul at Monterey.[160] Later this report was confirmed by Nunez, Chief Clerk of the Department of Foreign Relations, who assured Foster that their trial would soon take place. The Ministry also soon reported orders for greater vigilance on the frontier with a first movement against the Lipan raiders. So far these measures had been unsuccessful, Foster thought.[161] Fresh evidence of renewed effort to act against disorderly elements on the border was also to be seen in the decision of the Magistrate of the First Chamber of the Superior Tribunal of Coahuila in the case of Zeferino Avalos. A second sergeant in the Mexican army, Avalos was charged with killing Antonio Munoz, a blind Mexican, in Eagle Pass, Texas, was tried, convicted, and executed.[162]

Apparently also cooperation between local military and civil officials on both sides of the border showed gratifying signs of becoming stronger. The New York *Herald* on February 4, 1880, reported 180 Mexican troops under Colonel Casavantes on American soil in the Guadalupe mountains hunting marauding Indians. They had been invited into the

---

[158] *Report of Secretary of War for 1878*, p. 81.
[159] Foster to Evarts, October 16, 1878, Despatches MSS, LXIV.
[160] Foster to Evarts, March 1, 1879, *ibid.*, LXVI.
[161] Foster to Evarts, April 11, 1879, *ibid.*
[162] Foster to Evarts, December 18, 1879, *ibid.*, LXIX.

United States by the governor of New Mexico to cooperate in the search for the Indians, according to the report of a Mexican consul in Arizona.[163] In July, 1881, Morgan reported a raid on the Texas side of the river about thirty-six miles below Eagle Pass. Three Mexicans, Cristobal Lopez, Ramon Hernandez, and one other not known had taken by force Caledonia Rodriguez and her son into Coahuila. At Morgan's request, on behalf of his government, the Mexican Ministry of Foreign Relations secured the release of the prisoners through the efforts of the governor of Coahuila. Steps were then taken to punish the perpetrators.[164]

On the Arizona border in the fall of 1878 Colonel Willcox reported up to a " recent period " a tacit understanding between United States and Mexican troops for ignoring the border in pursuing raiders. When a body of United States troops had been located on the American side near the border, tending to drive the marauding Indians into Mexico, Mexican forces had moved to the border on their side, thus catching the marauders between two fires. He thought that the Mexican troops were showing " more energetic efforts . . . to hunt out the Apache." A new order of the Mexican Federal Government, communicated through Governor John P. Hoyt of Arizona, now forbade troops of either country to cross the border. But so fairly had the Mexican forces behaved that the American forces had been instructed to observe the line unless further raids were found to take place. If the vigilance of the Mexican troops were relaxed, however, or the Indians in Mexico were to escape this vigilance and again raid back into the United States, then it might again be necessary to pursue them.[165]

Further evidence of Mexican action is to be seen in a report by Treviño early in June 1878 that Mexican troops had

---

[163] *Se communica a las autoridades militares de los Estados del Norte, que no puedan pasar tropas mexicanas a territorio norte americano en persecución de los indios bárbaros February 19, 1878– May 26, 1880*, Photostats Mexican Archives MSS.
[164] Morgan to Blaine, July 1, 1881, Despatches MSS, LXXII.
[165] Annual Report Col. O. B. Willcox, Department of Arizona, September 13, 1878, in *Report of Secretary of War for 1878*, pp. 193-194.

routed a band of Lipans near Santa Rosa, Coahuila, killing six and capturing a hundred.[166]   A few months later the governor of Coahuila reported that Treviño " *con fuerzas federales numerosas y ciudadanos del Estado, muy prácticos en el terreno* " had proceeded against the rest of the Lipans and Mescaleros in the hope of freeing the border permanently from roving bands of these two tribes.[167]   A few weeks later still General Francisco Naranjo, second in chief of the Division of the North, reported to the Mexican Ministry of War and Marine that three columns of Mexican troops were moving against the Indians.   In a skirmish with the Indians one of their number had been captured who promised to serve as guide to the troops,[168] and within a few days General Treviño was said to have captured fourteen raiders, including James Gibson, an American, near Zaragoza, Coahuila.[169]

This note of hopefulness, due to increased cooperation, was reflected in a more optimistic view of the situation by United States army officers. Sheridan in October 1878 characterized the border situation as essentially unchanged until the past few months. " I think now," he reported, " that the Mexican Government is making more exertion to suppress lawlessness than heretofore.   If it does not succeed, I would recommend that Congress pass an act that, from and after a certain fixed time, if depredations in Texas are not discontinued, a force of troops be sent across at certain points and kept there until depredations entirely cease.   The moral effect of such Congressional action would, in my opinion, prevent all future trouble." [170]   In his report of the following year Sheridan said:

---

[166] *Correspondencia con el General Treviño con la Legación en Estados Unidos relativos a la persecución de los indios bárbaros de la frontera del norte April 29–December 28, 1878,* Enclosure G. Treviño Mexican Minister of War, June 5, 1878, Photostats Mexican Archives MSS.

[167] Enclosure H. Charles to Irinco Paz, September 7, 1878, *ibid.*

[168] Minister of War and Marine to Minister of Foreign Relations, November 18, 1878, *Memoria de la Secretaría de Estado del Despacho de Guerra y Marina presentada al Congreso de la Unión mexicana, 1878,* Annex No. 7, p. 67.

[169] *Ibid.,* p. 68.

[170] *Report of Secretary of War for 1878,* p. 39.

Nearly all of the vexatious conditions which have heretofore existed along the Rio Grande—the boundary line between our country and the Republic of Mexico—have ceased, owing to the active efforts of our own troops and those of the Mexican Government; an earnest and generally successful effort having been made upon both sides of the line to capture and destroy all raiding parties. Small parties of Indians occasionally succeed in evading the troops, and commit robberies and outrages upon the outlying settlements and mail routes; some of these parties at times entering Mexico from our side and others coming from that country into this.[171]

About the same time Ord wrote: " I respectfully invite attention to the earnest and successful efforts of the Mexican authorities—especially those of Generals Treviño and Canales —to suppress raiding from their side of the river; the condition of affairs which rendered necessary the Order of June 1, 1877, to cross the border, in my opinion, no longer exists, as the Mexican Government has shown its ability and determination to put a stop to such invasions of the United States." [172] Sherman quoted Ord's sentiments approvingly in his own Annual Report and commented upon the " comparative freedom from danger which has become habitual in that quarter of our country for two or three years, and have thereby aided materially in stimulating the great prosperity which now prevails in Texas." He spoke further of the large immigration to Texas moving the frontier west from Forts Richardson, Griffin, and Elliott [173] and helping thereby to diminish disorder.

After gaining a first-hand impression of the border at the end of the same year, Foster wrote: " I am gratified to be able to report that in my recent visit to the Mexican frontier States, I found a condition of peace and a better measure of order than is customary on the Rio Grande. . . . I found also that there was an improved state of feeling between the population on the opposing banks of the Rio Grande." He had " never doubted the good disposition of the administration of General Diaz in respect to the frontier

[171] Ibid., 1879, p. 44. See above ns. 146 and 147 for a different impression of the border situation.
[172] Annual Report Ord, October 1, in Report of Secretary of War for 1879, p. 93.
[173] Annual Report Sherman, November 1, 1879, ibid., p. 6.

relations " but internal turmoil, " the slender tenure by which
he exercised authority in the extreme States," the poverty of
the treasury, and other internal considerations caused neglect
of the boundary until Diaz saw from the attitude of the
United States the necessity of a vigorous border policy.
Foster felt that the firm attitude of the United States since
1877 " has had more to do with the comparative peace which
that region has enjoyed, than any voluntary action of the
Mexican Government. . . ." [174]

At the same time that military enforcement was on the
mend the new policy of the Mexican Government toward
growing pressure of American capital, railroad, and mining
interests, seeking an outlet in the vast virgin riches of Mexico,
served as a potent influence toward border peace. As already
noted, various organs of public opinion in Mexico, certain
powerful newspapers particularly, stood against the great
tide of gold and steel from the north. But they were too
weak or too late—at any rate, they lost. When Diaz had
been constitutionally inaugurated in 1877, public opinion in
Mexico was much divided on the policy of allowing United
States citizens to develop the resources of the country through
railroads, mines, and loans. A liberal policy in this regard
would mean the rapid infiltration of Mexico by American
capital and finally it was feared portions of the Republic
would be detached as Texas was thought to have been. Lerdo,
judging by his policy, had shared these doubts, but Diaz, if
he originally felt such fears, soon overcame them. The grim
warrior of Oaxaca, seated by the fortunes of war and his own
ability in the presidential chair, hoped that his native land
might become strong enough through material development
to take a place beyond the temptations and intrigues of the
great powers.[175] Such development would lead almost inevitably to action by American capitalists and business men,
since they were so near and so financially able.

Thus the whole question of American economic penetra-

---

[174] Foster to Evarts, December 27, 1879, *U. S. For. Rel. 1880-
1881*, p. 726.
[175] Romero, I, 117.

tion of Mexico in the late nineteenth and early twentieth centuries is bound up with the personal rule and personal character of General Porfirio Diaz. Estimates of Diaz differ as widely as the poles. He was one of the most powerful and striking personalities of the late nineteenth century without question, and like all powerful personalities he made for himself deep and bitter enmities and just as deep attachments. He was a power, but whether a power of darkness or of light is difficult to say without qualification. Born in humble surroundings in ˙Oaxaca September 15, 1830, just twenty years after Hidalgo's proclamation of independence, he grew to manhood in the momentous days of Santa Anna and Juárez. His father, apparently an obscure innkeeper, died when Diaz was young and his mother struggled valiantly alone to rear their family. *" El orden, el trabajo y la austeridad "* characterized Diaz' upbringing and his wants and habits remained simple to the end.[176] Rising at six, he ate a light breakfast and was ready for the saddle or for a hard day at his desk.[177]

Enemies and friends alike agreed that Diaz was rigorously self-disciplined physically and this was, in all probability, the reason for his long life and robust health. Diaz had the bearing of a natural leader of men. He never lost it and at eighty the " old warrior," clear-eyed, sat his horse with all the distinction of his youthful leadership. His forehead was high, sloping up to his stiff, white hair and jutting over his " deepset, dark, soul-searching eyes," his jaw was powerful, his chin massive, his mouth large, his neck short and powerful, his shoulders broad, his chest deep.[178] But with all his martial appearance his nostrils dilated sensitively with emotion on occasion like those of a high-strung race horse. Perhaps therefore Diaz was, as one of his friends and best-known

---

[176] Genero Garcia, *Porfirio Díaz. Sus padres, Niñez y Juventud,* p. 15.

[177] José F. Godoy, *Porfirio Díaz President of Mexico, the Master Builder of a Great Commonwealth,* p. 98.

[178] James Creelman, *Díaz Master of Mexico,* p. 2. Diaz *" porte era distinguido; su continente, aristocrático."* Pedro González-Blanco, *De Porfirio Díaz a Carranza,* p. 34.

biographers has said, romantic, warm-hearted, affectionate on
the one hand, yet on the other a stern ruler of his people. In
his home he was simple, honest, kindly,[179] in the field he was
an audacious, although not highly trained soldier.[180] He had
exceptional military ability without doubt [181] but he was not
the " *gigante de la lucha* " [182] which some of his most lauda-
tory friends claimed. He was a man of exceptional energy
and ability, an indefatigable worker,[183] of few but forceful
words,[184] of strong character and will.[185] His military—and
often civil—discipline was famed for severity [186] and he knew
how to make use of his bayonets in the creation of a new,
well-disciplined Mexico.[187] Ruthless in his punishment of
crime, he very often enforced efficiency at the muzzle of a
gun, but he brought a high degree of obedience to law and a
high degree of good order.[188]

So much for the lights of Diaz' nature ; unfortunately there
were many shadows. The picture of Diaz as a benevolent,
firm ruler, possessed of all the manly virtues was sedulously
painted in the brightest colors by his friendly biographers.

---

[179] Ethel Brilliana Tweedie (Mrs. Alec), *Porfirio Díaz, Seven Times
President of Mexico*, p. 63.
[180] F. de la Colina, *Madero y el Gral. Díaz*, pp. 11 ff.
[181] See M. Antonio Z. de Blanco, *General Don Porfirio Díaz, Presidente de la República Mexicana*, p. 6.
[182] Leopoldo Batres, *Recordatorio del Gral Díaz*, p. 1.
[183] Tweedie, pp. 312-313.
[184] *Ibid.*, p. 325.
[185] *Ibid.*, p. 2.
[186] Ignacio M. Escudero, *Apuntes históricos de la carrera militar del Señor general Porfirio Díaz presidente de la República Mexicana*, p. 23. It was said that " *Porfirio*.......*ejercia una influencia
absoluta sobre los solados* . . ."
[187] Juan Pedro Didapp, *Despecho político, Díaz y Mariscal*, II,
146.
[188] See Caspar Whitney, *What's the Matter with Mexico?* p. 78.
Sometimes, in spite of his knowledge of the Mexican nature, Diaz
carried his paternalism to lengths that brought its ultimate defeat.
He never attended bull fights and tried stubbornly to have them
abolished by law. In this he was unsuccessful, since the love of the
Mexican people for this pastime was too deeply rooted even for Diaz.
W. E. Carson, *Mexico, the Wonderland of the South*, p. 106. During
a serious outbreak of typhus in Mexico City Diaz ordered every peon
in the city to take a bath once a week. A series of riots resulted.
Peons were dragged by the police through the streets to the public
bath houses kicking and shouting " *No jabon! No jabon!* ". *Ibid.*,
p. 137.

Other writers, however, have left a much more sombre impression. Diaz was held to be disingenuous and intriguing. Although a fortunate military man and audacious soldier, he was said to have neither knowledge of political science nor illustrious patriotism.[189] Graft and corruption were thought to honeycomb the Mexican Government [190] and he was said to have placed his own puppets in power.[191] Freedom of the press seems to have been practically unknown. When Diaz came into office he was charged with having lodged some of the most turbulent opposition editors in Belem Prison, usually reserved for desperate criminals. After a week on bread and water they were said again to have been brought before the President whereupon their attitude was found to have changed. Many of the newspapers finally were thought to have been subsidized by the government and the others refrained from serious attacks through fear of the consequences.[192] As to Diaz' treatment of the peons many gruesome stories are told, but their authenticity is hard to vouch for. Their great number and frequent repetition would seem to indicate, however, some measure of truth. In order to stamp out crime or revolution, Diaz officials apparently resorted to bloody methods. If a crime were undiscovered in an Indian village the local *jefe de operaciones* would have the men of the village lined up and a number chosen at random to be shot and a warning then issued that for the next crime one man out of five would be shot. If a peon rebelled his life was forfeit.[193] More than 10,000 Mexicans were said by one foreign critic to have been shot during the Díaz régime,[194] while a friendly critic estimated the number at 3,000 lives.[195]

---

[189] Colina, pp. 11, 46.

[190] F. de la Colina, *Porfirio Díaz*, p. 21. Diaz was termed " *pérfido, hipócrita y traidor.*" *Ibid.*, p. 7.

[191] Carlo de Fornaro, *Diaz Czar of Mexico*, p. 13.

[192] Carson, pp. 143-144.

[193] Ernest Gruening, *Mexico and Its Heritage*, p. 65.

[194] *Ibid.*, p. 61.

[195] Mario G. Moreno, *El régimen Porfirista en México; su apoteosis*, p. 21. Moreno also admits that the suffrage was suppressed and liberty of thought discouraged under Diaz. He thinks, how-

Probably most of these statements pro and con, if stripped of their partiality, in many cases of their enthusiasm and their bitterness, would be found to contain a measure of truth. It can accurately be said that Diaz was a man of energy, tenacity, of methodical, temperate, and vigorous habits. His mind was simple and direct, his will clear. In mind and body he was first of all a soldier. The Presidency was to him " not a prize to be enjoyed, but a redoubt to be stormed, and then held by sleepless vigilance and the same hard fighting that was needed to win it." He was " a highly capable guerrillero," an organizer, a general, and a man of government.[196] He was, as his last great adversary, Madero, said, an incarnation " *de un principio: el del poder abso-luto. . . .*" [197] Personalism, or dictatorial government, " the pressure of a strong man " had been characteristic of Mexico from " time immemorial." Personalism was never better exemplified than in the strong person of Porfirio Diaz.[198]

Using this strong personal power to the full Diaz' chief permanent accomplishments were the establishment of order and the opening up of the natural resources of the country. Foster held that he " gave the country a long era of peace and order. He forced Congress to grant liberal concessions for railroads connecting with the United States. He established protection and security to life and property. He restored public confidence. He brought about a great development of the resources of the country. Under his régime, commerce, internal and foreign, flourished beyond the dream

---

ever, the gain to Mexico through better order, stiffened morale, and greater national wealth was worth the cost. See also Charles Lincoln Phifer, *Diaz the Dictator*, pp. 53-54.

[196] David Hannay, *Diaz*, p. 92. This work by a careful English student is probably the most authoritative and impartial life of Diaz.

[197] Francisco I. Madero, *La sucesión presidencial en 1910*, pp. 93 ff. Madero wrote this book in 1908, two years before the beginning of his successful revolution against Diaz.

[198] Ramon Beteta, " The Government of Mexico," in *Mexico* (Lectures before the Inter-American Institute of Pomona College and Claremont College and the Pacific Southwest Academy of Political and Social Science, February 9, 10, 11, 1928), pp. 7-16.

of the most hopeful." [199] Whether or not the people of Mexico generally benefitted by this Diaz program is doubtful.

In so far then as this Indian population, which was often not less Indian because of a slight admixture of European blood, was concerned, there is nothing to show that the long Administration of President Diaz did any lasting good or supplied any promise of improvement. There is not even evidence that the President as much as wished to raise its moral and intellectual level. This neglect of what ought to have been treated as an elementary duty cannot surely be counted to him for righteousness. But before we join those who condemn him wholly let us remember that " a man is only a man." He cannot shake himself quite free from the inherited dispositions of the society he lives in. If he could he would only become alien to it and incapable of governing. It may look discreditable to Diaz that though he was largely of Indian descent himself, and could profess pride in his Mixteca ancestry, he did nothing for his red kinsmen. But Juarez was a pure blooded Zapoteca, and he did no more. He, too, married a Creole wife, and forgot his people and his father's house. The truth is that the Mexican Indian who has risen in the world, and the mestizo, who is half, or more than half, European, alike wish to be even as the Creoles of Spanish descent—to rank as whites. [200]

At any rate the fact remains that Mexico, a poor country, found itself in the shadow of a rich and powerful neighbor. Diaz opened the flood gates, with the railroad builders as the first to respond. As a matter of fact they had already brought pressure to bear to bring about a receptive frame of mind. When Diaz was first recognized the foreign trade of Mexico was small and chiefly with Europe, the small volume of trade with the United States being due mainly in all probability to lack of communication. In the '70's the only regular communication was by steamer to New York, once every three weeks from Vera Cruz. Later in the same decade a steamship service to New Orleans was established with sailings twice a month. [201]

By that time, however, American business men were awaking to the possibilities furnished by Mexico as a market and source of raw materials. Diaz had not been long in office before American commercial delegations, on two occasions, visited Mexico City. The first of these was entertained by Diaz with a dinner in the National Palace " at which time he expressed the deep interest he felt in the development and

[199] Foster, I, 116.   [200] Hannay, p. 286.   [201] Foster, I, 108.

enlargement of the commercial relations of the two countries. But their visit did not materially increase the trade." [202] In January 1879 an excursion party made up of American tourists and business men largely from St. Louis, Milwaukee, Cincinnati, Wheeling, and other cities landed at Vera Cruz. They were met by an official committee at the port and escorted to Mexico City where they were entertained and instructed with a round of excursions, dinners, and a grand ball. [203] This visit " also had little influence upon the existing trade conditions." [204] In the meantime in the fall of 1878 Zamacona had represented his government at an Industrial Exposition in Chicago and had been paid marked courtesies, General Sheridan and other high United States officials calling upon him. He was followed through the Exposition by an assemblage " as numerous as that of the President " who opened the festivities, *El Diario Oficial* feeling that this showed the " sympathy with Mexico " of the manufacturers of the northwest and the " farming population in the environs of Chicago." [205]

Senator Morgan, of Alabama, analyzed this " very decided " interest of American business men in Mexico in an interesting letter to Foster about the same time. Mexico stood as " one of the best fields of enterprise " for American commerce. The United States, he thought, must show that its sentiments toward Mexico were " not rapacious but . . . inspired with respect, good will, and a desire to increase our prosperity by adding to theirs." Morgan was eager to see Mexico City connected by rail with the American railway system. To that end he suggested that Mexico should grant a concession to a good company organized under its own laws, the United States engaging to guarantee by treaty the payment of Mexican bonds issued to finance the project. In return the United States was " to be indemnified for [its] risk

[202] *Ibid.*, p. 109.
[203] Foster to Evarts, February 7, 1879, *U. S. For. Rel. 1879*, p. 796; Foster, I, 109.
[204] *Ibid.*
[205] Foster to Evarts, October 9, 1878, Enclosure *El Diario Oficial*, October 8, 1878, Despatches MSS, LXIV.

and also be allowed such privileges of trade which would furnish an inducement to the engagement." [206]

Still others in official position in the United States soon swelled the chorus of interest in Mexican trade. Sherman wrote as follows to Rear Admiral C. R. P. Rodgers, Commanding the Pacific Squadron, in October 1878:

> You asked me to ascertain and convey to you my judgment of the general feeling and purpose of our Government towards Mexico. I have seen the President and the Secretary of War, but Mr. Evarts is absent; so has been the Secretary of the Navy, but he is now here. My opinion is that no·one in authority, nor any considerable part of our people want war with Mexico or with any other country on earth. . . . The stealing and marauding on our frontier are simply local provocations which probably are inevitable and incidental to the character of the frontier inhabitants on both sides of the national boundary. These are irritating, but not a just cause of war unless sanctioned by the Central Government, or [the] . . . result of criminal neglect. I do not think the President or the Secretary of State charge the Diaz Government with privity or neglect, and they therefore do not intend to allow this the only existing cause of a sharp diplomatic correspondence to grow into a casus belli. . . . We do not wish to embody into our Union any more Mexican Territory or any more Mexican people.

Sherman thought that the "stimulation of trade, commerce, and friendly inter-communication" was "the full share [of Rodgers] towards our own prosperity and towards the maintenance of peace." He added: "Please consider these rather my own opinions than those of others in authority." [207]

By early June 1881 Secretary Blaine was able to report better relations between the two countries as "especially visible in the rapidly extending desire on the part of the citizens of this country [the United States] to take an active share in the prosecution of those industrial enterprises for which the magnificent resources of Mexico offer so broad and promising a field, and in the responsive and increasing disposition which is manifest on the part of the Mexican people to welcome such projects." With the growing stability of the Mexican administration Blaine felt the time ripe for again calling attention "to those general precepts which in the

[206] Senator John F. Morgan to Foster, September 27, 1878, John W. Foster Papers MSS.
[207] Sherman to Rodgers, October 13, 1878, W. T. Sherman Letter-book MSS.

judgment of the President should govern relations between the two Republics." The " chiefest endeavor " of the American Minister must be to cultivate " friendly feeling, political sympathy, and correlated interests " between the two states. Mexico, Blaine thought, was now so stable that she could " offer to foreign capital that just and certain protection without which the prospect even of extravagant profit will fail to tempt the extension of safe and enduring commercial and industrial enterprise." Therefore while:

. . . carefully avoiding all appearance of advocating any individual undertaking which the citizens of the United States may desire to initiate in Mexico, you will take . . . the opportunity which you may deem judicious to make clear the spirit and motive which control this movement in the direction of developing Mexican resources, and will impress upon the government of Mexico the earnest wish and hope felt by the people and government of this country that these resources may be multiplied and rendered fruitful for the primary benefit of the Mexican people themselves; that forms of orderly, constitutional and stable government may be strengthened as domestic wealth increases and as the conservative spirit of widely distributed and permanently vested interests is more and more felt; that the administration of Mexican finances, fostered by these healthful tendencies, may be placed upon a firm basis; that rich sections of the great territory of the Republic may be brought into closer intercommunications—in a word, that Mexico may quickly and beneficently attain the place toward which she is so manifestly tending as one of the most powerful, well ordered, and prosperous states in the harmonious system of the Western Republics.[208]

Possibly in reply to these instructions Morgan wrote that from the beginning of his tenure of office he had urged that " the United States has no disposition whatsoever to deprive Mexico of a foot of her territory " but that United States capital was the logical source for developing Mexico. He had stressed in his communications with the Mexican Government the value to Mexico of American capital, fully secured, in developing the country's " matchless resources " and he had tried especially to show the value of railways in this connection.[209]

Economic considerations were not the only ones thought of when the possibility of having American railroads spanning

---

[208] Blaine to Morgan, June 1, 1881, Instructions MSS, XX.
[209] Morgan to Blaine, August 13, 1881 (Confidential), Despatches MSS, LXXIII.

the border was discussed. As early as 1875 Richardson, in charge of the American Legation, had written to Secretary Fish that the time was excellent for investment in Mexico in railroads which would thus

give to the United States complete possession of the commerce of the northern and central States of Mexico. And the effect will be greater still. The completion of a railroad across the Rio Grande, a road across the Sonora and Arizona frontier, and a third road which would necessarily follow from Colorado and New Mexico into Chihuahua, Duranga, and Zacatecas will forever put an end to all lawless border troubles, and link the two republics in lasting peace, iron bands, and commercial interests, which neither border raiders, revolutions, filibusterers nor ambitions can ever break.[210]

"Protection, Reciprocity, Rail Roads, solve the Mexican problem," Senator Maxey wrote to Sherman in 1879.[211] Ord also was interested in railroads across the border. "I get letters from Generals Treviño and Canales," he wrote Sherman, "and have I think succeeded in interesting them in the matter of railroads. Treviño (who is to be González' Secretary of War)[212] is one of the progressive men of the country. . . ."

Thus American commercial and strategic considerations joined forces in exerting pressure upon Mexico to permit her markets and raw materials to be linked with those of the United States by means of railroads meeting at the border. Diaz seems to have become completely convinced of the necessity and desirability of railroads in Mexico built with American capital, for his policy came to be that of giving a subsidy to any railroad company without investigating the responsibility of the concern. If the road were built the country would stand to gain, if it were not built, then the subsidy would never be paid.[213] In rendering an account of his stewardship later at the end of his second term in 1888 Diaz said: "*Le Mexique avait besoin, avant tout, de moyens de communication faciles et rapides. . . . La situation géo-*

[210] Richardson to Fish, December 22, 1875, *ibid.*, LV.

[211] Maxey to Sherman, October 30, 1879, W. T. Sherman Papers MSS, L.

[212] González served one term in the presidency of Mexico, 1880-1884, when Diaz withdrew under the Constitution.

[213] Romero, I, 118.

graphique du Mexique et ses ressources naturelles lui assurent dans l'avenir de hautes destinées." [214]

Therefore within three years after the recognition of Diaz concessions to Americans provided for construction of five railroads in Mexico aggregating over 2,500 miles and carrying subsidies of over $32,000,000.[215] So rapid was this expansion that Foster, writing from St. Petersburg, where he was American Minister in 1881, warned against a too great and sudden rush of capital into Mexican railroads. He wrote to Plumb:

> I have noticed with considerable interest the fever in the United States on railroad construction in Mexico. I was prepared for a reasonable amount of enthusiasm, as the development in that direction has always been the popular idea in the United States, but I can only account for the fever now raging by the plethora of money among our capitalists, coupled with the exaggerated notions prevalent as to the riches of Mexico. I have always been somewhat credulous as to the paying capacity of Mexican railroads connecting with our frontier, and it can hardly be that that country will justify two of those competing lines as now seems to be contemplated. . . . I sincerely desire to see Mexico peaceful and prosperous and to this end will be glad to see railroad construction succeed. But I think that American capitalists are sadly in need of some better information than they appear to be receiving as to the difficulties likely to be encountered, . . . severity, politics, etc. When difficulties are upon them, they may turn to those able to advise.[216]

In spite of a few such forebodings railroad construction to the border and into Mexico went forward with a rush in the late '70's and early '80's. The Southern Pacific had been extended eastward as far as Yuma, Arizona, in 1877 and in 1881 was built to Deming, New Mexico, and El Paso, Texas, connecting at Deming with the Atchison, Topeka and Santa Fe. Trackage rights were obtained over the former by the

---

[214] *Rapport du général Porfirio Diaz . . . à ses compatriotes* (traduction du " Courrier du Mexique ").

[215] Powell, *Railroads of Mexico*, p. 116. John Bigelow, investigating Mexican railroad possibilities at the request of Samuel J. Tilden, called attention to the staggering size of the subsidies assumed by a relatively weak Mexican Government, to the lack of suitable public lands, danger in too many competing lines, and the undeveloped state of business in the region opened by the railroads. Bigelow's arguments were answered by Romero and by various American financial writers interested in Mexico as a field of investment.

[216] Foster to Plumb, March 16, 1881, Plumb Papers MSS, XIII.

Santa Fe from Deming to Benson, Arizona, and a branch from Benson reached Nogales, Arizona, in 1882. The Texas and Pacific in 1882 made a junction at Sierra Blanca, Texas, with the Southern Pacific which had come east from El Paso. The International and Great Northern reached the border at Laredo in 1882. In 1883 the Galveston, Houston, and San Antonio connected with the Southern Pacific and by means of a branch from Spofford, Texas, reached Eagle Pass the same year.[217] Meanwhile work was also progressing rapidly south of the border. Despite opposition by Alfredo Chavero, " a prominent public man, a supporter of the Diaz Administration, and Speaker of the Chamber of Deputies " and some other eminent men [218] the Mexican Congress under the firm guiding hand of Diaz rapidly granted concessions to American interests for railroad building toward the northern frontier [219] as well as from east to west. These grants were all issued with the stipulation that the roadbed would revert to Mexico at the end of 99 years.[220] Thus foreign capital and railroads grafted a youthful, growing mode of transportation upon the primitive trunk of Mexico, and stimulated the growth of cities.[221]

To the frontier the railroad brought increased settlement and helped bring peace. Scouts drove the Indians before the oncoming construction squads and an " almost unparalleled " emigration followed in the wake of the railroad,[222] new towns springing up at the magic touch of the wand of steel.[223]

---

[217] Powell, pp. 120-121. See also Annual Report Col. O. B. Willcox, Commanding Department of Arizona, September 11, 1880, in *Report of Secretary of War for 1880*, p. 206.

[218] Foster, I, 110; Foster to Evarts, May 29, 1878, *U. S. For. Rel. 1878*, pp. 550-551.

[219] See for a discussion of these concessions Powell, pp. 109 ff; Foster to Evarts, May 29, 1878, *U. S. For. Rel. 1878*, pp. 550-552; Foster to Evarts, December 16, 1878, *ibid., 1879*, p. 765; Foster to Evarts, January 28, 1879, *ibid.*, pp. 776-778; Foster to Evarts, August 16, 1879, *ibid.*, pp. 826 ff; Morgan to Blaine, July 30, 1881, *ibid., 1881*, pp. 780-781; Foster, I, 111.

[220] Romero, p. 118.

[221] Frank Tannenbaum, *The Mexican Agrarian Revolution*, pp. 143-144, 146-147.

[222] *Report of Secretary of War for 1880*, p. 56.

[223] Rister, p. 295.

" The coming of the railroad marked the passing of an epoch. The land of sage brush and cactus was isolated no longer; through the very heart of it ran two of the new trade routes binding together the eastern and western coasts of the nation. The railroad brought settlers and capital." [224]

As railroads and settlements thus began to dot the border more thickly, the region came to lose the more lawless aspects of the frontier. In addition, the growing power of Diaz, as already remarked, together with his apparently increased determination, led to more effective military cooperation on the border. Occasional serious outbreaks like those of Victorio and Geronimo marked the '80's. In the long run, however, the forces toward peace became progressively more powerful than those toward continued lawlessness. As a result the United States Government early in 1880 took important action on the Order of June 1. In a memorandum which he left at the State Department Zamacona referred to previous conversations on the matter and to the statement in President Hayes' Message of December 1879 that he hoped the Order might be repealed without detriment to either country. " The state of public opinion in Mexico is becoming painfully alive to the fact that these orders, in spite of the improved condition of affairs on the border and of the Presidential indication of early repeal of them, were still in force," Zamacona declared. His own position was becoming delicate since: " The impression was arising in Mexico that he was lax in his duty in not pressing for repeal." [225]

Within a few weeks the Order was repealed, Evarts writing Foster of " the decision of this government to consider the instructions contained in the order of June 1, 1877, from the War Department, contemplating and providing for a direction to General E. O. C. Ord, that under certain circumstances therein set forth he might pursue raiders across the border into the Republic of Mexico for the purpose of punish-

---

[224] R. H. Gabriel, *The Lure of the Frontier*, p. 298.
[225] Memorandum left with Hay by Zamacona in the absence of Secretary Evarts, February 19, 1880, Notes from the Legation MSS, XXVI.

ing them and recapturing stolen property, as no longer opera-
tive." [226] Zamacona reported the satisfaction of his government at this action, which had been desired so long and so
ardently and added that the decision of the United States in
this matter " dispels the only cloud on our northern horizon
and will raise to its full height the feeling of mutual confidence which has for some time past been developing." [227]
" The President," Ruelas wrote, " has been informed of that
measure, which was dictated by the Government of the United
States in justice to Mexico and sees in it a proof of the desire that the relations between the two republics may be
sincere and cordial." [228]

While the border situation was not entirely satisfactory
thereafter, as it had not been before, at least a new " espíritu
du fraternidad," new " relaciones de amistad " now marked
the contacts of the two countries along the boundary.[229] Diaz'
semi-annual message to the Mexican Congress for April 1880
definitely showed this new spirit. Several of his previous
messages, although conciliatory, had not been hopeful of
permanent border agreement, so long as the Order of June 1
was in force.[230] With its repeal Díaz " Discurso " took on a
markedly different tone. He said in part:

Las relaciones con los Estados Unidos de América son en la actuali-
dad cordiales y satisfactorias. El Gobierno de dichos Estados acordó
por fin la derogación de la orden de 1° de Junio de 1877; y al
tributar ese homenaje a la justicia y a la ley internacional, ha hecho
desaparecer un peligro permanente para la paz entre las dos Re-
públicas y un obstáculo que se venía oponiendo a la perfecta inteli-
gencia, al desarrollo y porvenir económicos entre ambas naciones.[231]

---

[226] Evarts to Foster, March 1, 1880, U. S. For. Rel. 1880-1881,
p. 735.

[227] Zamacona to Evarts, March 10, 1880, Notes from the Legation
MSS, XXVI.

[228] Neill to Evarts, April 12, 1880, U. S. For. Rel. 1880-1881,
p. 744.

[229] " Memoria que en cumplimiento del precepto constitucional
presenta al décimo Congreso de la Unión," Memoria de la Secretaría de Relaciones Exteriores, 1881, p. 6.

[230] For the text of Diaz' Semi-Annual Messages see Ricardo Rodrí-
guez, Historia auténtica de la administración del Sr. Gral. Porfirio Díaz, I, Discurso, September 16, 1877, pp. 18 ff; Discurso,
April 1, 1878, pp. 23 ff; Discurso, September 17, 1878, pp. 31 ff.

[231] Ibid., Discurso ante el Congreso de la Unión, April 1, 1880, pp.
65 ff.

Withdrawal of the Order of June 1 was thus greeted with enthusiastic approval by the Mexican Government but it did not bring for some time permission to cross into Mexico in pursuit of raiders. As already noticed, the scourge of Victorio and his warriors was at its height in the spring of 1880 and in June Hay telegraphed Morgan that: " Colonel Hatch telegraphs . . . great bulk hostile Indians have crossed Mexican line and are now in mountains of Chihuahua. Hatch says State authorities Chihuahua are willing that he should cross line. The President desires that you ask authority for that purpose from Mexican Government immediately." [232] Morgan's answer was that the Mexican Minister of Foreign Relations " after consultation with the President declines consent to American troops to cross Mexican frontier in pursuit Indians mentioned in your despatch. Tried to persuade him." [233] The Mexican executive did not find itself empowered under the Constitution, Ruelas told Morgan, to permit " entrance of foreign troops into the territory of the federation." A significant statement, however, held out a great measure of hope. Ruelas asserted that the Mexican Senate could if it wished authorize such unilateral crossing. The Mexican executive was still empowered to grant permission only if the crossing were reciprocal. Any other arrangement would exceed the powers granted it by the Senate.[234]

Apparently Ruelas dropped this hint as to possible Mexican action in response to a forceful presentation of the American point of view by Morgan. The United States Government, Morgan said, felt that:

The hands of these people [the Indians] are lifted against all men. They will destroy in Mexico as they have destroyed in the United States. It is as much in the interest of Mexico that they should be captured as it is in the interest of the United States. They are now within reach of our troops. They may easily be captured. This opportunity lost, another may not occur. The frontier between

---

[232] Hay to Morgan, June 18, 1880 (Cipher Telegram), Instructions MSS, XX.

[233] Morgan to Hay, June 20, 1880 (Cipher Telegram), Despatches MSS, XXXII.

[234] Morgan to Evarts, June 29, 1880, Enclosure No. 6, Ruelas to Morgan, June 23, 1880, *U. S. For. Rel. 1880-1881*, pp. 760-761.

the two countries is so extended that it is difficult to guard it from
end to end. . . . Mexico need apprehend no unpleasant complications from the temporary presence of United States troops upon her
soil. They will go there, if at all, simply in the pursuit of robbers
and murderers, and these captured they will immediately retire.[235]

Morgan claimed that Ruelas in reply went so far as to make
specific Diaz' stand. The latter was said to consent to crossing on the following terms: (a) that this consent would not
serve as a precedent, (b) that Mexican troops should be
allowed in turn to cross into the United States in pursuit of
the particular Indians in question.[236] After holding out
this encouragement, however, the Mexican Government suffered a change of heart, in the opinion of Morgan. The
Minister of Foreign Relations asserted that Morgan had
" misapprehended " his previous statements. It was in vain,
Morgan said, to argue " the impolicy as well as the unfriendli-
ness " of this " sudden change of views on the part of the
President and the denial of the authority the President of
the United States asked at his hands." [237]

Meanwhile the United States Government chafed under
the continued delay of the Mexican Government in the matter
of permission for crossing. Evarts wrote that " the President greatly regrets that the Mexican authorities should not
have permitted the operations of our troops on her soil for
the purpose of inflicting just punishment, if possible, upon a
marauding band of Indians, whose depredations are a source
of constant annoyance to the peace of both countries." The
flight of Indians across the border from the United States
" involves, in the apprehension of this government, an urgent
obligation on the part of the Mexican Government to disarm
these Indians, and a responsibility for any future inroads
upon our territory they may make." [238]

---

[235] Enclosure No. 5, Morgan to Ruelas, June 21, 1880, ibid., pp.
759-760.
[236] Morgan to Evarts, June 29, 1880, Enclosure, A Memorandum
of an interview Morgan and Ruelas, June 19, 1880, Despatches
MSS, LXX. This memorandum is omitted in U. S. For Rel.
[237] Ibid. This portion of the despatch is also omitted from
U. S. For. Rel.
[238] Evarts to Morgan, June 26, 1880, U. S. For. Rel. 1880-1881,
pp. 756-757.

Several months later Evarts again telegraphed urgently: " Victorio after renewed attacks on our troops escapes pursuit over border. Press upon Mexico necessity allowing our troops to pursue across border or assume responsibility of harboring and yet not disarming him." [239] In reply to these pressing requests Diaz in the same month asked the consent of the Mexican Senate, under the Mexican Constitution, for United States troops to cross in pursuit of Victorio and within a few weeks obtained the desired permission [240] for three months although only in reciprocal form. By the action of the Senate the Mexican executive was authorized to permit reciprocal passing by the troops of both countries when " in close pursuit of a band of savage Indians." Such pursuit was to be made only in the desert portion of the frontier with an understanding to be sought with the American Government as to what part of the border was to be considered desert. The pursuing force which entered foreign territory was to retire to its own soil as soon as the band pursued should be defeated or its trail lost. Abuses were to be punished by the government to whom the troops belonged under their own laws as if they occurred on their own soil.[241] Although substantial powers on reciprocal crossing were thus again in the hands of Diaz, not until the summer of 1882 was an agreement actually reached, as will be seen in the next chapter.

[239] Evarts to Morgan, September 14, 1880 (Cipher Telegram), Instructions MSS, XX.
[240] Morgan to Evarts, September 22, 1880 (Cipher Telegram), Despatches MSS, LXXI.
[241] Morgan to Evarts, October 16, 1880, Subenclosure Office of the Secretaries of the Chamber of Senators of the Congress of the Union Section 2, Secret Bureau, *U. S. For. Rel. 1881-1882*, pp. 746-747; Rippy, *The Southwestern Historical Quarterly*, XXIV, 314.

CHAPTER IV

GROWING PEACE AND ORDER, 1881-1910

As the long fingers of the railroad reached toward the border and settlements became larger and more frequent, the disorders of frontier days slowly retreated before them. Moreover, American and Mexican cooperation, officially sanctioned in 1882, served to hasten the coming of relative peace. Indian outbreaks, cattle raiding, smuggling, and other forms of frontier lawlessness gradually came to be less serious and finally in the early '90's practically ceased, only an occasional flare of disorder appearing as a reminder of unhappier days.

Before this much-desired condition, however, the '80's were to be marked by further savage Indian raids. In 1881 Nana with the remnants of Victorio's band, noted above, led his warriors in a series of bloody forays from Mexico back into the United States and in September of the same year Juh and Nahdi with some Chiricahuas again fled their reservation and were forced by the troops into Mexican territory. There in April 1882 they were joined by Geronimo and the rest of the hostile Chiricahuas of the San Carlos reservation with Loco and a band from the Ojo Caliente reservation. With these forces Geronimo harried the American border and committed equally serious or even more serious depredations in northern Chihuahua.[1] Early in 1882 Zamacona reported word from the Mexican consul at Tucson, Arizona, that the escaped Chiricahua Indians had invaded and had committed depredations in several districts of northern Sonora, including those of Ures and Arispe. The United States was asked to exercise increased vigilance over the reservations in Arizona.[2]

In reply Frelinghuysen reported that he had asked the secretaries of war and of the interior " to adopt every proper measure in accordance with the request of the Mexican Gov-

---

[1] *U. S. Bureau American Ethnology Bulletin No. 30*, p. 65.
[2] Zamacona to Frelinghuysen, February 18, 1882, *U. S. For. Rel. 1882-1883*, p. 409.

ernment in the premises." [3]   Secretary of War Robert T. Lincoln responded that in the absence from Washington of the General of the Army " instructions will be sent direct to the commanding general Military Division of the Pacific, to take all possible steps to prevent the incursions of these Indians." [4]   The Commissioner of Indian Affairs, speaking for the Interior Department, placed most of the onus of the Indian situation on the Mexican local border authorities. He claimed that it " has been the aim of this office to fully and heartily co-operate with the Mexican authorities in any and all efforts that might be made to put a stop to raiding of renegades upon the border." He asserted further that not all the Indians mentioned by Zamacona " belong to reservations under the supervision of this bureau." Some were renegade Indians who refused to return since Mexican local authorities " induced them to remain in Mexico for the purpose of carrying on trade with them for stolen property." [5]

In the light of this situation strong diplomatic pressure was again brought to bear upon the Mexican Administration to permit American troops to cross in pursuit of the Apache marauders. At first Diaz refused to submit such a proposition to the Mexican Senate unless permission were given to Mexican troops to cross under similar circumstances,[6] the Mexican position being stated succintly by Mariscal:

. . . I have the honor to say to your excellency that, as is known, it belongs to the Senate of Mexico to grant the permission asked for, and considering that that body has twice felt it to be its duty to refuse a similar request except upon the condition of reciprocity, and under certain . . . measures of precaution necessary to both

[3] Frelinghuysen to De Cuellar, March 1, 1882, ibid., p. 409.
[4] Frelinghuysen to Romero, March 13, 1882, Enclosure Lincoln to Frelinghuysen, March 6, 1882, ibid., p. 410.
[5] Frelinghuysen to Romero, March 15, 1882, Enclosure, S. J. Kirkwood to Frelinghuysen, March 8, 1882, subenclosure H. Price, Commissioner of Indian Affairs to Kirkwood, March 7, 1882, ibid., p. 411. Raids from Arizona into Sonora by " marauders styling themselves cowboys " were reported late in 1881. Romero to Frelinghuysen, April 6, 1882, Enclosure U. S. Marshal J. W. Evans for Arizona Territory to Gov. Luis E. Torres, of Sonora, October 12, 1881, ibid., p. 412.
[6] Morgan to Frelinghuysen, May 5, 1882 (Cipher Telegram), Despatches MSS, LXXVI.

countries, conditions with reference to which the Government of the United States has returned no answer whatever, the President does not consider it proper . . . to consult the said house upon the subject on this occasion, while, at least, he is not informed that said government is disposed to grant a similar request, under similar circumstances, to Mexican troops.

Diaz had, however, sent orders through the Mexican Secretary of War "that within the Mexican territory, they [the Indians] be pursued with the greatest vigor, and to capture them . . .; and that should they succeed in recrossing the frontier prompt advice be given thereof to the United States forces to the end that they be able to attack them without loss of time." [7] Meanwhile Colonel Mackenzie and Lieutenant Colonel Forsyth had arrived at a satisfactory unofficial working agreement with the Mexican forces in Sonora. "The very successful result obtained from the indefatigable pursuit of the Apaches by Lieutenant-Colonel Forsyth," Sheridan wrote, "is due to the careful management of Colonel Mackenzie and Lieutenant-Colonel Forsyth, in keeping scouts in Mexico to watch the Indians and making special and satisfactory arrangements for the co-operation of the Mexican military commanders on the border." [8]

Very soon, moreover, Diaz reversed his position and gained permission from the Mexican Senate for United States troops to cross into Mexican territory, such permission to apply to Lower California, Sonora, and Chihuahua as far east as El Paso. In this region hostile Indians were to be pursued on the same terms as those in the instructions of October 15, 1880. The orders were to date, for six months from May 12 and were to go into effect as soon as word was received that the United States had accepted them. [9] But in spite of former eagerness on the part of the United States, negotiations dragged along for several months, Sherman in Washington impatiently urging that the agreement be made. He thought

[7] Morgan to Frelinghuysen, May 6, 1882, Enclosure No. 2, Mariscal to Morgan, May 4, 1882, *U. S. For. Rel. 1882-1883*, p. 389.

[8] Frelinghuysen to Romero, May 12, 1882, Sub-Enclosure Telegram Sheridan to R. C. Drum, Adjutant General U. S. A., May 4, 1882, *ibid.*, p. 420.

[9] Morgan to Frelinghuysen, May 13, 1882 (Telegram), Despatches MSS, LXXVI.

that "the terms proposed by the Mexicans minister in his communication of May 12, 1882, for mutual passage of national troops across the border in pursuit of hostile Indians are just and fair and should be accepted pure and simple. When so accepted instructions to our Department Commanders bordering Mexico should be made to conform." [10] Evidently the Secretary of War agreed with him, since Frelinghuysen wrote to Morgan:

> Acknowledging the receipt of your telegram of the 13th ultimo, in relation to the reciprocal passage of troops across the border when in pursuit of hostile Indians, I have now the pleasure to inclose, for your information, a copy of a letter from the Secretary of War, of the 31st ultimo, wherein he announces that the proposed terms or conditions upon which such passage may be made are acceptable to the General of the Army and to himself. [11]

At the same time Mexican troops in the field were pressing relentlessly against the Apaches, who had escaped from San Carlos, and against their fugitive brethren, with whom they were making common cause in Mexico. Romero reported a serious clash late in April between Mexican forces under Colonel Lorenzo Garcia and Indians thought to have escaped from Arizona reservations. Combined columns under Colonel Garcia and Major Louis Ceroso in northern Chihuahua were said to have "utterly routed a band of Apaches who had just been carrying on plundering operations in the United States, taking from them their booty, which consisted of horses and mules. . . . Some of the Indians escaped, fleeing in the direction of Casas Grandes." The Mexican loss was given as three officers and eighteen men killed and two officers and eight men wounded. [12] A few weeks later Mexican troops fought a band of Juh's Apaches in northern Chihuahua, during which thirty-six of the Indians were reported killed and ten taken prisoner, while fifty animals were captured. The

---

[10] Sherman Endorsement May 26, 1882, on communication from State Department referring to previous correspondence upon the subject of reciprocal crossing, W. T. Sherman Endorsements MSS.

[11] Frelinghuysen to Morgan, June 6, 1882, *U. S. For. Rel. 1882-1883*, p. 390.

[12] Romero to Frelinghuysen, June 1, 1882, Enclosure Gen. I. G. Carbo to Mexican Minister of War (undated), *ibid.*, p. 421.

survivors of the band were pursued into the Sierra Madre mountains.[18]

These efforts of Mexican forces to destroy the marauding Apaches were enthusiastically acclaimed in Washington where Frelinghuysen quoted Sherman as saying: " In my judgment the Mexican Government and the Mexican troops are entitled to our thanks for their gallantry and successful actions against our common enemies, the Apaches." With this view Secretary of War Lincoln heartily agreed: "Concurring," he said, " in the views of the General of the Army, that the Mexican Government and its troops are entitled to the thanks of this department, I have the honor to request that the same may be appropriately tendered." Frelinghuysen did so tender to Romero the appreciation of both the State and the War Departments.[14]

The Mexican action was paralleled by similar vigorous steps against the Apaches on the American side of the line. Acting Adjutant General George D. Ruggles summarized the Juh outbreak in April 1882 as follows:

(a) April 17 Juh and a band of sixty marauding Apaches returned secretly from Mexico to the San Carlos Reservation and compelled the remainder of the Chiricahuas—some 40 men and 300 women and children—to leave the reservation with him.

(b) April 18 the entire band left the reservation killing Indian chief of police Sterling and a police sergeant who tried to bar their way.

(c) April 18-20 the Indians fled in the direction of Fort Thomas killing ten men, women, and children on Eagle Creek as they fled. They were pursued by Lieutenant Colonel Schofield of Fort Thomas but his advance guard was forced to return, when its ammunition was exhausted.

(d) April 20 Captain Gordon and 119 men of the 6th Cavalry sought to intercept the Indians. Lieutenant-Colonel Forsyth with four troops of the 4th Cavalry at Separ, New

---

[18] Romero to Frelinghuysen, June 22, 1882, *ibid.*, p. 423.
[14] Frelinghuysen to Romero, July 12, 1882, *ibid.*, p. 434.

Mexico, was reported "on the alert to cooperate." General McDowell ordered Harris' troop of the 1st Cavalry to report to General Willcox in Arizona and "immediate steps were taken to use all the troops in the Department of Arizona available."

(e) April 24 Forsyth attacked the Indians "in an impregnable position" in Stein's Peak Range, New Mexico. The troops lost five killed and five wounded, while two of the Indians were killed and several were wounded.

(f) On April 28 Captain Tupper with troops G and M of the 6th Cavalry struck the Indians near Cloverdale. Twelve or fifteen Indians were killed, including Loco's son, and seventy head of stock were captured. The troops lost one man killed and two men wounded. Forsyth and Tupper then united their columns and pursued the Indians across the line where they were attacked by Mexican troops as already noted.[15] Thus a greater degree of cooperation between border

---

[15] Frelinghuysen to Romero, July 20, 1882, *ibid.*, pp. 434-436. In his Annual Report for 1882 Willcox enlarged upon the difficulties of campaigning against the hostile Apaches. While the troops were busy driving the Indians in upon San Carlos one company of Indian scouts under Lieutenant Cruse had mutinied. Five of the mutineers were subsequently captured or gave themselves up. Three of these were hung, two were sent to prison on Alcatraz Island, California. Willcox said further that the revolting Indians had threatened to kill the San Carlos Indians if they did not follow the former on the warpath. He spoke of the troops in the Department of Arizona as totally inadequate to handle the whole situation. He reported only 1,184 regulars in the entire department. These few men were expected to guard the borders of the San Carlos Reservation (containing 4,550 square miles), protect settlers, railroad construction, and a section of the border stretching from Yuma to the New Mexican line, a distance of 382 miles. He spoke also of the difficulties in such a vast region of obtaining true reports of Indian depredations and the exact whereabouts of the depredators. Beside the Indians' own cunning and mobility many of the settlers were new to the region and ignorant of frontier lore and Indian fighting. This state of affairs helped give rise to wild rumors which only served to confuse the situation and send the troops off on false scents. In spite of these difficulties, however, Willcox asserted that railroad construction within the Department had not been interrupted for a single day by Indian raids since the spring of 1878. Work at mills and mines had been suspended for this cause only a few days in a few remote places. During those four years the population of the Territory had doubled, increasing from 40,000 to 80,000. He thought that the country might well feel proud of the young officers of the 3rd and 6th Cavalry and of the 12th Infantry, which

forces was developing even before the two governments had successfully completed their negotiations for a reciprocal agreement.

Here matters stood when the two governments took one of the most important steps in the history of the border disturbances by signing a two-year reciprocal crossing agreement. Not only did this agreement prove important for the years 1882-1884, but being renewed from time to time it became a major feature of border policy. This important document, signed July 29, 1882, provided " that the Regular federal troops of the two Republics may reciprocally cross the boundary line of the two countries, when they are in close pursuit of a band of savage Indians," with the qualification that pursuit should occur only in desert or unpopulated parts of the border.

Unpopulated regions were defined as those points at least two leagues distant " from any encampment or town of either country." Article III stated that no crossings should take place from Capitan Leal on the Mexican side of the Rio Grande, 20 Mexican leagues (52 English miles) above Piedras Negras, to the mouth of the Rio Grande. Article IV provided that the commander of troops which crossed the border in pursuit of Indians was to give notice when he crossed, or if possible before, to the nearest military commander or civil authority of the country whose territory he was entering. Article V said: " The pursuing force shall retire to its own territory as soon as it shall have fought the band of which it is in pursuit or have lost its trail. In no case shall the forces of the two countries, respectively, establish themselves or remain in the foreign territory for any time longer than is necessary to make the pursuit of the band whose trail they follow." Article VI provided that abuses committed by the troops of one country on the soil of the other country should be punished by the government to which the forces belonged. Article VII stated the reverse of the

---

regiments had operated for various lengths of time in his Department. *Report of Secretary of War for 1882*, pp. 146-151.

previous question. In case offenses were committed by the inhabitants of one country against forces of the other within its territory the government of the country whose inhabitants had committed the offenses was responsible only for denial of justice in the punishment of the guilty. This agreement, by the terms of Article VIII, was to remain in force for two years, although it might be terminated on four months' notice by either government. Ratification by neither Senate was to be necessary for carrying the agreement into effect. Permission had already been granted to the executive by the Mexican Senate and the Constitution of the United States did not require consent of the Senate for an agreement of this form.[16]

That the new agreement was gratifying to the military on the disturbed section of the border in Arizona may be seen from the Annual Report of Willcox: " Our troops and the people of Arizona hail with rejoicing the recent treaty effected between the two governments on this subject. It is what all military commanders along the line have long contended

---

[16] Malloy, *Treaties, Conventions*, I, 1144-1145; Davis to Morgan, August 18, 1882, *U. S. For. Rel. 1882-1883*, pp. 396-397. By a supplementary agreement the time involved was changed from two to one year. Malloy, I, 1145-1146. Occasionally international matters have been adjusted without the formality of a treaty and without ratification by the United States Senate. One method used is the protocol, an agreement between the State Department and a foreign office reduced to writing. It is not a treaty, so far as the United States is concerned, and does not become the supreme law of ·the land. Thus a protocol is neither a treaty nor a law and is binding in a moral sense only, and then probably only upon the administration making it. Charles H. Butler, *The Treaty-Making Power of the United States*, II, 370-371, n. Another authority says that the President of the United States through his constitutional power to " receive ambassadors and other public ministers " and to negotiate treaties becomes the " sole organ " of the government in communicating with foreign powers. As such he has, without the Senate, certain powers of making foreign agreements, in theory only temporary, or specific in scope, or binding the executive alone, but in practice, by precedent, binding other departments of the government and through interpretations of treaties and international law binding the state as a whole. Thus he disagrees with Butler. Further the President's " power as Commander-in-Chief permits him to conclude agreements in time of peace as well as war." The mutual pursuit agreements with Mexico (above) are cited as examples. Quincy Wright, *The Control of American Foreign Relations*, pp. 242, 243, 246.

for." [17]   Fortunately for the more thickly populated Texas border, where the reciprocal crossing agreement did not apply, the Indian outbreaks burned themselves out in the desert border country and did not extend as far south and east as the Rio Grande. " Everything is smooth in the running of the Department of Texas," Sheridan reported in June 1882.[18] General Augur who had succeeded Ord in command of the Department of Texas in 1881 wrote: " There have been occasional reports that bands of hostile Indians have appeared in the northwestern part of this department but in every instance investigation has proved them incorrect." Some smugglers and horse thieves disguised as Indians had operated across the border from each country, he thought, but measured in terms of previous disorder the Rio Grande border had been comparatively quiet during. 1882.[19]

In furtherance of the letter and spirit of the new agreement Romero in Washington reported word from his government that it had " given orders to the military commanders on the frontier to act in concert with the commanders of the United States forces in pursuit of the savages." [20]   The Indian menace, however, was difficult to down in spite of the new agreement. In December 1882, four representatives and senators of Chihuahua appealed to Diaz to correct what they considered " the alarming situation of the people on the frontier." They complained bitterly of American reservation policies. The United States had freed " millions of slaves " but " the fact that it is unwilling or unable to disarm those hordes that so cruelly murder its own citizens and ours, is also a subject of wonder." [21]   Frelinghuysen on the other

---

[17] Annual Report Major General O. B. Willcox, Commanding Department of Arizona, August 31, 1882, in *Report of Secretary of War for 1882*, p. 149.

[18] Sheridan to Sherman, June 28, 1882, W. T. Sherman Papers MSS, LVIII.

[19] *Report of Secretary of War for 1882*, p. 106.

[20] Romero to Frelinghuysen, September 5, 1882, *U. S. For. Rel. 1882-1883*, p. 438.

[21] Romero to Frelinghuysen, January 20, 1883, *ibid. 1883*, pp. 681-683. H. Price, Indian Commissioner, in his Annual Report Octo-

hand felt that " stringent provisions in each Republic rendering it as far as possible impracticable for the Indians to
dispose of their booty in the territory of the other would be
a salutary measure." [22] Romero agreed but wanted to know
some practical means of settling the troublesome question of
sale of booty.[23]

At the same time Frelinghuysen defended American reservation practice. He referred to the report of Brigadier General George Crook in command of the Department of Arizona on the escape of Apache bands from San Carlos reservation, claiming that since a series of conferences with the
Apaches in the fall of 1882, no depredations had taken place
for which the San Carlos Indians or other reservation Indians in Arizona were responsible. He asserted further that
since Juh and Geronimo and their Chiricahua Apaches had
fled in 1881 and early 1882 no Indians had left the reservation. He had placed, he said, on each Indian " capable of
bearing arms " a brass or tin identification tag. A daily
count of the Indians was also taken. He felt the organization at San Carlos to be so perfect that an Indian could not
leave without the fact becoming known almost before he
reached the Gila river. Crook added: " Nothing would give
me greater pleasure than to cooperate or combine with him
[Reyes] in operations to force to submission the persistently
hostile Chiricahua Apaches." [24]

As additional evidence that the Indian raiding problem
was difficult to solve, even after the agreement, there arose a
demand among military men, apparently on both sides of the
border, that they be permitted to depart from the letter of
the agreement where necessary. General Schofield in com-

---

ber 10, 1882, felt that one cause of conflict between Indians and
whites was uncertain reservation boundaries. He wished them sur-
veyed. *Report of Commissioner of Indian Affairs for 1882*, p. 5.
    [22] Frelinghuysen to Romero, April 9, 1883, *U. S. For. Rel. 1883*, p.
686.
    [23] Romero to Frelinghuysen, April 11, 1883, *ibid.*, p. 689.
    [24] Frelinghuysen to Romero, April 10, 1883, *ibid.*, pp. 687-688.
See also *Depredaciones cometidas en territorio mexicano por Indios
bárbaros de los Estados Unidos 1877-1884*, Romero to Secretary of
Foreign Relations, May 5, 1883, Photostats of Mexican Archives
MSS.

mand of the Military Division of the Pacific (which included
the Department of Arizona) said that he had held

consultation with the general officers in command of the Mexican
forces in Sonora and Chihuahua. We all recognize the fact that a
literal construction of the terms of the present convention between
the United States and Mexico will bring about failure in the settlement of pending Indian hostilities. It is all important that we on
the ground be permitted to vary these stipulations to the extent
required by the best interests of the two Governments, and I urgently
request that immediate steps be taken to bring about this desired
result. With this point of view Frelinghuysen evidently heartily
agreed since he urged the Mexican Government to grant " its permission to conclude [such] an understanding with me . . ." [25]

Sherman sensed the difficulties in the path of such a
project for he wrote to Schofield: " It is not possible or prac-
ticable to alter or amend the agreement made with the Mexican Government as to the co-operation of the troops . . . on
. . . the national border. That agreement is all the Mexican
laws will permit, and there is no time for their Congress to
modify laws to suit the private judgment of local commanders." [26] Objection to any such modification came also
from the Mexican Government. The Secretary of Foreign
Relations quoted Diaz as holding that there could be no
modification of the " aforesaid arrangement without a fresh
authorization thereto from the Chamber of Senators. . . ."
The Mexican Foreign Office awaited full word of the modi-
fications proposed by the United States before deciding on a
suitable course.[27]

What the United States Government desired most of all
was apparently an extension of the time limit of the agreement rather than the liberalizing of its terms. John Davis,
Acting Secretary of State, wrote Romero in May 1883 that
" the object in view [by the United States] was not so much
to confer upon the respective military commanders powers
enabling them to depart from the general stipulations of that
agreement, as to permit them to continue the active operations now begun beyond the time fixed by the supplementary

[25] Frelinghuysen to Romero, April 24, 1883, *U. S. For. Rel. 1883*,
pp. 690-691.
[26] Enclosure. Sherman to Schofield, April 19, 1883, *ibid.*, p. 692.
[27] Romero to Frelinghuysen, April 26, 1883, *ibid.*, p. 693.

protocol of September 21, 1882, for the termination of the arrangement." [28] In reply Romero wrote two days later quoting the Mexican foreign office: " When the minister of the United States shall have prepared, in due form, negotiation for extension of treaty for crossing of troops, the matter shall receive special attention." [29] As an outcome of these negotiations a new agreement was signed on June 28, 1883, by United States Minister P. H. Morgan and José Fernandez, official mayor of the Mexican Department of Foreign Relations, providing for prolongation of the original crossing agreement and the protocol in modification thereof until August 18, 1884.[30]

During 1883 close cooperation of the troops of the two countries plus the rapid development of the border country brought unusual quiet to the region. Secretary of War Robert T. Lincoln pointed out in his Annual Report that a condition of peace characterized border relations except for the expedition of Brigadier General Crook into the Sierra Madre mountains of northern Mexico where he fought the Apaches still on the warpath and took many prisoners including fifty-two male Indians. He reported also an agreement reached by the War and Interior Departments whereby police control of the Indians on the San Carlos reservation was to be intrusted to General Crook. General Sherman felt that if Crook were allowed to manage the Indians in his own way all troubles with them would cease [31] and Crook in his Annual Report asserted that he had persuaded many of the hostile Apaches to return to San Carlos and settle on land of their own choice within the reservation.[32] For the same year Brigadier General R. L. MacKenzie reported few depredations within the District of New Mexico, a few minor forays by Navajos stealing ponies being the only disturbances which

---

[28] Davis to Cayetano Romero, May 7, 1883, ibid., pp. 693-694.
[29] Cayetano Romero to Davis, May 9, 1883, ibid., pp. 695-696.
[30] Malloy, I, 1157-1158.
[31] Report of Secretary of War for 1883, p. 5.
[32] Annual Report Crook, Commanding Department of Arizona, September 27, 1883, ibid., p. 145.

he considered worthy of note.[33]   Unusual quiet also reigned on the Texas border, Brigadier General C. C. Augur reporting that there was " no reason to believe that a hostile Indian has been within the limits of this Department during the past year." [34]   Sheridan went even farther than his subordinates and expressed his opinion that use of troops against Indians in his Division would " soon cease."   However new railroad construction into Mexico must be guarded for some time, he thought.[35]

So successful did the reciprocal agreements prove that they came to be regularly extended with very little discussion from 1882 to 1886, with the exception of a brief interval from August 18 to October 31, 1884.[36]   About the middle of July 1884 the Mexican Minister at Washington was instructed by his government to inquire of the United States whether it desired to renew the agreement for reciprocal crossing of the border.   The Mexican Government was ready to negotiate as soon as Morgan were empowered.[37]   Within a few days Morgan received such authorization.[38]   The Mexican Government however hesitated to extend the agreement for so long a period as two years and negotiations dragged until at last the Mexican point of view prevailed.   In October the Mexican Minister of Foreign Relations reported that the Mexican Senate had authorized the President to extend the agreement of July 29, 1882 " upon the same terms " for one additional year.[39]   The point was conceded by Frelinghuysen in a telegram of October 25 and by W. Hunter, Acting Secre-

---

[33] Annual Report McKenzie, Commanding District of New Mexico in the Department of Missouri, September 26, 1883, *ibid.*, p. 137.

[34] Annual Report Augur, Commanding Department of Texas, September 21, 1883, *ibid.*, p. 145.

[35] Annual Report Sheridan, Commanding Division of the Missouri, October 17, 1883, *ibid.*, p. 105.

[36] Rippy, " Some Precedents of the Pershing Expedition into Mexico," *Southwestern Historical Quarterly*, XXIV, 314-315.

[37] Morgan to Frelinghuysen, July 16, 1884, Despatches MSS, LXXXIII.

[38] Davis, Acting Secretary of State, to Morgan, July 31, 1884, Instructions MSS, XXI.

[39] Morgan to Frelinghuysen, October 19, 1884, Despatches MSS, LXXXIV.

tary of State, in his instructions of October 30 [40] and in response to these new instructions Morgan signed a one-year
extension October 31.[41]   Thus only during the period between August 18, 1884, when the old agreement expired, and
October 31, when the new agreement was made, was the
border unprotected by a reciprocal crossing agreement.

Opportunity to use the extended agreement came during
1885 when the Apaches began again to become troublesome
on the border.   During the summer of 1884 the War Department had assumed police control of the San Carlos reservation and the Apaches on the reservation were placed in the
sole charge of General Crook who began to train them in
agricultural pursuits.   As the result of the efforts of Crook
and other representatives of the War Department during
the summer and fall of 1884, the Indians of the reservation
not only remained peaceful but raised and harvested over
4,000 tons of grain, vegetables, and fruits.[42]   Early in 1885,
perhaps because of the curtailment of Crook's powers and
growing friction between military and civil authorities which
distracted the administration of San Carlos, nearly half of
the Chiricahuas fled the reservation, raiding along the borders
of Arizona and New Mexico and murdering during the following year and a half, seventy-three whites and many
friendly Apaches.[43]   Under their skilled leader, Geronimo,
and with several ponies to a man, these fierce warriors and
skillful horsemen and marksmen kept the border of New
Mexico and Arizona in a state of feverish alarm for many
months.[44]   Great herds and good crops surrounding the reservation gave the marauders a sphere of action until these areas
became devastated.   Then they began to lengthen their radius.

---

[40] W. Hunter, Acting Secretary of State, to Morgan, October 30,
1884, Instructions MSS, XXI.

[41] Morgan to Frelinghuysen, October 31, 1884, Despatches MSS,
LXXXIV; Malloy, I, 1158-1159.

[42] U. S. Bureau of American Ethnology Bulletin No. 30, p. 65.

[43] Ibid.   See also Rodriguez, Historia auténtica, Discurso, September 16, 1885, I, 121, for an official statement of the Apache troubles
by President Diaz to the Mexican Congress.   The Secretary of War
in his Annual Report for 1888 (pp. 5-7) estimated the escaped
Apaches at one-fourth of the total.

[44] Report of Secretary of War for 1885, p. 129.

Thus in spite of the renewal of the reciprocal crossing agreement for another year from November 1, 1885,[45] the Geronimo uprising became one of the most serious which the border had ever experienced. From May 1885 to September 1886 the escaped Apaches shot and tortured their victims, burned buildings, and ran off stock. In his Annual Report for 1888 the Secretary of War called this the most " bloody and savage " raid in border history. Seventy-two persons were killed on the United States side of the line and twenty-four were killed in Mexico by the raiders.[46] Not until September 1886 were the Apaches finally conquered by Brigadier General Nelson A. Miles. Then Geronimo and most of his band surrendered and the captured Apaches were sent to Florida, far from the scene of their depredations. They were transferred thence to Mt. Vernon, Alabama, and finally to Fort Sill, Oklahoma. Some of the hostile Indians were never captured and as late as November 1900 attacked a Mormon settlement in Chihuahua.[47]

This raid gave rise to few international complications, for the troops on both sides of the line pursued the raiders desperately and for the most part with good cooperation. Only one instance of serious friction developed during the course of the arduous campaign. In January 1886, a United States force, composed mainly of Indian scouts under Captain Emmet Crawford, surrounded a camp of hostile Chiricahuas near Teopar, 50 miles southwest of Nacori, Mexico. The soldiers, wearing moccasins, crept stealthily toward the Indian camp under cover of night and would probably have effected a complete surprise if the braying of the startled Indian burros had not given the alarm. A running fight ensued in which no Indians were captured and casualties were unknown. At daybreak the next morning a body of

[45] Bayard to Jackson, October 6, 1885, Instructions MSS, XXI; Jackson to Bayard, October 17, 1885, Despatches MSS, LXXXVI.
[46] Report of Secretary of War for 1888, pp. 5-7. Another report put the number as seventy-three whites in the United States. See n. 43, above.
[47] U. S. Bureau American Ethnology Bulletin No. 30, pp. 65-66.

about 150 ununiformed Mexican soldiers, apparently nacionales, poured a hail of bullets into the American forces. Captain Crawford and Lieutenant Maus were standing about fifty yards in front of the American position. The Mexicans, according to Lieutenant Maus, agreed to cease firing but thereupon moved to a higher hill and reopened their fire and the troops replied. Captain Crawford fell with a mortal head wound and one Indian scout was severely wounded and two scouts and an interpreter were slightly wounded. The Mexicans, Maus estimated, lost four killed and five wounded. Maus reported further: " They [the Mexicans] seemed very sincere in their regrets and signed a paper stating all was a mistake."

The death of Crawford led to an immediate demand on the part of the United States that the Mexican Government thoroughly investigate. " You will . . . ask a searching examination into the facts of this unfortunate occurrence," the Acting Secretary of State wrote to Jackson, " with a view to locating the responsibility therefor, and preventing the recurrence of like ' accidents ' in the border operations against the hostiles which the two Governments have undertaken in their common and joint interest." [48] Although the uncertain morning light might have excused " the first surprise and attacking volley at daylight," the later firing could not be justified by any such claim which could " have no possible value . . . after the conference in the open in daylight, when the nationality and friendly mission of Captain Crawford were plainly announced, and when the white signal of a parley was displayed. It is difficult to conceive how the allegation of a ' mistake ' could be soberly made under such circumstances." [49] This demand was duly conveyed by Jackson to Mariscal, Mexican Minister of Foreign Relations, and the latter reported an investigation already in progress.[50]

---

[48] James D. Porter, Acting Secretary of State, to Jackson, February 2, 1886, *U. S. For. Rel. 1886*, pp. 570-573, Enclosure, Telegram Brigadier General George Crook to Sheridan, January 27, 1886, embodying report of First Lieutenant M. P. Maus, January 21, 1886.

[49] *Ibid.*, Instructions MSS, XXI; see also Rippy, *Southwestern Historical Quarterly*, XXIV, 315.

[50] Jackson to Bayard, February 16, 1886, *U. S. For. Rel. 1886*, pp.

Late the next month the United States Government again made earnest representations on the subject of Crawford's death.[51] Bayard enclosed a supplementary report by Lieutenant Maus in which the latter claimed that after the death of Crawford he, Maus, had been detained in the Mexican camp. He was later released, he asserted, in exchange for some of the horses which the American troops had captured from the Indians. Maus varied his earlier report somewhat, asserting that the first attack was a mistake but that the later attack, in which Crawford was killed, was " deliberate, dishonorable and treacherous." [52] This accusation was supported by statements of other members of the American force engaged and Bayard felt that the depositions and the Maus report showed " hostility . . . unmistakably " on the part of the Mexicans after the death of Crawford when the identity of the American forces was fully known. He was confident that the Mexican Government would continue its investigation and execute justice firmly. In reply to the suggestion that the Indian scouts be abolished because of their easy confusion with hostile Indians he said: " To abandon the employment of Indian scouts for this especial service would appear to be to relinquish the best known means of giving peace to the border land between Mexico and the United States, and safety to the inhabitants of both countries." [53]

The Mexican Government delayed some time in making an official statement to the United States Government on the Crawford case. In the meantime Diaz in his semi-annual message to the Mexican Congress, delivered on April 1, 1886, maintained that Crawford's death had been the result of a mistake—" habia sido unintencionalmente causada por nues-

---

573-574; Jackson to Bayard, February 23, 1886, Enclosure Mariscal to Jackson, February 18, 1886, ibid., pp. 574-575.

[51] Bayard to Jackson, March 20, 1886, ibid., pp. 575-584.

[52] Enclosure Lieutenant Maus to Captain C. S. Roberts, February 23, 1886, with supporting statements including those by 2nd Lieutenant W. E. Shipp, 10th Cavalry, Thomas Horn and William Harrison, Chief of Scouts, and Concepcion, sergeant Co. E. Battalion of Scouts, ibid., pp. 576-584.

[53] Ibid., Instructions MSS, XXI.

tra fuerza." [54] Morgan, the American Minister, complained
that the delay of the Mexican Government in replying to the
note of February 15 on Crawford's death was " unduly pro-
tracted." Diaz in his message to Congress had excused the
Mexican troops on the technical ground that the United
States Indian scouts were not included under the convention for reciprocal crossing of the border by regular forces.
Morgan denied that such forces were irregular. He insisted
that they were enlisted for just such work—" regularly enlisted, paid, armed and commanded." [55] Mariscal on the
other hand disputed the American claim that Crawford's
command was engaged with Apaches the day before the clash
with the Mexican troops. He said that only one attack was
made by the Mexicans on the scouts and then only after the
scouts had first fired on the Mexicans. No insignia of a military character was worn by the American officers, Mariscal
claimed. Further the Mexican commander Santana Perez
denied asking Maus for provisions. Mariscal admitted and
justified the detention of Maus, who was said to have been
out of uniform. The horses demanded of him were said to
have been stolen by the Indian scouts. Mariscal further
accused Crawford's scouts of a number of murders and robberies in northern Mexico.[56]

About the same time the moderate Romero at the Washington legation took up the question with the United States
Government. He thought the attack a mistake and that the
" Chihuahua volunteers " making up the Mexican force involved had thought the Indian scouts " rebel Indians." He
asserted that the Chihuahua volunteers were under less strict
discipline than the regular Mexican forces. Therefore the
orders of their officers to stop firing were not obeyed, but
neither were the orders of Lieutenant Maus to the Indian
scouts to the same end. He held that the theory that the

---

[54] Rodriguez, I, 127-128.
[55] Morgan to Bayard, April 14, 1886, Enclosure, *U. S. For. Rel.
1886*, pp. 585-586.
[56] Morgan to Bayard, May 25, 1886, Enclosure Mariscal to Morgan, May 19, 1886, *ibid.*, pp. 587-589.

Mexicans had attacked to obtain supplies was unlikely since the Mexicans involved were "peaceable citizens who had armed themselves to defend their lives and property and could not think of exposing them, especially as the Scouts occupied a very strong position. . ." A second theory, that the volunteers sought to capture the scouts in order to present them to the Mexican Government for a purported reward of $400 apiece was equally untenable, Romero said. He denied that there was any such reward offered or any Mexican federal law providing for such an offer. A Chihuahua state law of May 25, 1842, provided a reward of $250 for each Indian captured under arms, $200 for every armed Indian killed in action, $150 for every female Indian or Indian child under fourteen captured. These rewards, however, were to apply only to " barbarous " Indians.[57]

Official investigation by General Crispin S. Palomares purported to show certain new angles to the situation. C. Leivas, Prefect of the District of Moctezuma, Sonora, swore to depredations by Crawford and his men. He asserted that on December 21, 1885, Captain Crawford and 150 men killed a number of beeves belonging to Messrs. Woodward and Pinazo near Capadchuache. The Indian scouts of Crawford's force while encamped near Güeverache were said to have ridden into the town of Guasabas while intoxicated and to have committed "numberless disorders." Gendarmes had to be called to quell the disorder and one Indian was arrested, only to be released later on demand of Maus. Another deposition claimed that when the Americans passed through Granados eleven cattle were killed. A total of thirty-seven Mexican and one Amerian depositions testified as to various disorders by the Indian scouts—the alleged murder of Francisco Lavandera and Tomas Moreno, cattle thefts, and the burning of sugar cane and fences. The depositions also maintained that Crawford had been killed through " a positive mistake." The Indian scouts were easily confused with hostile Apaches,

[57] Romero to Bayard, May 5, 1887, Notes from the Legation MSS, XXXV.

it was claimed.[58]   So confused were the facts in the case that the United States at last accepted the findings of the Mexican Government that the unfortunate tragedy had been an accident.[59]

Meanwhile when Crawford fell Lieutenant Maus went forward with his superior's plans, and arranged with Geronimo to meet General Crook near the border. About two months later they met at El Canon, twenty-five miles south of the line. Strongly intrenched and well supplied the Indians would surrender only on acceptance by the military of one of two propositions. The first proposition was that they should be sent East, taking their families if they so desired. The second was that they should be allowed to return to their reservation with their former peaceful status as wards of the Government. Crook accepted the first proposition and the party started for Fort Bowie but his course was disapproved by President Cleveland. Before word of Washington's attitude could reach the border, however, Geronimo, Natchez and twenty men and thirteen women escaped to the mountains during the night of March 29. The rest of the Apaches, some sixty strong, were sent to Florida.

Because of this escape and the course of the whole campaign Sheridan cast doubt upon the trustworthiness of the Indian scouts. Crook, who had organized the scouts in question, asked to be removed from command and Brigadier General Miles was put in his place.[60]   Miles relentlessly pursued Geronimo over 1,300 miles, attacking and breaking up his camps and allowing him no rest until he and his followers surrendered, whereupon they were also sent to Florida.[61]

[58] Morgan to Bayard, June 12, 1886, *U. S. For. Rel. 1886*, pp. 657 ff.

[59] Rippy, *The Southwestern Historical Quarterly*, XXIV, 315.

[60] *Report of Secretary of War for 1886*, pp. 9-12.

[61] *Ibid.*, pp. 12, 13-14. Diaz felt that in the capture of Geronimo much credit was due to the cooperation of the Mexican troops. Rodriguez, Semi-Annual Message of April, 1887, I, 164. At the same time Mexican officials denied charges in the Washington *Post* that the Apaches had been provoked, sustained, and aided by the Mexicans. Romero to Secretary of Foreign Relations, October 8, 1886. Enclosure Cayetano Romero *Memorándum Cargos Contra México con motivo de la sublevación de los Indios Apaches capi-*

After Geronimo's power was thus destroyed Indian depredations along the border fell off decidedly. Although small
outbreaks occurred from time to time Brigadier General
Miles could report in 1888 that the Department of Arizona,
so beset by Indian raids earlier, had experienced no disturbances "worthy of mention."[62]

Again in 1890 Apache disorders on the Arizona and New
Mexico border led to a reciprocal crossing agreement to take
the place of the previous agreement which had not been renewed when it lapsed November 1, 1886.[63] Due to the sad
experiences with Indian scouts in the Crawford case and later
in the pursuit of Geronimo a significant article was inserted
providing that such scouts with the United States forces
should not cross the border, except as guides or trailers un-
armed, and not exceeding two scouts to a company or separate command. This agreement was to remain in force not
longer than one year from June 25, 1890.[64] In 1892 it was
renewed for another year in order to facilitate the pursuit of
the Apache outlaw "Kid" who had escaped into Sonora.[65]
The pursuit was unsuccessful for "Kid" disappeared from
view after May 1893 and did not again put in an appearance
until the summer of 1896.[66] In the latter year the two governments signed the last of their reciprocal agreements during the period under discussion in this work. This reciprocal agreement of 1896 was to stay in force until Kid's band
was "wholly exterminated."[67]

---

taneados por Gerónimo October 2 to November 9, 1886, Photostats
Mexican Archives MSS. See also *Informes de la Embajada en
Washington relativa a rendición de los Indios Apaches capitaneados
por Gerónimo April 11, 1887, to February 27, 1890, ibid.*

[62] Annual Report Miles, September 8, 1888, *Report of Secretary
of War for 1888*, p. 127.

[63] Malloy, I, 1162-1163, 1170-1171.

[64] *Ibid.*, pp. 1170-1171.

[65] *Ibid.*, pp. 1171-1174; Dougherty to Foster, November 17, 1892,
Despatches MSS, CXIV; Dougherty to Foster, November 22, 1892
(Telegram Cipher), *ibid.*; Dougherty to Foster, November 28, 1892,
ibid.; *Report of Secretary of War for 1892*, pp. 80 ff.

[66] Rippy, *Southwestern Historical Quarterly*, XXIV, 315.

[67] Malloy, I, 1177-1178; Romero to Olney, June 2, 1896, Notes
from the Legation MSS, XLIV. See also Sepulveda to Olney, June
18, 1896, Despatches MSS, CXXVIII; Foster to Dougherty, November 8, 1892, Instructions MSS. XXIII.

During the absence of " Kid " the border became so quiet
that the General commanding the Department of Colorado
(which then included Arizona) was able to report a single
insignificant act as the only Indian depredation in his Department during the year. A ranchman near Monument,
Arizona, had seen an Indian and a squaw trying to steal a
horse from a neighbor. He had fired and wounded the
squaw.[68] Miles, who had come to chief command of the
Army, spoke in similar encouraging vein in his Annual Report for 1895. He said: ". . . the outbreaks and depredations incident to Indian hostilities have been avoided during
the past five years." He thought that this almost complete
state of peace throughout the Indian country (which included most of the border) was due to the efficiency of the
troops.[69] Brigadier General Wheaton, commanding the Department of Colorado, reported in 1896 that operations in
Arizona had dwindled to scouting movements against petty
thievery and other minor affairs perpetrated by small groups
of Apaches, skulking at night across the border from Mexico
into Arizona.

Although the American side of the border was thus relatively free from Indian raids during 1896 one serious raid
occurred on the Mexican side, apparently by Indians from
the United States. The customs house at Nogales was attacked by forty-five to fifty Yaqui raiders who seemed to have
come from the United States. The American General thought
that they were probably religious fanatics, followers of Santa
Teresa de Caborda. Armed with rifles, pistols, and bows and
arrows, they sacked the customs house, their booty including
about $20,000 worth of arms and ammunition. Immediately

---

[68] *Report of Secretary of War for 1894*, p. 140.

[69] *Report of Secretary of War for 1896*, p. 63. The Annual Reports
of United States military men having to do with the border during
the '90's show this growing state of peace by their subject matter.
For the most part they leave off talking about Indian raids and have
to do mainly with the condition of the posts, with lyceums, gym-
nasiums, messes, laundries, water pipes, etc. Railroads also occupy
a more and more important place in these reports. For the question of claims arising out of Indian depredations see Gresham to
Gray, February 11, 1895, Instructions MSS, XXIII.

a number of American citizens crossed the line and aided the Mexican citizens against the marauders. In the ensuing fight six Mexicans and eight Indians were killed, one Indian was wounded, and three were captured and the shattered remnants of the band apparently crossed against onto American soil. Although United States troops searched thoroughly they apparently scattered and could not be discovered.[70]

A few random Indian raids occurred in the following years but the era of widespread border terrorism by the Indian had definitely passed. In 1897 Brigadier General Otis, then commanding the Department of Colorado, reported complaints by cattlemen in the Baboquivari mountains southwest of Tucson that Papago Indians were constantly stealing their stock, also asserting that the Mexican stockmen of Sonora feared these Papagos. Although two troops of the Seventh Cavalry investigated, the Indians denied the raids and nothing definite was learned.[71] Early in the next year about forty Papagos raided from the United States into Mexico attacking some of the mines at El Plomo in Sonora. The Mexican Government asked for their punishment and that steps be taken to prevent a recurrence of the raiding.[72] Indian Bureau officials denied that Indians engaged in the raid had brought back stolen cattle into the United States to any greater extent than Mexican and American whites. It was thought that Mexican citizens had made misleading statements.[73] Later still in 1903 the United States consul at Nogales reported a claim for damages against the Mexican Government filed by C. F. Dawson of the United States Graphite Company for "losses sustained in a raid by marauding Indians." Clayton, the American Minister at Mexico City, was instructed to bring the alleged attack to the attention of the Mexican Gov-

---

[70] *Report of Secretary of War for 1896*, pp. 145-147.

[71] Annual Report of Elwell S. Otis, Commanding Department of Colorado, September 10, 1897, in *ibid., 1897*, p. 171.

[72] Aspiros to Hay, July 11, 1899, Notes from the Legation MSS, XLVI. See Hay to Clayton, November 21, 1898, Instructions MSS, XXIV.

[73] *Report of the Commissioner of Indian Affairs for 1899*, p. 77.

ernment so that the perpetrators could be punished and re-currence of the attack prevented.[74]

Another annoyance and danger continued to harass certain sections of the border during this period, although in diminishing quantity. As contrasted to Indian forays, thefts of horses and cattle by whites raiding across the border were fairly common occurrences and civilian posses from each country apparently often crossed the line in pursuit of these marauders. For instance Sheriff Tumlinson of Dimmitt County, Texas, rode across the boundary in pursuit of horse thieves in the summer of 1885. The governor of Texas reported that Tumlinson hoped for the " aid of local authorities in their capture, that he was well received and that his efforts were fruitless to overtake the bandits." Bayard thought that the Mexican Government could not well object to this action by Tumlinson because of " countless instances in which Mexican citizens with arms cross into the United States. . . ." [75] In answer to protests by residents of El Presidio, Webster, Foley, and Buchel counties in Texas at alleged raids, said to have been committed by Mexican outlaws sheltering in Chihuahua, the Mexican Government assured the United States Government that it " watched constantly and with especial care the boundary line of the Rio Grande " with municipal and police officers, federal troops, and revenue guards.[76]

There were also white raiders going in the opposite direction and one of the most troublesome bandits was Catarino Garza who from Texas carried on a series of raids into Mexico. In response to complaints of the Mexican Government the State Department reported " strong endeavors to break up bands of malcontents of whom the minister [Mariscal] complains." [77] Evidently these assurances were not suffi-

---

[74] Hay to Clayton, June 9, 1903, Instructions MSS, XXV.

[75] Bayard to Jackson, November 7, 1885, *ibid.*, XXI. See also Jackson to Bayard, August 6, 1885, Despatches MSS, LXXXVI.

[76] Romero to Blaine, May 6, 1891, Notes from the Legation MSS, XXXIX.

[77] Blaine to Ryan, December 29, 1891, Instructions MSS, XXIII; Blaine to Romero, December 15, 1891, Notes to the Legation MSS,

cient, as an immediate reply from the Mexican Government protested to the Government of the United States " for permitting Catarino Garza to establish on the territory of this country [in Texas] his general headquarters and camp in which he holds a prisoner and organizes invasions of Mexican territory." [78] United States forces were quickly in the field against Garza, broke up his camp in Texas and dispersed his band. The Mexican Government sent " expressive thanks " for the action of the troops.[79]

Several months later, however, Garza and his bandits reappeared on the Texas border with the outlaws attacking a small detachment of Mexican troops opposite San Ignacio, Texas, escaping immediately thereafter and crossing the border where they took refuge in Texas.[80] In their flight they carried away fifty horses and some arms and ammunition belonging to the Mexicans.[81] The Mexican representations growing out of this new raid by Garza were received by Foster, then Secretary of State, and must have reminded him of the many similar notes he had presented to the Mexican Government during his years of residence there as United States Minister. He adopted the usual formula and promised that the United States would seek to fulfill its " international

---

IX. See Romero to Blaine, January 3, 1892, Enclosure cablegram Mariscal to Romero, December 30, 1891, Notes from the Legation MSS, XL, for a Mexican proposal for cooperative military action against Garza.

[78] Romero to Blaine, January 4, 1892, *ibid*. The prisoner was said to be Abelardo Dominguez of Guerrero City, Mexico, whom Garza was said to have been holding incommunicado for twenty-six days. Romero to Blaine, January 6, 1892, *ibid*.

[79] Ryan to Blaine, January 8, 1892, Enclosure No. 3, Mariscal to Ryan, January 8, 1892, Despatches MSS, CXI; Ryan to Blaine, February 18, 1892 (Telegram), *ibid*.

[80] Romero to Foster, December 13, 1892, *U. S. For. Rel. 1893*, p. 424.

[81] Romero to Foster, December 14, 1892, Enclosure Ormelas to Romero, December 13, 1892, *ibid*., p. 425. The Mexican soldiers were in stables unprepared for attack and before they could gain their weapons their quarters were on fire. Two officers and four soldiers were killed and several were wounded, Captain Segura and several wounded soldiers being thrown into a burning building. Twenty Mexican soldiers and women and children were driven to the United States side of the border. The bandits were reported to number about 130. *Report of Secretary of War for 1893*, pp. 140-141.

obligations " in these raids in spite of the long border, thin population, and difficult terrain.[82]

Further difficulties in pursuit of bandits were set forth at length by Foster in another note to Romero a little later. The bandits, Foster thought, were

organized secretly in Texas and do not appear as organized bodies until the moment of crossing the Rio Grande, too late for attack by United States troops. Likewise, after committing depredations in Mexico and upon returning to Texas, they disperse and scatter over the country, either individually or in small parties, making pursuit difficult, if not impossible, as they never present an object of attack by troops on American soil. The Commanding General of the department of Texas, has put in the field all of his available force in pursuit of the returned bandits, and three troops of cavalry, fully mounted and equipped, have been ordered from Fort Riley, Kans., at great expense and inconvenience to the Department, for service on the Mexican border.

He complained that the United States received " little cooperation or assistance from the Mexican side of the border." [83]

This remark brought a quick retort from Romero. " I must say . . . that the Government of Mexico will take proper care of its extensive frontier, and that it will spare no pains in doing so, as is shown by the fact that the outlaws have been obliged to return to this country after their various raids, never having remained for more than a few hours in Mexican territory, whither they go for the sole purpose of robbing and plundering." [84] The raids, Mariscal wrote from Mexico City a few days later, had continued for months and were the work of 200 such bandits, asserting further that " a large portion of the [United States] federal force " had been withdrawn from the region of the border. He pointed out that the Rio Grande was fordable in many places and this factor could be overcome only by " a sufficient number of soldiers well distributed " along the frontier. Cooperation of United States and Mexican forces was necessary—" some fords might be guarded by the troops on one bank, and

[82] Foster to Romero, December 15, 1892, U. S. For. Rel. 1893, p. 427.

[83] Foster to Romero, December 27, 1892, ibid., pp. 429-430.

[84] Romero to Foster, December 28, 1892, ibid., pp. 430-431.

others by those on the opposite bank " and he thought that the agreement as to reciprocal crossing should be extended to outlaws.[85]   After Foster had replied to the charge of insufficient United States troops on the Texas portion of the border by stating that there were 1,800 regulars on or near the Rio Grande,[86] Romero continued the debate with an official statement of the Mexican Department of State, War, and Marine which placed 1,884 Mexican troops on the Texas border from Paso del Norte, Chihuahua to Bagdad, Tamaulipas.[87]

Romero gave point to this note by sending to Foster a clipping from *The New York Times* of a despatch from San Monterey, Mexico, showing that the Mexican force on the frontier consisted of 2,727 men.[88]   Foster then turned to the military and sent Romero a communication from Major General Schofield, commanding the United States Army to Secretary of War Elkins.   Schofield held the United States military force on the border to be " as large in proportion to the service required as the aggregate strength of the Army will permit, and it is believed as large as the international obligations of the United States require."   He thought that the bandits should be captured primarily by Texas authorities or by United States marshals.   " In this work the troops can only aid the United States marshals as part of their posse."   Since the bandits were being sought for murder, cattle theft, arson, and other offenses under state laws and for violation of federal neutrality laws Mexican forces could not be inducted into the posse.   Therefore no reciprocal agreement as to crossing the border in the Texas region in order to enforce these laws could be carried out,[89] the situation thus being distinctly different from that involved in the agreement for pursuit of Indians.

---

[85] Mariscal to Romero, December 31, 1892, *ibid.*, pp. 431-433.

[86] Foster to Romero, January 4, 1893, *ibid.*, p. 435.

[87] Romero to Foster, January 12, 1893, Enclosure, Mexican Department of State, War, and Marine detailed report, December 26, 1892, *ibid.*, p. 437.

[88] Romero to Foster, January 1, 1893, *ibid.*, pp. 434-435.

[89] Foster to Romero, January 23, 1893, Enclosure Schofield to Elkins, January 17, 1893, *ibid.*, pp. 439-440.

Fortunately very soon active cooperation between the United States troops and civil authorities against the bandits began to bring excellent results. Francisco Benavides, who led the attack on the Mexican outpost opposite San Ignacio, and two other important bandit leaders were captured about a month after the attack on the Mexican post.[90] Closely pressed by the troops the bandits rapidly surrendered, were captured, or were killed during 1893,[91] the troops using native Texans as scouts and often operating through "a mass of dense chaparral and cactus," doing brave and persistent work in running their quarry to earth.[92]

Another great border problem, that of stock "rustling," so true of any vast, thinly settled region where stock ranges at large, and especially true of a border country with all of its political and racial complications, continued during this period as a fruitful cause of irritation. In 1882 Romero protested that a herd of stolen Mexican cattle had been sold by the Collector of Customs at San Felipe del Rio, Texas, as smuggled goods, although evidence was presented to him of their ownership by Mexicans. Romero felt that this action constituted "an outrage upon the property of Mexican citizens . . . and it hopes the United States Government will do all in its power to redress said outrage."[93] In line with Romero's protest the United States Treasury Department

<hr>

[90] Foster to Romero, February 1, 1893, Enclosure telegram of Brigadier General Frank Wheaton, Commanding the Department of Texas, to Adjutant General, January 25, 1893, *ibid.*, pp. 440-441.

[91] W. Q. Gresham to Romero, April 21, 1893, *ibid.*, p. 447; Alvey A. Adee, Acting Secretary of State, to Romero, April 27, 1893, *ibid.*, p. 447; Gresham to Romero, May 3, 1893, *ibid.*, p. 448; Gresham to Romero, August 5, 1893, *ibid.*, p. 456; Josiah Quincy to Romero, August 12, 1893, *ibid.*, p. 456.

[92] *Report of Secretary of War for 1893*, pp. 141-142. Questions of extradition and citizenship not covered in this study were involved in the cases of the bandit leaders Ochoa and Rasures. For Ochoa see Romero to Gresham, November 15, 1893, Notes from the Legation MSS, XLI; Romero to Gresham, February 12, 1894, *ibid.*, XLII; Sherman to Clayton, August 17, 1897, Instructions MSS, XXIV. For Rasures see Romero to Bayard, August 25, 1886, Notes from the Legation MSS, XXXV; Jackson to Bayard, August 13, 1886 (Telegram Cipher), Despatches MSS, XC; Jackson to Bayard, August 27, 1886, *ibid.*

[93] Romero to Frelinghuysen, July 7, 1882, Notes from the Legation MSS, XXIX.

issued a circular providing that if cattle were seized for customs irregularities the Treasury be informed.[94]

Nor were the charges one-sided. In 1885, Morgan reported to the Mexican Government " the complaint of several citizens of Dimmitt County Texas " to Governor Ireland of Texas concerning the loss of considerable stock. The animals were said to have been taken to Mexico where they were sold. Morgan claimed " that for several years past stock consisting of horses, cattle, and sheep have been systematically stolen from that county [Dimmitt] and vicinity in small numbers and taken into the republic of Mexico by the citizens of or persons under the protection of that Republic." He claimed that no punishment had been meted out by Mexican authorities. In the last raid Morgan asserted that three Americans near the border had lost 10, 29, and 18 horses respectively and an undetermined number of cattle and claimed that a sheriff and five men had pursued the robbers across the border, but that Mexicans had fired upon them. Mariscal replied that he had ordered the governor of Coahuila to investigate " with all possible despatch " and to " take such steps as to him may seem proper to put an end to the causes giving rise to complaints of this nature." [95]   The governor of Coahuila stated that an investigation by the judge of the Court of Records in the Rio Grande District of Coahuila seemed to show an entirely different situation than Morgan claimed to exist. He thought that instead of stealing cattle residents of the Mexican side of the Rio Grande had been " the innocent victims of persecution and assassination " perpetrated by the inhabitants of Dimmitt County, adding that the American accusations were vague and in general undated. He claimed that numerous bandits had been

---

[94] Romero to Frelinghuysen, July 8, 1882, *ibid.* Romero in this note acknowledged Frelinghuysen's Note to the Legation of July 7 including an excerpt from a communication of the Treasury Department to the State Department July 1, 1882. In a note in 1884 Romero suggested, under his instructions, commissioners to be appointed by the governors of states on both sides of the line to inventory stolen stock stopped at the frontier. Romero to Frelinghuysen, May 7, 1884, *ibid.*, XXXIII.

[95] Morgan to Frelinghuysen, March 3, 1885, Despatches MSS, LXXXV, Enclosure Morgan to Mariscal, February 13, 1885, *ibid.*

prosecuted in Mexico following raids into the United States, and noted that the cases of Pedro Letechipia and Pedro Garcia were pending in the Supreme Court of Chihuahua.[96]

Fortunately with growing settlement, improved transportation, and the coming of relative peace and good order, stock "rustling" was reduced to a minimum. A few minor cases arose from time to time but without important diplomatic consequences. In 1894 for instance T. N. Paschal, a member of Congress from Texas, communicated to the State Department a letter from J. C. Loving, Secretary of the Texas Cattle Raisers Association. Loving claimed that unsuccessful efforts had been made to recover a horse stolen by unknown persons and said to be held by Mexican authorities in Ciudad Porfirio Diaz. Gray, the American Minister, was asked to make representations on the subject to the Mexican Government.[97]

The stock problem had still another angle which was brought about by border conditions, that of cattle straying through the great unfenced areas of the border region and in their search for grass and water wandering without heed across a man-made international line, or even fording the winding, muddy river designated as part of the boundary between the two countries. Attempts were made repeatedly to arrange for reciprocal return of cattle which strayed across the border and such an agreement was signed on July 11, 1888. Apparently, however, the opposition of the Mexican border states was too strong and this agreement was never ratified by the Mexican Senate.[98]

Due to this failure to frame a convention acceptable both

[96] Jackson to Bayard, August 6, 1885, Enclosure No. 3, Mariscal to Jackson, July 17, 1885, ibid., LXXXVI.

[97] Edwin F. Uhl, Acting Secretary of State, to Gray, June 16, 1894, Instructions MSS, XXIII.

[98] Jackson to Bayard, July 7, 1886, Despatches MSS, XC; Connery to Bayard, November 4, 1887, ibid., XCIV; Ryan to Blaine, August 13, 1890, ibid., CV; Ryan to Blaine, September 26, 1890, ibid.; Ryan to Blaine, October 31, 1890, ibid.; Alvey A. Adee, Acting Secretary of State, to Ryan, May 25, 1891, Instructions MSS, XXIII; Wharton, Acting Secretary of State, to Ryan, June 17, 1891, ibid.; Ryan to Blaine, June 2, 1891, Despatches MSS, CIX; Ryan to Blaine, July 25, 1891, ibid.; Foster to Ryan, July 15, 1892, Instructions MSS, XXIII.

to the United States and Mexico great inconvenience was experienced by stockmen. In the spring of 1897 twenty-five cattlemen of New Mexico petitioned the United States Government to bring influence to bear on the Mexican Government to modify Mexican laws. They claimed that they were practically prevented from rounding up their stray cattle and horses by oppressive Mexican laws. If they used American horses in Mexico they had to pay excessive duties, the only alternative being purchase of Mexican horses.[99] Such appeal proved impracticable, however, because "it appears that the legislátion of the United States is not sufficiently elastic in this regard to offer Mexico any substantial reciprocal privileges for the exemptions which the petitioners seek." [100] Thus the American stockmen were thrown back upon the necessity of making what arrangements they could with Mexican officials directly. In August 1897 Joseph S. Carter, a United States citizen, claimed that he had been imprisoned and other obstacles placed in the way of his recovery of cattle which had strayed into Mexico. He claimed that he had been damaged to the extent of $5,000 by his imprisonment and the loss of his cattle, and he asked permission through the State Department to remove his stock. This was granted by the Mexican Government and an extension of time also, after the State Department had again interceded in Carter's behalf.[101]

Equally unsatisfactory was the situation as to cattle passing through customs houses of the two countries. Aspiroz in Washington complained to Hay that American customs authorities at Eagle Pass were confiscating and selling cattle,

[99] Clayton to John Sherman, June 9, 1897, Enclosure Consul Buford to Clayton, June 3, 1897, Despatches MSS, CXXX.

[100] Sherman to Clayton, July 9, 1897, Instructions MSS, XXIV.

[101] Sherman to Clayton, August 26, 1897, ibid.; Sherman to Clayton, October 22, 1897, ibid.; Sherman to Clayton, December 6, 1897, ibid.; Sherman to Clayton (Telegram), December 28, 1897, ibid. For disputes as to American cattlemen entering Sonora to recover their cattle in the annual roundups see Hay to Clayton, June 10, 1899, ibid., XXV; Clayton to Hay, July 7, 1899, Despatches MSS, CXL; Clayton to Hay, August 5, 1899, ibid., CXLI; Clayton to Hay, August 15, 1899, ibid.; Clayton to Hay, January 16, 1900, ibid., CXLIII.

which had strayed into the United States from Mexico, unless the owner paid the import duty.[102]   American cattlemen on their side complained just as vigorously of alleged discriminations against them by Mexican customs officials at Sasabe, Sonora.   The Americans claimed that they were only allowed a ten-day permit to search for their cattle and that $4.50 was charged for the permit.   In contrast to these regulations Mexican cattlemen coming into the United States on the same mission were only charged twenty-five cents for a ten-day permit and were allowed an extension to thirty days. Furthermore, it was claimed that Mexican customs officials had finally prevented the entrance of American cattlemen on any pretext.[103]

To these complaints the Mexican Treasury officials answered that Mexican customs officials only required a verbal petition with a declaration that the petitioner was really a stockman and a bond to the extent of $3.00 to guarantee payment of duties.   Then a customs house permit was issued for ten days for twenty-five cents, renewable up to thirty days.[104]   The Americans, however, maintained that the situation described by the Mexican Treasury Department was no longer true and that " during the last two years local authorities have positively and absolutely refused us entrance into Sonora with our American horses and saddles and we have been compelled to buy and hire horses to look after our interests." [105]   A special permit from the Treasury Department was required in each individual case for the use of American horses.   As Nogales was the only telegraph office along the Sonora border often two or three days were con-

[102] Aspiroz to Hay, July 22, 1899, Notes from the Legation MSS, XLVI.
[103] Clayton to Hay, January 16, 1900, Enclosure No. 1, Marteny to Clayton, December 17, 1899, Despatches MSS, CXLIII; Hay to McCreery, February 19, 1900, Instructions MSS, XXV; Hay to Clayton, April 27, 1900, ibid.; McCreery to Hay, March 24, 1900, Despatches MSS, CXLIV; McCreery to Hay, May 11, 1900, ibid.
[104] Clayton to Hay, October 13, 1900, Enclosure No. 4, Mexican Department of the Treasury to Department of Foreign Affairs No. 6596, ibid.
[105] Clayton to Hay, November 15, 1900, Enclosure No. 1, W. M. Marteny (Arivaca, Arizona) to Clayton, November 7, 1900, ibid., XLVIII.   See also Clayton to Mariscal, November 14, 1900, ibid.

sumed in sending the request and receiving an answer. In order to obviate this delay orders were issued by the direction of Diaz "empowering Collectors of Customs of Frontier Customs houses from Tijuana, Lower California to Ciudad Juárez, Chihuahua to grant, when petitioned, temporary permits for 10 days, under the same conditions as those which this Department has granted in each case." [106] The Mexican Treasury Department in answering asserted that inquiry at the customs house at Nogales showed that American stockmen had always been permitted to enter to collect stock with horses and saddles for ten days in line with the Treasury Department's orders. Inquiry of Tijuana revealed, it was said, that up to that time no American had asked permission to collect stock. Officials of the customs houses were reported as saying that if such permission should be asked it would be granted.[107]

Wrongful use of authority by civil and military officials of one country operating in the other also was an occasional source of friction during the period under discussion in this chapter. In one important instance Lieutenant Gutiérrez of the Mexican army committed an offense on the American side of the line at Nogales, Arizona. He was arrested and imprisoned by United States civil authorities, whereupon Colonel Arvizu, Lieutenant Gutiérrez' superior officer, brought his soldiers across the border, effected a rescue and returned to Mexico. Thereupon the United States demanded that the rescued prisoner be restored and the rescuers be captured and punished by Mexican authorities.[108] Diaz himself admitted the main contentions of the United States [109]

[106] McCreery to Hay, February 20, 1901, Enclosure No. 6, Secretary of the Treasury to Foreign Office, February 8, 1901, *ibid.*, CXLIX. See for further complaints by American stockmen of Mexican customs regulations Hay to Clayton, July 18, 1901, Instructions MSS, XXV; Clayton to Hay, August 6, 1901, Enclosure Clayton to Mariscal, August 6, 1901, Despatches MSS, CLI.

[107] Clayton to Hay, October 30, 1901, Enclosure No. 4, Secretary Treasury to Department Foreign Affairs Section 1, *ibid.*, CLII.

[108] Manning to Bayard, March 9, 1887, *U. S. For. Rel. 1887*, pp. 693-694.

[109] Manning to Bayard, April 5, 1887, Enclosure Speech of President Diaz on the opening of the second period of the 13th Mexican

but the Mexican Government requested the United States not to insist on the delivery of Gutiérrez, who had in the meantime been arrested, since suitable punishment in Mexico was promised.[110] To this the United States agreed, promising to suspend judgment while awaiting results of the Mexican court martial.[111]

As a result of the court martial Colonel Arvizu, Lieutenant Gutiérrez, and a private named Valenzuela were sentenced to death, a sentence which was upheld by the Supreme Military Court.[112] This was apparently more than had been expected and at the strenuous request of the United States Government this sentence was finally commuted to twenty years' imprisonment.[113] A somewhat similar case of crossing by Mexican troops occurred shortly thereafter at Eagle Pass, where a Mexican officer and three soldiers crossed the border and arrested an alleged Mexican deserter. On receiving protests from the United States the Mexican Government promised investigation and " condign punishment." [114] Ultimately only the Captain in command was punished on the ground that the others were acting under his orders, but he received the severe sentence of ten years' imprisonment and the loss of his commission, decorations, and military awards.[115]

Congress April 1, 1887, *ibid.*, pp. 702-708. See also Manning to Bayard, March 8, 1887 (Telegram Cipher), Despatches MSS, XCII; Manning to Bayard, March 9, 1887, *ibid.*; Manning to Bayard, March 12, 1887, *ibid.*

[110] Manning to Bayard, April 6, 1887, *U. S. For. Rel. 1887*, p. 709; Manning to Bayard, April 6, 1887 (Telegram Cipher), Despatches MSS, XCIII.

[111] Bayard to Manning, April 8, 1887, *U. S. For. Rel. 1887*, p. 710.

[112] Manning to Bayard, May 5, 1887, *ibid.*, p. 719; Manning to Bayard, May 23, 1887, Enclosure No. 1 Mariscal to Manning, May 21, 1887, Despatches MSS, XCIII; Connery to Bayard, October 31, 1887, *ibid.*, XCIV.

[113] Bragg to Bayard, April 21, 1888 (Telegram Cipher), *ibid.*, XCV; Bragg to Bayard, April 28, 1888, Enclosure Mariscal to Bragg, April 27, 1888, *U. S. For. Rel. 1888*, p. 1188; Bayard to Bragg, March 22, 1888, Instructions MSS, XXII.

[114] Bragg to Bayard, April 14, 1888, Enclosure No. 1 Mariscal to Bragg, April 13, 1888, Despatches MSS, XCV; Bragg to Bayard, April 10, 1888, Enclosure No. 2, *El Diario Oficial*, April 2, 1888, Address of President Diaz at the opening of the 4th period of the 13th Mexican Congress, April 1, 1888, *ibid.*

[115] Blaine to Ryan, December 14, 1889, Instructions MSS, XXII.

The punishment was not so severe when the cases were reversed. In 1893, John Roberts, deputy sheriff of Nogales, Arizona, crossed the border in pursuit of a Mexican, although the evidence showed that he had been warned that he was on Mexican soil. The escaping Mexican was overtaken, severely beaten, and dragged back across the boundary. Once in Arizona he was sentenced to a fine of $60 or to sixty days' imprisonment. The Mexican Government demanded the punishment of Roberts and his accomplices and an indemnity to be paid to Garcia, the captured Mexican.[116] Nothing seems to have come of this incident.

Occasionally other acts of violence marked border relations but following the last Indian outbreaks of the late '80's no disturbance of serious proportions developed along the international boundary, previously so harassed by raiding Indians and white desperadoes. On a few occasions shots were fired across the line endangering lives but apparently taking none.[117] The alleged murder of an American soldier at Ciudad Porfirio Diaz in 1904 led to a brief exchange of correspondence but the case was dropped when the investigation by Mexican police showed that the death had been due to a fall rather than to foul play.[118]

The situation growing out of the Spanish-American War was potentially more dangerous. Serious complications along the border might have developed from the activities of Spanish sympathizers in Mexico if the war had not been of such brief duration. The alertness of Mexican officials in arrest-

---

[116] Romero to Gresham, September 6, 1893, *U. S. For. Rel. 1893*, p. 457.

[117] For several occasions when shots were alleged to have been fired from the American side of the boundary into Mexico see Romero to Foster, August 29, 1892, Notes from the Legation MSS, XL. For shots alleged to have been fired into the United States from Mexico on one occasion see Olney to Ransom, January 30, 1896, Instructions MSS, XXIII.

[118] Clayton to Hay, April 18, 1904, Enclosure No. 4 Governor of Coahuila to Secretary of Foreign Affairs of Mexico, April 6, 1904, Despatches MSS, CLXIX; McCreery to Hay, May 9, 1904, *ibid.* Numerous cases arose on the border involving the questions of extradition and citizenship. These cases, such as those of Martinez and Oberlander, cannot be considered here because their main significance lies along lines which do not fall within the scope of this study.

ing a Spaniard named Marti and several other members of an alleged band of Spaniards and Spanish sympathizers at Nuevo Laredo early in April 1898 also aided in clearing up a situation which might have proved troublesome.[119] The Mexican Secretary of the Interior wrote to the governors of the border states urging them to redouble their efforts so that Mexican neutrality should not be violated.[120] This request was repeated in substantially the same terms by the Ministry of War and Marine to army commanders.[121] Although fear was felt " along the border of attacks . . . by Spanish sympathizers from Mexico," [122] none materialized and the war was soon over, ending the likelihood of any such action.[123]

The most important question remaining to be considered involved the Free Zone and the smuggling incident to it. In a new tariff act passed on January 24, 1885, the Free Zone, previously restricted to the state of Tamaulipas, was extended to the whole frontier and for a distance of 20 kilometres from the boundary line.[124] Although extended in area the franchises of the Free Zone were limited considerably and these limitations caused an outcry from the border region affected, with such political pressure being brought to bear on the Mexican Congress that the limitations were suspended and very liberal regulations adopted March 1, 1887. The next tariff act, that of June 12, 1891, marked a new era so

---

[119] Clayton to Sherman, April 5, 1898, *ibid.*, CXXXIV. This arrest occurred before war was declared on April 19.

[120] Clayton to Sherman, April 30, 1898, Enclosure No. 4, *El Diario Oficial*, April 26, 1898, *ibid.*

[121] Clayton to Sherman, May 6, 1898, Enclosure No. 2, *El Diario Oficial*, April 30, 1898, *ibid.*

[122] Day to Clayton, May 25, 1898, Instructions MSS, XXIV. See also Clayton to Day, May 21, 1898, Despatches MSS, CXXXV; Sherman to Clayton, April 26, 1898, Instructions MSS, XXIV.

[123] For further correspondence on the question of possible raids by Spanish sympathizers from Mexico into the United States, especially from the Free Zone, see Clayton to Sherman, May 3, 1898, Enclosure Clayton to Mariscal, May 3, 1898, Despatches MSS, CXXXIV; Clayton to Sherman, May 3, 1898, Enclosure Clayton to Mariscal, May 3, 1898, *ibid.* (another despatch of the same date) ; Day to Clayton, May 13, 1898, Instructions MSS, XXIV; Day to Clayton, June 1, 1898, *ibid.*; Day to Clayton, June 2, 1898, *ibid.*; Day to Clayton, June 3, 1898, *ibid.*; Day to Clayton, June 10, 1898, *ibid.*

[124] Romero, *Mexico and the United States*, I, 440.

far as the Free Zone was concerned, Article 696 imposing on
all goods coming to the Free Zone, previously free of duty,
a tax equal to 10 per cent of the duties levied on similar
goods coming into other parts of Mexico. A decree of the
Mexican Treasury Department of May 12, 1896, raised the
10 per cent to 18½ per cent. Another decree of the Treasury Department of June 4, 1896, established an additional
municipal duty of 1½ per cent upon import duties.[125]
Thus the Free Zone ceased to be "free," although the
duties imposed throughout the period under consideration
were lower than those on similar goods imported into the
rest of Mexico. But probably the worst blow which the
Mexican Government dealt the Free Zone came in the Tariff
Act of 1891 with the provision that "the commodities manufactured in the Zone, whether of foreign or domestic raw
materials should pay import duties coming into Mexico,
out side of the Free Zone." [126]

Whether or not these various changes in relation to the
Free Zone aided materially in the battle against smuggling
is doubtful.[127] One Mexican writer felt that modification
of the Free Zone actually turned many inhabitants of the
Mexican side of the boundary into "*contrabandistas.*" He
thought beside a contraband trade on a considerable scale
that goods were bought on a small scale by Mexicans and
smuggled into Mexico from the United States.[128] The

[125] *Ibid.*, pp. 440-441. See also for correspondence on extension of
the Free Zone Blaine to Morgan, July 27, 1887, Instructions MSS,
XX; Hitt, Acting Secretary of State to Morgan, September 15,
1887, *ibid.*; Romero to Bayard, February 10, 1888, *U. S. For. Rel.
1888*, pp. 1266-1281.

[126] Romero, p. 441. Romero thought that the new regulations of
1891 made "a privileged zone" rather than a Free Zone. Romero
to Blaine, November 20, 1891 (Unofficial), Notes from the Legation
MSS, XL.

[127] 55th Cong., 2d sess., *H. Rept.* No. 702, III, 1. See also on the
question of smuggling, Frelinghuysen to Cayetano Romero, September 15, 1883, Notes to the Legation MSS, VIII; Blaine to Ryan,
February 3, 1891, Instructions MSS, XXIII; Blaine to Ryan, March
18, 1891, *ibid.*; Blaine to Ryan, January 28, 1891, *ibid.*; Blaine to
Ryan, February 11, 1891, *ibid.* For alleged smuggling of Chinese
from Mexico into the United States, see Hill to Clayton, September
24, 1901, *ibid.*, XXV; Loomis to Clayton, May 24, 1905, *ibid.*, XXVI;
Root to Amenbassy, July 2, 1906 (Cipher Telegram), *ibid.*

[128] Ulises Irigoyen, *En pro de la Zona libre*, pp. 3, 7.

number of cases of smuggling which continued to find their way into the Instructions and Despatches of the State Department would seem to bear out this conclusion.[129]   One Mexican proposal was that customs guards on each side of the border should cooperate in a strict examination of goods carried through border points. It was further suggested that employees of each customs service should be stationed in the customs houses " of greater importance such as Nogales, Ciudad Porfirio Diaz, Laredo, and Matamoras " in order to watch " unofficially " for violation of customs regulations of their own country.[130]

Such a remedy, of course, failed to take into account the fact that most of the smuggling took place in great, practically uninhabited regions far removed from customs houses. As late as March 1907 Creel, the American Ambassador to Mexico, reported troublesome smuggling along the Arizona border.[131]   Root referred Creel's despatch to the governor of Arizona Territory, the Secretaries of War, Treasury, Commerce and Labor, and the Attorney General with the request that precautionary measures against smuggling be reapplied along the Arizona border.[132]   The Secretary of the Interior thereupon requested the governor of Arizona to reapply precautionary measures and the Secretary of the Treasury similarly instructed the collector of customs at Nogales, Arizona.[133]   The Acting Attorney General reported that his investigation convinced him of the fact of smuggling but that the nature of the country made prevention difficult.[134]   In spite of the difficulties Governor Kibbey of Arizona Territory reported to the Secretary of the Interior early in the next month that sheriffs of the border counties

---

[129] Uhl, Acting Secretary, to Butler, January 15, 1895, Instructions MSS, XXIII; Gresham to Gray, November 28, 1894, ibid.; Uhl to Butler, January 10, 1895, ibid.; Hay to Clayton, January 11, 1905, Instructions MSS.

[130] Clayton to Hay, February 17, 1905, Enclosure No. 4 Secretary of Treasury to Sécretary Foreign Affairs, 1st section, February 8, 1904, Despatches MSS, CLXXVI.

[131] Creel to Root, March 13, 1907, U. S. For. Rel. 1907, pp. 846-847.

[132] Root to Creel, March 20, 1907, ibid., p. 847.

[133] Bacon, Acting Secretary of State, to the Mexican Ambassador, April 6, 1907, ibid., p. 848.

[134] Acting Attorney General H. M. Hoyt to Root, April 26, 1907, ibid., p. 851.

and rangers had practically suppressed the traffic.[135] Thus
another vexed question steadily diminished in importance.

As already suggested this growing peace and order of the
border was bound up with rapid settlement, with railroad
building, with the increased stability of Diaz in Mexico, and
with a growing spirit of cooperation between the two countries. American capital, largely invested in railroads and
mines continued to pour into Mexico, closely linking together
the fortunes of the two countries. Nationals of other countries invested freely in various fields but American dollars
built the main lines of communication.[136] No doubt Mexico
recognized the " importance of extending the facilities of
communication between its own component states and with
neighboring countries, as conducive to the strength and prosperity of Mexico," Blaine wrote to Morgan in a long instruction in 1887. Charters in the future should not be limited
by a " narrow and suspicious jealousy of foreign capital it
[Mexico] so greatly needs." Previous Mexican railroad charters, it was said, had contained " provisions . . . to the effect
that all capital, stockholders and employees engaged in the
enterprise are to be considered Mexican in all matters touching their operations within the Republic, and that they are not
to maintain their claims as foreign, even when alleging a
denial of justice. This limitation would of itself, be almost
sufficient to prohibit all such undertakings; and even if
accepted by over-sanguine speculators, might only too probably lead to discussions and issues with foreign governments
not conducive to maintaining that international cordiality so
much to be desired." Later in the same despatch Blaine
urged Morgan to prepare the ground for a new commercial
treaty between the United States and Mexico.[137] But about
two years later Blaine told Romero in Washington that
reports that the United States was trying to acquire Lower

[135] Root to Mexican Ambassador, May 7, 1907, Enclosure Kibbey
to Secretary of Interior, April 23, 1907, ibid., pp. 848-849.
[136] Ramon V. Williams, Chancellor of the Mexican Consulate General in the United States, The Mexican Trade Directory, p. 9. See
also Morgan to Frelinghuysen, April 25, 1883, U. S. For. Rel. 1883,
pp. 635 ff.
[137] Blaine to Morgan, June 16, 1887, Instructions MSS, XXII.

California "were of no importance whatever, since public opinion did not favor further acquisitions, and that, even if any future administration should favor them, he thought that it would meet with no support in the country for such a design." [138]

This pressure of American business interests, backed in some cases by the insistence of their government and coupled with Diaz' eagerness to see Mexico develop quickly, led to widespread granting of concessions to American mining and railroad interests at an even more rapid rate than in the previous period.[139] On the American side of the border as early as 1882 Pope reported that scarcely a pass in New Mexico was not traversed by a railroad. Some of these passes led toward the border. Fort Stanton was the only post in the Territory not on or accessible to a railroad.[140] On the Mexican side,

---

[138] Memo. interview Romero and Blaine, June 6, 1889, Notes from the Legation MSS, XXXVIII. See also Ryan to Wm. F. Wharton, Acting Secretary of State, August 25, 1889, Despatches MSS, C; *Proposición presentada a la Legislatura de Arizona para abrir negociaciones con el Gobierno de México con objeto de adquirir territorio mexicano en el Golfo de California April 13-October 27, 1893*, Photostats Mexican Archives MSS. Hay later denied a newspaper rumor to the effect that a Yaqui chieftain had declared the independence of Sonora and the latter's annexation to the United States as "so entirely and obviously without possible foundation as hardly to merit formal contradiction." Hay to Clayton, April 6, 1900, Instructions MSS, XXV. See also Conger to Root, July 27, 1905, Despatches MSS, CLXXIX; McCreery to Root, August 23, 1905, *ibid.*

[139] Powell, *Railroads of Mexico*, p. 119. See for copy of concession granted for one of the most important railroad projects connecting the two countries during this period Charter of the Mexican International Railway Company (summary) December 5, 1888, Plumb Papers MSS, XIV.

[140] Annual Report Brevet Major General John Pope, Commanding the Department of Missouri, October 2, 1882, *Report of the Secretary of War for 1882*, p. 101. As the railroads increased, demand for troops on the border was heard from at least one railroad official. C. P. Huntington of the Southern Pacific wrote Sherman in 1882 that border posts from Fort Yuma east and down the Rio Grande should be strengthened. "You are aware that the Southern Pacific lies close to the frontier all the way from the California line to Eagle Pass in Texas, and that the Galveston, Harrisburg and San Antonio Road, which has become virtually a continuation of the former, skirts the frontier for more than 1500 miles. Being large owners in both roads I and my friends have naturally some concern in the degree of protection which the Government may extend to property so situated, as well as in the carriage of troops themselves and their supplies." Huntington to Sherman, November 15, 1882, W. T. Sherman Papers MSS, LIX.

as Hannay says, during the '80's "the whole question of 'works' was becoming predominant . . . and whoever had the general direction of them stood fair to be the most important man in the country." [141] Even during the four years Gonzalez was in the presidency, this man was Diaz.[142] From 1884 to Diaz' final overthrow in 1911 there was little question as to who was leading Mexico in the path of foreign investment.

Thus as railroads began to span the border, connecting the two countries, and American capital flowed more and more extensively into Mexico an era of peace and good feeling marked the last twenty years or more of Diaz' relationships with the United States. Border troubles decreased almost to the vanishing point and cordiality replaced the strain and suspicion so frequently evident earlier.[143] At last old and tired, Diaz relaxed his former strong grip and his régime was overthrown. In the meantime, however, the forces of greater population, better transportation, and increased good will had apparently ended to all intents and purposes border disorder.

---

[141] Hannay, *Diaz*, pp. 217-218.

[142] Diaz served as Minister of Works for about a year under González. During this time González in a letter to Foster rather naïvely admitted his administration's dependence upon Diaz. After asserting that growing foreign investment showed American and European confidence in Mexican stability and reiterating the need of Mexico for more railroads in order to bring about a social and economic revolution in Mexican life, González said frankly: "El nombramiento del Sr. general Díaz quiere decir que seguimos unidos como siempre, y su aceptación demuestra claramente que somos republicanos. Por otra parte, el mismo Señor general Díaz tiene el patriótico empeño de ver concluídas, si es posible, las importantísimas mejoras ferro-carrileras que inició, y ningún puesto más a propósito que el de la Secretaría de Fomento que ya desempeña." González to Foster, December 3, 1880, Foster Papers MSS. Foster thought that Diaz' régime in Mexico was a period of "unparalleled prosperity" but that he should have retired at the end of his second term in order to give his nation training in self-government. Foster, *Memoirs*, I, 106. The fact that González was born in a border rancho, del Moquete, near Matamoras (see Salvador Quevedo y Zubieta, *Manuel González y su gobierno en México*, p. 30) may have accounted in a measure for his interest in railroad development in Mexico by American capital.

[143] After Diaz' fall the succeeding confused period brought more border disorders culminating in the raid of Villa on Columbus, New Mexico, in 1916 and Pershing's expedition into Mexico in pursuit, but these disorders were temporary.

BIBLIOGRAPHY

MANUSCRIPT SOURCES

Doolittle, James R., Papers, Library of Congress.
Foster, John W., Papers, Library of Congress.
Hayes, Rutherford B., Papers, Fremont, Ohio.
Mexican Despatches; Instructions; Notes to the Mexican Legation; Notes from the Mexican Legation, 1875-1906. U. S. Department of State.
Photostats of the Mexican Archives, Library of Congress (24 packets of material dealing with the border situation).
Plumb, Edward Lee, Papers, Library of Congress.
Sherman, John, Papers, 1868-1880, Library of Congress.
Sherman, General W. T., Records and Papers, 1870-1882, Library of Congress.
Washburne, Elihu B., Papers (Autograph Letters Foreign Diplomats vol. 100), Library of Congress.

OFFICIAL PRINTED SOURCES

Mexico

Anales del Ministerio de Fomento de la República Mexicana (Annual Reports for 1877-1882, 1887, 1888, 1891, 1898), Mexico City, 1877 ff.

Correspondencia diplomática relativa a las invasiones del territorio mexicano por fuerzas de los Estados-Unidos de 1873 a 1877, Mexico City, 1878. This is a Mexican Government publication.

Cuestión americana—negocios diplomáticos con los Estados Unidos—notas y documentos relativos (edición oficial), Guadalajara, 1873.

Documentos relativos al establecimiento de la Zona Libre en la frontera de Tamaulipas, Mexico City, 1869.

Exposición de la Secretaría de Hacienda de los Estados-Unidos mexicanos de 15 de enero de 1879, Mexico City, 1879.

Memoria de la Secretaría de Relaciones Exteriores (Annual Reports for 1871, 1873, 1875, 1878, 1881, 1885).

Memoria de la Secretaría de Estado del Despacho de Guerra y Marina presentada al Congreso de la Unión mexicana (Annual Reports for 1875, 1877-1881, 1883-1886, 1886-1890, 1896-1899, 1900, 1900-1901), Mexico City, 1901.

Memoranda y notas relativas cambiadas entre el Ministerio de Relaciones Exteriores y el Ministro Plenipotenciario de los Estados Unidos, Mexico City, 1877. This is an official Mexican publication.

Memorias de Porfirio Díaz, 1830-1867, 2 vols., 2d ed., Mexico City, 1922-1923.

Reciprocidad comercial entre México y los Estados Unidos, Mexico City, 1890.

Rodriguez, Ricardo, *Historia auténtica de la administración del Sr. Gral. Porfirio Díaz,* 2 vols., Mexico City, 1904. Contains text of Diaz' semi-annual messages to the Mexican Congress.

187

Secretaría de Relaciones Exteriores la emigración y protección de Mexicanos en el extranjero, Mexico, 1928.

Tratados y convenciones concluídos y ratificados por la República mexicana desde su independencia hasta el año de 1896 acompañados de varios documentos que les son referentes (segunda parte, edición oficial), Mexico City, 1896.

United States

Congressional Record, Washington, 1873 ff.

Harrison, Carter H., *Speech on the Texas Border Question July 12, 1876,* Washington, 1876.

House Documents.
    24th Cong., 1st sess., Doc. No. 256.
    45th Cong., 1st sess., Ex. Doc. No. 13.
    45th Cong., 2d sess., Misc. Doc. No. 64.
    46th Cong., 3d sess., Doc. No. 1.
    48th Cong., 1st sess., Doc. No. 86.
    56th Cong., 2d sess., Doc. No. 181, Pt. 3.
    59th Cong., 2d sess., Doc. No. 817.

House Journal.
    45th Cong., 2d sess.

House Reports.
    44th Cong., 1st sess., Rept. No. 343.
    45th Cong., 2d sess., Repts. of Committees, vol. 3, Rept. No. 701.

Hubbard, R. B. (Governor of Texas), *Letter to President Hayes January 8, 1878,* Austin, 1878.

Interior, Department of, *Reports of the Commissioner of Indian Affairs, 1876-1910.* These reports are published as separate documents, also as House documents.

Malloy, William M., *Treaties, Conventions, International Acts, Protocols and Agreements between the United States of America and Other Powers,* 2 vols., Washington, 1910.

Maxey, S. B., *Rio Grande Frontier* (Speech in the Senate, November 14, 1877), Washington, 1877.

Moore, John Bassett, *A Digest of International Law,* 8 vols., Washington, 1906.

Report of the Committee of Investigation sent in 1873 by the Mexican Government to the Frontier of Texas (translated from the official edition made in Mexico), New York, 1875. The official Mexican edition is called *Informe de la Comisión pesquisidora del norte al ejecutivo de la unión en cumplimiento . . . de la ley de 30 de setiembre de 1872,* Mexico City, 1874.

Report of United States Commissioners to Texas appointed under Joint Resolution of Congress May 7, 1872, Washington, 1872.

Richardson, James D. (editor), *A Compilation of the Messages and Papers of the Presidents,* 10 vols., New York, 1896-1899.

———, *A Compilation of the Messages and Papers of the Confederacy,* 2 vols., Nashville, 1905.

Schleicher, Gustave, *Protection of the Texas Frontier* (Speech in the House of Representatives June 30, 1876), Washington, 1876.

Senate Documents.
    40th Cong., 1st sess., Doc. No. 20.

44th Cong., 2d sess., Doc. No. 31.
50th Cong., 1st sess., Doc. No. 130.
52d Cong., 1st sess., Doc. No. 8.
52d Cong., 1st sess., Doc. No. 149.
55th Cong., 2d sess., Doc. No. 247.
55th Cong., 3d sess., Doc. No. 51.
62d Cong., 2d sess., Doc. No. 404.
66th Cong., 2d sess., Doc. No. 284.
Senate Reports.
42d Cong., 1st sess., Rept. No. 39.
66th Cong., 2d sess., Rept. No. 645.
Special Report of Adjutant General W. H. King to Governor John Ireland of Texas, September, 1884, Austin, 1884.
State, Department of, *Papers Relating to the Foreign Relations of the United States,* Washington, 1861 ff. Those for period after 1906 used especially.
War, Department of, *Reports of the Secretary of War of the United States, 1876-1910.* These reports are published as separate documents, also as House documents.
Wharton, Francis, *A Digest of the International Law of the United States,* 3 vols., Washington, 1886.

SECONDARY SOURCES

BOOKS

Apuntes biográficos del C. general Porfirio Díaz (ed. de la " Victoria "), Oaxaca, 1876.
Baerlein, Henry, *Mexico the Land of Unrest,* London, 1914.
Bancroft, H. H., *History of Mexico, 1516-1887,* 6 vols., San Francisco, 1883-1888.
Batres, Leopoldo, *Recordatorio del Gral Díaz,* Mexico City, 1925.
Beals, Carleton, *Porfirio Diaz Dictator of Mexico,* Philadelphia, 1932.
Bell, Edward I., *The Political Shame of Mexico,* New York, 1914.
Benedict, H. Y., and Lomax, John A., *The Book of Texas,* Garden City, 1916.
Blakeslee, George H. (editor), *Mexico and the Caribbean* (Clark University Addresses), New York, 1920.
Blanco, M. Antonio Z. de, *General Don Porfirio Díaz, presidente de la República Mexicana,* Mexico City, 1900.
Blumenkron, Fernando, *Porfirio Díaz en el destierro,* Mexico City, 1911.
Brown, John Henry, *History of Texas from 1685 to 1892,* 2 vols., St. Louis, 1893.
Bulnes, Francisco, *Charges against the Diaz Administration,* New York, 1916.
Butler, Charles H., *The Treaty-Making Power of the United States,* 2 vols., New York, 1902.
Callahan, James Morton, *American Foreign Policy in Mexican Relations,* New York, 1932.
———, *Evolution of Seward's Mexican Policy,* in " West Virginia University Studies in American History," Series 1, Diplomatic History, Nos. 4, 5, 6, Morgantown, 1909.
Carreño, Alberto Maria, *Mexico y los Estados de América,* Mexico City, 1922.

Carson, W. E., *Mexico, the Wonderland of the South*, New York, 1914.

Carter, Captain R. G., *The Mackenzie Raid into Mexico*, Washington, 1919.

Case, Alden B., *Thirty Years with the Mexicans: In Peace and Revolution*, New York, 1917.

Castrillo, José R. Del, *Historia de la revolución*, Mexico City, 1915.

Chase, Stuart, *Mexico, a Study of Two Americas*, New York, 1931.

Cole, Taylor, *The Recognition Policy of the United States since 1901*, Baton Rouge, 1928.

Colina, F. de la, *Madero y el Gral. Díaz*, Mexico, 1913.

———, *Porfirio Díaz*, Mexico, 1911.

Creel, George, *The People Next Door*, New York, 1926.

Creelman, James, *Diaz Master of Mexico*, New York, 1911.

Cubas, Antonio García, *The Republic of Mexico in 1876*, Mexico City, 1876.

Deaton, E. L., *Indian Fights on Texas Frontier*, Hamilton, Texas, 1894.

De Kay, John W., *Dictators of Mexico*, London, 1914.

De LaCombe, H. Mercier, *Le Mexique et les États Unis*, Paris, 1863.

Didapp, Juan Pedro, *Despecho político. Díaz y Mariscal*, 2 vols., Santander, 1906.

———, *Los Estados Unidos y nuestros conflictos internos*, Mexico City, 1913.

Dillon, E. J., *Mexico on the Verge*, New York, 1921.

Domenech, Robert, *Mexico y el imperialismo Norte Americano*, Buenos Aires, 1914.

Dunn, Frederick S., *Diplomatic Protection of Americans in Mexico*, New York, 1933.

Duval, John C., *The Adventures of Big-Foot Wallace*, Philadelphia, 1871.

Eckenrode, H. J., *Rutherford B. Hayes, Statesman of Reunion*, New York, 1930.

Elkins, Captain John M., *Indian Fighting on the Texas Frontier*, Amarillo, Texas, 1929.

Enriquez, Rafael de Zayas, *Los Estados Unidos Mexicanos*, New York, 1897

———, *Porfirio Díaz. La evolución de su vida*, New York, 1908.

Escudero, Ignacio M., *Apuntes históricos de la carrera militar del Señor general Porfirio Díaz presidente de la República Mexicana*, Mexico, 1889.

Fornaro, Carlo de, *Diaz, Czar of Mexico*, Mexico City, 1909.

Foster, John W., *Diplomatic Memoirs*, 2 vols., Boston-New York, 1909. The Mexican Government published a part of Volume I of Foster's *Memoirs* dealing with Mexico in a Spanish edition, *Las memorias diplomáticas de Mr. Foster Sobre Mexico* (Ministerio de Relaciones Exteriores, Archivo Histórico Diplomático Mexicano Numero 29), Mexico City, 1929.

Fyfe, H. Hamilton, *The Real Mexico*, New York, 1914.

Gabriel, Ralph Henry, *The Lure of the Frontier*, New Haven, 1929.

Gannett, Henry, *Modern History and Present Distribution of North American Indians*, New Lork, 1881.

García, Genaro, *Porfirio Díaz. Sus padres, Niñez y Juventud*, Mexico City, 1906.

Garland, Hamlin, *The Book of the American Indian*, New York, 1923.

Godoy, José F., *Porfirio Diaz President of Mexico, the Master Builder of a Great Commonwealth*, New York, 1910.

Goebel, Julius, Jr., *The Recognition Policy of the United States,* in "Columbia University Studies in History, Economics and Public Law," LXVI, No. 1, New York, 1915.

González-Blanco, Andres, *Un déspota y un libertador,* Madrid, 1916.

González-Blanco, Pedro, *De Porfirio Díaz a Carranza,* Madrid, 1916.

Gruening, Ernest, *Mexico and Its Heritage,* New York-London, 1928.

Hannay, David, *Diaz,* New York, 1917.

Hernandez, Fortunato, *Un pueblo, un siglo y un hombre,* Mexico City, 1909.

Howland, Charles P., *Survey of American Foreign Relations 1928,* New Haven, 1928-1931.

Iglesias, José Maria, *La cuestión presidencial en 1876,* Mexico City, 1892.

Inman, Samuel Guy, *Intervention in Mexico,* New York, 1919.

Irigoyen, Ulises, *En pro de la Zona libre,* Juárez, 1920.

Johnson, Willis F., *America's Foreign Relations,* 2 vols., New York, 1916.

Lane, Ralph Normal Angell, *What Can Military Force Do in Mexico?* World Peace Foundation Pamphlet Series, April to May, 1914, IV, No. 3.

Leupp, Francis E., *The Indian and His Problem,* New York, 1910.

Madero, Francisco I., *La sucesión presidencial en 1910,* San Pedro, 1908.

Manero, Antonio, *El antiguo régimen y la revolución,* Mexico City, 1911.

Manning, W. R., *Early Diplomatic Relations between the United States and Mexico,* Baltimore, 1913.

Marcy, R. B., *Thirty Years of Army Life on the Border,* New York, 1866.

Martínez, Concepcion (editor), *Album onomástico,* Mexico City, 1897.

Morales, Vicente y Caballero, Manuel, *El Señor Root en México,* Mexico, 1908.

Moreno, Mario G., *El régimen Porfirista en México; su apoteosis,* Mexico City, 1913.

Obregón, T. Esquivel, *México y los Estados Unidos ante el derecho internacional,* Mexico, 1926.

O'Shaughnessey, Edith (Mrs. Nelson O'Shaughnessey), *Intimate Pages of Mexican History,* New York, 1920.

Paxon, F. L., *The Independence of the South American Republics,* Philadelphia, 1916.

Paz, Ireneo (editor), *Biografía del C. general Porfirio Díaz,* Mexico City, 1884.

Phifer, Charles Lincoln, *Diaz the Dictator,* Girard, Kansas, 1910.

Pickrell, Annie D., *Pioneer Women in Texas,* Austin, 1929.

Porfirio Díaz y su obra, Mexico City, 1908.

Powell, Fred Wilbur, *The Railroads of Mexico,* Boston, 1921.

Priestley, H. I., *The Mexican Nation, a History,* New York, 1923.

Quevedo y Zubieta, Salvador, *Manuel González y su gobierno en México,* Madrid, 1928.

Rabago, J. M., *Historia del gran crimen,* Mexico City, 1897.

Ramsdell, C. W., *Reconstruction in Texas,* "Columbia University Studies in History, Economics, and Public Law," XXXVI, No. 1, New York, 1910.

Rapport du général Porfirio Diaz président des États-Unis mexicans à ses compatriotes (traduction du "Courrier du Mexique"), Mexico City, 1889.

Rebolledo, Miguel, *México y los Estados Unidos,* Mexico City, 1917.

República Mexicana y su regeneración por el Señor general Porfirio Díaz, Mexico City, 1910.

Rippy, J. Fred, *The United States and Mexico*, New York, 1928.

Rister, Carl C., *The Southwestern Frontier 1865-1881*, Cleveland, 1928.

Rives, G. L., *The United States and Mexico, 1821-1848*, 2 vols., New York, 1913.

Rock, James L., and Smith, W. I. (editors), *Southern and Western Texas Guide for 1878*, St. Louis, 1878.

Romero, Matias, *Mexico and the United States*, 1 vol., New York, 1898.

————, *Railways in Mexico*, Washington, 1882.

————, *Speech read on 65th Anniversary of the Birth of U. S. Grant, April 25, 1887*, New York, 1887.

Santibañez, Enrique, *México y sus relaciones internacionales*, Mexico City, 1917.

Sherman, W. T., *Memoirs of*, 2 vols., New York, 1875.

Smith, Clinton L., and Smith, Jefferson D., *The Boy Captives*, Bandera, Texas, 1927.

Smith, Justin, *The Annexation of Texas*, New York, 1911.

————, *The War with Mexico*, New York, 1919.

Smithsonian Institution, U. S. Bureau of Ethnology, *Handbook of American Indians North of Mexico*, Part I, Bulletin No. 30, Washington, 1912.

Sowell, A. J., *Early Settlers and Indian Fighters of Southwest Texas*, Austin, 1900.

Starr, Frederick, *In Indian Mexico*, Chicago, 1908.

————, *Mexico and the United States*, Chicago, 1914.

Steele, James W., *Frontier Army Sketches*, Chicago, 1883.

Stone, Will Hale, *Twenty-four Years a Cowboy and Ranchman*, Hedrick, Oklahoma Territory, 1905.

Stuart, Graham H., *Latin America and the United States*, New York, 1923.

Tannenbaum, Frank, *The Mexican Agrarian Revolution*, New York, 1929.

Turner, John Kenneth, *Barbarous Mexico*, Chicago, 1911.

Tweedie, Ethel Brilliana (Mrs. Alec), *Porfirio Diaz, Seven Times President of Mexico*, London, 1906.

Velasco, Alfonso Luis, *Porfirio Díaz. Estudio biográfico*, Mexico City, 1892.

Whitney, Caspar, *What's the Matter with Mexico?* New York, 1916.

Wilbarger, J. W., *Indian Depredations in Texas*, Austin, 1889.

Williams, Charles R., *The Life of Rutherford Birchard Hayes*, 2 vols., Boston-New York, 1914.

————, *Diary and Letters of Rutherford B. Hayes, Nineteenth President of the United States*, 5 vols., (Ohio State Archeological and Historical Society, Hayes Series, III-VII), Columbus, 1922-26.

Williams, Ramon V., *The Mexican Trade Directory*, New York, 1888.

Wooten, Dudley G. (editor), *A Comprehensive History of Texas, 1685-1897*, 2 vols., Dallas, 1898.

Wright, Quincy, *The Control of American Foreign Relations*, New York, 1922.

Zaragoza y Escobar, Antonio, *El ' Monroismo " y el general Porfirio Díaz*, Havana, 1896.

ARTICLES

Beteta, Ramon, "The Government of Mexico," in *Mexico* (Lectures before the Inter-American Institute of Pomona College and Claremont College and the Pacific Southwest Academy of Political and Social Science, February 9, 10, 11, 1928), Pomona, 1929.

Hackett, Charles W., "The Recognition of the Diaz Government by the United States," *Southwestern Historical Quarterly*, XXVIII, 34-56, July, 1924.

Lewis, William Ray, "The Hayes Administration and Mexico," *Southwestern Historical Quarterly*, XXIV, 140-154, October, 1920.

Rippy, J. Fred, "Border Troubles along the Rio Grande, 1848-1860," *Southwestern Historical Quarterly*, XXIII, 91-112, October, 1919.

———, "Some Precedents of the Pershing Expedition into Mexico," *Southwestern Historical Quarterly*, XXIV, 292-316, April, 1921.

Tansill, Charles C., "War Powers of the President of the United States with Special Reference to the Beginning of Hostilities," *Political Science Quarterly*, XLV, 1-35, March, 1930.

Winkler, E. W. (editor), "The Bryan-Hayes Correspondence," *Southwestern Historical Quarterly*, XXV ff.

INDEX

Alvarez, General, 25, 29.
American Border Commission Report, 16.
Areola, raids of, 113.
Arvizu, Colonel, and Gutiérrez affair, 178-179.
Aspiroz, on alleged confiscation of Mexican cattle, 176.
Augur, Brigadier General C. C., describes border conditions, 158.

Bayard, demands investigation of Crawford affair, 162.
Benavides, Francisco, capture of, 173.
Biddle, Major James, reports Arizona territory free of Victorio's raiding, 111.
Blaine, James G., deprecates alleged expansionist policy by U. S., 44; reports better relations between two countries, 136; favors new commercial treaty, 184, 185 n.
Bonito, Chief, flees into Mexico to join Victorio, 112.
Border Smuggling, 12, 13. See Free Zone and Zona Libre.
Bullis, Lieutenant, crosses Rio Grande, 62.
Bryan, Colonel Guy M., strong influence on Hayes, 31, 31 n.; advice on Mexican recognition, 32; opposes expansion into Mexico, 46 n.

Carter, Joseph S., and stock rustling, 176.
Charles, Governor of Coahuila, on Indian raids, 113-114.
Cochise, flees Ojo Caliente reservation, 108.
Coke, Senator Richard, opposes Free Zone, 102.
Conkling, Senator Roscoe, opposes Hayes' non-recognition policy, 79.
Cortina, Juan N., and filibustering, 13.

Cox, Representative of New York, demands reasons for failure to recognize Diaz, 78; introduces resolution asking for recognition, 79-80.
Creel, U. S. Ambassador to Mexico, reports smuggling on Arizona border, 183.
Crawford, Captain Emmet, attacks raiding Indians, 160; death of, 161-162.
Crook, Brigadier-General George, and reservation conditions, 155; policing of Indians, 157; training of Indians, 159; and Geronimo, 165.

Davis, John, on reciprocal crossing, 156-157.
de Cuellar, José T., protests Order of June 1, 1877, 55; complains of alleged Mexican revotionary organizations on American soil, 94-95.
Diaz, Porfirio, overthrows Lerdo, 16-17, 17 n., 18-19; provisional president, 23 n.; and Treaty of 1868, 24, 24 n.; constitutional president, 25, 28 n.; and Grant Administration, 27; recognition of by Germany, Spain, Salvador, Guatemala, and Italy, 29, 29 n.; and Foster, 36; on infiltration of American capital, 38; and proposed sale of Mexican territory, 45; on recognition, 49-50, 73-74; on Order of June 1, 54-55, 57, 57 n.; counter - revolutionary attempts against, 59-60; reinforces border, 60; and Hayes Administration, 69; denies responsibility for border conditions, 71; and Extradition Treaty of 1861, 72; concerning proposed abolition of Free Trade, 69 n., 75; recognition of by U. S., 80; modification of Free Zone, 101; personal characteristics of, 130-132; interest

195

agreement for joint action of troops, 49; protests Order of June 1, 54; pleased with new order to Ord, 59; demands disavowal of act of Shafter, 63; demands recognition before settlement of claims, 69; agrees on compromise for crossing, 75; reports band of alleged revolutionists at Laredo, 95; asks U. S. to prevent revolutionary expeditions from California, 98.

Victorio, succeeds Cochise as leader of Indian marauders, 108-109; killed, 110.

Wheaton, Brigadier General, commanding Department of Colorado, reports border free of raids, 167.

Willcox, Colonel, commanding

Department of Arizona, reports raiding expedition near Sonora line, 97; requests return of Indians escaped to Mexico, 122; reports cooperation on border, 126; difficulties on border, 151, 151 n.; approves reciprocal crossing, 153.

Zamacona, sent to U. S. to seek recognition, 76; protests gathering of Mexican revolutionists in Texas, 95, 95 n.; reports raid of Lerdist forces, 96; reports crossing of officials from Texas, 100; visits Chicago, 135; asks repeal of Order of June 1, 1877, 141; reports Indian raids, 146.

Zona Libre. See Free Zone.

Zuloaga, Juan M., on raids from Texas, 115.